LOST FOUND KEPT: A MEMOIR

Lost Found Kept: A Memoir
By Deborah Derrickson Kossmann

Winner of the 2023 Aurora Polaris Award

Copyright © January 5, 2025 Deborah Derrickson Kossmann

No part of this book may be used or performed without written consent of the author, if living, except for critical articles or reviews.

Derrickson Kossmann, Deborah
1st edition

ISBN: 978-1-949487-33-6
Library of Congress Control Number: 2024939541

Interior design by Natasha Kane
Cover design by Joel W. Coggins
Editing by David Groff

Trio House Press, Inc.
Minneapolis
www.triohousepress.org

For Marc—with all my love

"I came to explore the wreck,
The words are purposes,
The words are maps.
I came to see the damage that was done
And the treasures that prevail."
—Adrienne Rich
Diving into the Wreck

"How should we be able to forget those ancient myths that are at the beginning of all peoples, the myths about dragons that at the last moment turn into princesses; perhaps all the dragons in our lives are princesses who are only waiting to see us once beautiful and brave. Perhaps everything terrible is in its deepest being something helpless that wants help from us."
—Rainer Maria Rilke
Letters To a Young Poet

Table of Contents

Prologue — 5

Part I - Lost
Chapter 1: A Path Around — 9
Chapter 2: Charm Bracelet — 20
Chapter 3: Drawdown Warning — 30
Chapter 4: What We Hold On To — 42
Chapter 5: Going in — 57
Chapter 6: Bullies I Love — 70

Part II - Found
Chapter 7: Building Myself — 89
Chapter 8: Shit Show — 114
Chapter 9: The Garden — 135
Chapter 10: When You See Fit — 154
Chapter 11: Thirty-Yard Dumpster — 173

Part III - Kept
Chapter 12: Family Secrets — 197
Chapter 13: Barren — 213
Chapter 14: What Remains — 220
Chapter 15: At the Center — 239
Chapter 16: A House is Not a Home — 252

Epilogue: The Star-filled Dark — 266

Acknowledgments — 271
About the Author — 275

Prologue

Twirling on lush lawn, I'm pretending to be an astronaut in outer space, circling the blue and green Earth, trying to spot the tiny dot where I came from.

"Dizzyland!" my younger sister and I yell as we play this game. We fall in the grass laughing, waiting for the feeling to pass so we can stand up and fly all over again.

I learn about astronomy from my mother. At night she sets up my grandfather, Nonno's, telescope in the backyard.

"Look," she says, "here's the Big Dipper over there!" She pushes down my head a little to help me look through the lens as she adjusts the tilt.

"Can you see Canis Major? It's supposed to be a big dog barking."

She explains to my sister and me about the constellation of Cassiopeia, who in Greek mythology had her kingdom destroyed by a sea monster. My mother knows many stories about myths, different religions, and magic. She's told us that she believes brownies and fairies are real, and sometimes we look under a plant when she is gardening to see if they have been there like in the books we read together. A little statue of a birthday fairy appears on the dining room table with the gifts for our special day.

As she does with many of her stories, my mother leaves out a part of the Greek myth: Cassiopeia's daughter, Princess Andromeda, was left bound to a rock as prey for that sea monster. But the princess escaped her fate with the help of Perseus who married her. She became her own star in the night sky.

"After Cassiopeia's kingdom was destroyed," continues my mother, "she was left to circle the north celestial pole chained to her throne, half her time upside-down and clinging to it so she wouldn't fall off."

My mother looks up at the sky. "It's so beautiful," she sighs. "One light connects to another, so there's always a picture for us."

I squint through the glasses I wear for my nearsightedness. I don't always succeed in glimpsing the pattern, but I don't want to disappoint her.

I nod as she points in the dark.

"Yes," I say, "I can see it too."

PART I - *LOST*

Chapter 1 - A Path Around

There are two houses in my story, a "before" house and an "after" house, both in Cherry Hill, New Jersey, a second ring suburb of Philadelphia, Pennsylvania. The nearby Cherry Hill Mall was one of the first indoor malls in the country and was one of four malls within twenty minutes of my neighborhood. I did not, as a college friend once joked, have that "growing up in the mall pallor" but certainly could have, given how much time we spent in all of them.

Cherry Hill was home to Garden State Park, the first horse racetrack to be licensed by the state. It burned to the ground in April 1977 during my junior year in high school. As we stood in our front yard listening to the wailing sirens, black ash from six miles away fell from the cloudless sky like a freak snowfall. Cherry Hill was also known for the famous Latin Casino nightclub where singer Jackie Wilson collapsed from a heart attack in 1975. There are not too many other interesting things to say about the town. It was only a little more than an hour from the coast and everyone spent some or all summer "down the shore." You could always find decent bagels and diner food. Kaminski's had the best cheese fries.

Our first house was at 315 South Woodstock Drive in the Glenview neighborhood on the east side, where I lived between the ages of six and twelve. My mother, Faith, would always say this had been her favorite house. It had been the builder's and included amenities like air conditioning and a finished attic.

Our second house was one neighborhood over in Brookfield, a slightly less upscale address because it bordered I-295 and was across the highway from the Melitta factory that roasted coffee. It was a short bike ride through the development, maybe ten minutes or less, from my first house. We moved to 137 Willowbrook Road when I was thirteen and my sister, Melissa, was nine, after the divorce. This remained my mother's house after we both grew up and left home.

 I'm remembering my adolescence there. I had my own bedroom and hated the pink shag carpeting. I can almost hear the *Saturday Night Fever* soundtrack blasting at my high school graduation party as we drank beer and danced in the backyard.

 It's a hot and sticky day in early July 2016 when I pull up and park on the street in front of the Willowbrook Road house, looking around to make sure my mother's dinged-up Toyota isn't parked in the crumbling driveway. Old mail, circulars, and some plastic bags seep out of the closed garage door. A waterlogged pile of newspapers is solidified near the empty trash can beside the house. The front door is covered with ivy, and I can barely see past the untrimmed arborvitae for a glimpse of the envelopes stuffed in the mailbox which hangs by one hook off the brick wall. All the window shades are closed. The living room windows are blocked by overgrown evergreen bushes that twist and turn against the house, hiding what's inside.

 I'm trying to remember the names of the neighbors, most of whom I haven't seen for thirty years. The Morgans in the red house with their wild little boys I babysat. Annette and Jeanette Barry, the shy Mormon twins around the corner, rode our bus and wore long skirts. Jim and Neola Reese, the first Black family in the neighborhood lived in the house next door since before we moved here in 1973. Across the street diagonally, the Gallaghers, where I know Kathy, our honorary younger sister, still lives with her mother and oldest brother. She had four brothers, but one, Joey, was killed in a car accident when I was in college.

I'm feeling wilted from the humid New Jersey summer and tired after the fifty-minute drive from Havertown, Pennsylvania, a suburb west of Philadelphia where I live. I'm glad my mother is not home, so I can get out of the car. Over the past twenty years or so, I would occasionally drive by the house on a stealth mission to see how it looked. I'd never linger, fearing she'd pop out and yell at me because I came by without her explicit permission. Nobody just "stops by" this house. My mother won't let anyone come near the outside, much less invite them in. The day she had her first breast cancer surgery seventeen years ago, she was waiting at the curb, bag packed, for me to take her to the hospital. Neither my younger sister, who lives nearby in Medford, New Jersey, nor I, have been allowed to have a key for years. I have not been inside my childhood home since 1987.

I don't want to be here now. Absentmindedly, I start my old habit of picking at the flesh on my thumb. I heard the question someone asks when I tell them about this. *How is it possible you haven't seen the inside of your mother's house for almost thirty years?*

"Well, it's complicated," I'd always answer. "You don't know my mother." Until today, keeping my mother's secret has been mostly convenient for my sister and me, even though it's strange to other people.

Through the years, Melissa and I have talked about what we will find when we're finally able to enter the house. The carcass of our old cat, Samantha? Hidden treasure like piles of crisp hundred dollar bills pressed under her mattress? Our husbands, who have never been inside, tease us after a few beers that they are just going to take matters into their own hands and "burn it down" when the time comes. My sister and I joke that if my mother dies, we hope it will happen when she's not at her house, so at least we'd be notified about it. There's worry beneath our laughter. We've respected her autonomy. It's her right to live as she chooses, including her decision to not allow anyone inside. But over the past year, there have been a series of incidents. First, there was her hospitalization for frostbitten diabetic feet after she shoveled the end of the driveway during a snowstorm. Then, there was the matter of her landline phone being turned off several times. Finally, she's told my brother-in-law, Ron, that she's running out of money. As I look at the filthy windows I'm asking, *were we wrong to let her live the way she wanted? Should we have done something sooner?*

It was never a bad house: three bedrooms, one and a half baths, an attic, kitchen, living room, dining room, and rec room downstairs next to a laundry room by the back door. A simple, white, split-level with some brick on the lower half, it had black shutters and a black front door. My mother placed a big brass knocker over a piece of wood to cover up the window and make the door more secure and private so you couldn't see in. I was in seventh grade, old enough to understand she was trying to keep my stepfather out.

"It looks nice," I'd told her when she asked me what I thought about the knocker.

Back then she did projects. And the house looked like all the other ones in the development, freshly painted, with a well-groomed lawn. The attached garage was big enough for a car and a clothes dryer, with some room left over for our bikes. The front porch was decorated with a frog statue and a frog planter with a geranium in it. Today I can see the planter from my car window, above the broken steps, empty of flowers and shoved back in the corner of the landing.

I walk up the driveway and around the side of the house. An unpruned tree leans over the chain link fence that somehow has been bent downward so the gate to the backyard doesn't work. I push back some big branches to squeeze myself through, trying not to tear my dress. A mosquito bites my bare calf, and I slap it, cursing.

I was supposed to be at a party this afternoon with my husband, Marc, but when I called my mother this morning to wish her a happy eighty-second birthday, I found her landline was disconnected for the fourth time in six months. My sister is out of town, so I have no way to tell my mother that our plans to celebrate her birthday tomorrow have changed except to drive twenty miles over here and leave her a handwritten message.

"Fuck," I blurt out. I slap another mosquito and step over more and more of those lumpy piles of newspapers that obstruct the path and are moldering into cement against the back wall of the house. Where once there was a yard with my mother's carefully planted flowers, now there is a jungle. I loved the pink, red, and yellow roses that separated our yard from the Reese's. It was my job to water those roses in the summer. I used to help weed around juniper shrubs on the little hill by the driveway, spread out in a pretty way so you wouldn't have to mow there.

I take a deep breath. *Do I really want to go further?* I don't have another way of communicating with her, so I don't feel like I have much choice. I've come this far today, so there's no point in backing out. I'll confess, I'm curious. *What is it like here?*

There's an empty, tall, blue recycling bin blocking the back door, and when I move it, I see most of the storm door's glass is gone. I open it and notice the door to the inside has broken glass, too, as though someone has put a fist through it. I flashback to the time my stepfather axed down the front door of the Woodstock Drive house after my mother locked him out. My mother has stuffed this door with yellowing newspaper and heavy, shredded plastic sheets. Mosquitos are starting to swarm out of the bin which is full of stagnant water, and I'm sweating and slapping them away from my face.

I've prepared a birthday card, which I've placed back into its plastic sleeve because it's supposed to rain, and I'm planning to tape it to the back door. My message inside the card is gentle. "Happy Birthday. Your phone is out again. Please call me about the time we are meeting tomorrow."

What I really wanted to write is, *Why the hell did I have to give up my plans and drive all the way here to reach you, and why can't you just pay your phone bill like a normal person, so I don't have to do things like slink around my old house like a criminal?* But as a private practice psychologist I know how to use words that don't escalate situations.

Twenty years ago, at a lunch, my mother turned to me and hissed, "I know you've been sneaking around the backyard trying to get in." I was shocked at the time since nothing could have been further from my mind than going back to this house. It had taken years of my own therapy to be able to leave it behind. Her paranoia was something I learned to tiptoe away from slowly, the way you would avoid a grizzly bear standing up on its hind legs. I'd never been sure when it would chase me down and devour me. I denied I'd been back, and she looked at me with disbelief. She will know I've been here now. And she'll know I've been "snooping" around because the last time my sister left her a note, she'd stuck it on the garage out front.

I keep looking over my shoulder. It's creepy behind the house under the gray sky, even though it's mid-afternoon on a Saturday.

"Who lives like this?" I say out loud.

I look at the wrecked door and start to tear up. Something is taking shape in the July humidity—a resolve, a rage, a sadness, a fear I don't fully understand. It's about what might be inside, but also what this house is telling me about my mother. I've seen pictures of houses like this. The dirty, covered windows, the tall weeds blooming all over the yard, the unopened mail— all signs of a life unraveling. I don't know what I should do about the way my mother is living. But it's clear to me that Melissa and I need to do something. My mother raised us. She was the parent who was there.

My mother sits like a tiny, musty Jabba the Hut in a wing chair at the local Barnes & Noble. She's picking at some scabs on her hands and telling me the doctor is checking her for autoimmune disorders because she's been having so much trouble with her allergies. It's a week or so after my foray outside the house and I've already broached the idea that perhaps my sister and I need to help her with the bill paying and money management because she's had so many issues with the phone. I tried not to sound pushy about it, despite my ominous feeling that this is becoming a crisis. She stared at me with narrowed eyes before looking away and saying we'd discuss it in a few weeks when she was feeling better. As I look at her more closely, I'm starting to understand it's likely the house that is making her sick.

This bookstore, and Ponzio's, the local diner, are my mother's favorite hangout spots. She has introduced us to the waitresses, whom my sister calls my mother's "paid friends." They all seem to love her, waving hello or stopping by the table and chatting while we're eating. My mother knows about their families and medical issues and asks after the girls who aren't working that day. My mother hasn't had a fridge or a working kitchen in years. She's mentioned that it doesn't matter because she hates to cook and eats all her meals out. She also has other haunts, like the movie theater. I know she's lonely. More and more of her "real" friends have died or become infirm. In the past, she'd talk about helping them with doctors' appointments and giving them medical advice from her nursing days. She was a very good RN back when she was working.

I sit in the wooden chair opposite her beside the magazine rack, and try to ignore the man who's sitting a few feet away typing on his laptop. It's like this space is my mother's living room and he's another visitor. I've brought her a little present, a book of poetry written by a friend who's given me an extra copy for her. My mother appreciates good poetry, such as the work of Linda Pastan or Mary Oliver. She has always been an avid reader. It's a bond we have. I also have another offering, a manila folder with sample Power of Attorney papers. I'm trying to be stealthy about my interventions to help, to avoid rousing that grizzly bear. She probably knows it's coming after our earlier conversation.

"How's Marc?" she asks, and I wonder, as the familiar irritation comes over me for the umpteenth time, why she never asks how *I* am or what *I'm* doing. It's been the same interaction for the past few years, so I've learned to accept it. After all, I'm not sure I really want to know how she's doing either.

"He's good. What are you reading? Anything I should borrow?" We chat for a few minutes about the new Louise Penny book coming out. Both of us love a literary mystery. Then, summoning my courage, I delve into the point of my visit.

"Melissa and I are worried about you not having a landline because you aren't using the cell phone we bought you last

Christmas…"

"Deborah," she snaps, using my full name so I know she's annoyed, "I'm working on it."

She shifts in her seat, glancing out the front window of the store to indicate she's finished with this topic.

"I've been thinking," I persist, moving on to the next topic that must be broached, "that it might be time to get a Power of Attorney and activate it, so we can help you with the bills," not adding that we need to tackle the house situation. One thing at a time.

"We *did* a POA," my mother says, her voice rising. "Don't you have that?"

I'm suddenly unsure, but then I remember that she had one done before her second mastectomy in 2001. *Why didn't I remember this?* Maybe it was because she had taken this step so begrudgingly. I recall that we'd gone to the bank together to put through the paperwork, so it was on file, but not activated.

"Well," I say, "how about you and Melissa and I go over to the bank then next week and you can put us on the account as signatories and I can start to help you with the bills?"

She looks away. I try and soften my request. "We can all have lunch at Ponzio's first."

"I don't really want to talk about this anymore," she says as she rummages in her purse. "I'm tired and I'm going to take an Advil."

She gets up as if she's in arthritic pain, rising slowly and bending her knees to make sure they will hold her, and then stalks toward the water fountain with a pill in her hand. I look at the chair where she was sitting and see a stack of four books on it, a magazine she's been reading, and some greeting cards. The man on his laptop is still sitting close by, staring pointedly at his screen to show he's not listening. I watch my eighty-two-year-old mother walking back toward me and try and see her like that man might. When I was a child, my mother, while short, had a voluptuous figure and shapely legs. She wasn't somebody who wore a lot of makeup, but she liked to put pink polish on her fingers and toes. She always wore her antique rings or an artistic beaded necklace. I remember the scent of her Wind Song perfume. She'd dab her neck and the inside of her wrists before she went out. Now she has shrunk several inches from age and arthritis and is tiny, maybe only five feet tall. Her black pants and light blue sweater are rumpled, and she wears a cat t-shirt underneath. Her short, cropped hair is silver-gray and a little greasy. She has good skin and not a lot of wrinkles, but her color is kind of pale, and she looks tired. She also smells a little ripe, but it's hot and humid out so maybe that's why.

Brushing the books, magazine, and cards aside, she settles back into the chair. She keeps picking at the raw spots on her hands. As her sweater gets pushed up, I can see she has the rash going up her arms as well. "Did I ever tell you how your grandmother threw out my stuffed cat?"

Somehow her mind has made this connection to our conversation about the bank appointment.

"Your grandmother...." She shakes her head. "I was little, and she just decided one day to throw it out because it was dirty. Can you imagine doing that to a child?" She continues, pulling her sleeve down so it covers her arm, "Then there was the bike she got rid of when I was in nursing school. I loved that bike and came home to get it and she'd just sold it without telling me."

I nod and make a sympathetic noise as if she's one of my therapy clients. I loved Nanna, but she's gone and I'm not going to do anything to upset or question my mother's reality about her.

I have long understood my family role, which is also, not surprisingly, what I continue to do as a psychologist—to hear the subtext, to understand what she and my clients are indirectly telling me. It's clear from her comments that as we start the process of addressing her house issues, I am going to "throw out her dirty stuffed cat" and she will feel bereft. She will feel I am cruel to her. I am as bad as the mother she hates sometimes. My insides shrivel at my anticipation of her anger as I try to stay present with her. Part of me doesn't want to be closer to her world, I just want to continue living in my own. But I know it's mostly through compassion for her that I will be able to do what needs to be done next, which at this point is getting the POA underway, so we can find out exactly what her current life really entails.

I lean over and kiss her cheek as I say goodbye and leave the bookstore. As I walk outside, my thoughts return to her house. *Maybe I've never really left.* I've been orbiting around it for years in the swirling vortex of love and memory and old misery at its gravitational center.

I look back through the big bookstore window and see my mother sitting there, closing her eyes to nap. Today, I'm beginning to understand what I'm afraid of. I'm terrified that the house is about to pull me in.

Chapter 2 - Charm Bracelet

Somewhere in an album, long buried in one of the many piles inside my mother's house, there is a picture from her second wedding. In it, my mother is wearing blue: a blue silk, sleeveless, sheath dress with matching azure shoes. Her hair is short, her lips very red and smiling. She's looking down at me. I'm almost three at the time, and my dress is the same sky blue, perhaps even cut from the same cloth. My dress is a little different from hers, though, with white trim over the breastbone, but our hair is short and cut the same way with our ears showing. I'm holding a little white purse and waving. Maybe it's just before or right after the ceremony.

Behind me stands my stepfather wearing a dark business suit of the kind men wore in 1963, at least my mother's men. He's smiling, too. Maybe it's because, as the ceremony began, I walked up the long aisle with the white runner, waved at him and said, "Hi, Howard." I don't call him "Daddy" then. It is July, and my sister, Howard's daughter, is at the wedding too. She's three months growing inside my mother's snug and somewhat sexy outfit. She will arrive before Christmas.

My "real" father, Malcolm, is not in this picture. He and my mother fell apart when I was two. By then my mother was sleeping with my stepfather, who lived upstairs from my parents' apartment. My mother claims Malcolm had an affair before she did, with the red-haired wife of a doctor he met while performing in community theatre. Malcolm is evident in my big-boned height and the way I walk, even at three years old, my feet hitting the floor in the same way, with heavy clomps as if I'm stamping something down. The color of my eyes came from him. They shift from a green, springtime earth color to something darker.

"You look like him," my mother would later say. "You have his sense of humor."

I'm told Malcolm said goodbye to me before he left. My memory of this interaction is blank. How could my recollection be otherwise? At that age, I had no words of my own. I understood only the words people spoke to me. I see myself as I must have looked then: pixie haircut, tights, those black buckled shoes with thick soles. I am holding a long, stuffed cat. My "lovey," as my mother called it. Would a two year old cry if her father left? Would she remember being held up in the air and watching her father smile when she laughs and reaches for his nose? Would she forget how he kissed the top of her bumped head or put her softly to bed?

When I am older, I realize I do have a memory of what happened. It resides deep in my body, and I feel it each time I am left. It's pure pain—a slow, seeping sadness that doesn't have any words. My parents treated each other badly. Faithlessly forgetting what was breaking, what *could* break between them.

In the picture from the wedding, it's early in my mother and stepfather's relationship, and we look happy. There are other pictures, like the one taken a year after my sister is born while we are on vacation at Padre Island. It's right after I am given a special present, a silver charm bracelet with only one charm, a silver heart engraved "Debbie and Daddy" with the date underneath. I am adopted and Howard becomes my real daddy. I remember the blinding sunlight as we walked along the white expanse of beach that stretched on and on past the hotel to the Gulf.

But it won't last. I remember this without any pictures or

keepsakes. One of my first memories: Daddy throwing the checkbook at my mother, screaming that all she wanted was a rich man, that it wasn't his fault he was fired, as she backed away into the corner of the bedroom. Then the sound of his hand against her face before he left, and the word "bitch" spoken under his breath. And my mother, face down on the white bedspread, crying so hard it was as if she was laughing. I'd heard her laugh like that with me, sometimes, with the edges all rough. I wanted to be like her, so I throw my four-year-old self down on their bed, my face pressing against the raised bedspread pattern, and I laugh or cry too, the same hard sound rising into my throat and clawing its way out.

In the beginning of my new family, we move a few times because my stepfather keeps changing jobs. From Rochester, Minnesota where I'd been born, to Lincoln, Nebraska where my sister is born, to Omaha. Soon after this, like settlers seeking a new life, we go to Houston, Texas where everything will be better. Before we do, we vacation at the Connecticut lakeside cabin of Daddy's cousin, Aunt Jan. We find an orange kitten there and my mother tells me I can name him.

"Whiskers," I say.

"Thomas," my mother says, "His middle name can be Whiskers."

The kitten climbs up the terrycloth bib of my new baby sister, Missy, while my mother is feeding her buttered toast. Tommy licks her face, and she laughs and laughs. Tommy will be mine, a furred brother.

Aunt Jan's daughter, my new second cousin, tells me there are bogeymen back in the woods. I don't like it when it gets dark in the early evening because I know those scary things are out there. I sit on Daddy's lap then, and we listen to the radio, singing a song that is my favorite. "Polly-Wolly-Bing-Bang," we shout together. He is lifting his knee up and down and I can swing on it. Sometimes I stand with my back to him and put my bare feet on his oxford shoes. I hold my arms up so I can walk in big steps like he does. I love to look down on those shoes and see the circles made with the little holes.

A boy, with a name I don't remember, stays in the cabin next door. We play hide and seek together. One day he gives me a gold necklace with a locket and tells me he will marry me. I am excited about this because I want to get married like Mommy and Daddy. I shyly show my mother what he's given me, and she marches with me over to his cabin where she gives it back to his mother. He looks sad when his mother yells at him for taking it.

On the walk back to our cabin, my mother holds my hand and explains, "You're almost five and way too young to get married." She laughs and gives me a hug. "When you're a much bigger girl, then you'll marry a good husband who will give you nice jewelry like Daddy did for me."

Daddy takes me out sailing on the lake in a little boat. My mother makes him put the orange life jacket on me with the straps across my chest. It smells like old water. When we are out on the lake and the wind picks up, he starts to yell. The boat rolls from side to side and he keeps telling me to move to one side or the other or to sit very still. He can't control either the boat or his temper. We come close to tipping over. Fear blows along with us in large windy waves.

In Texas, I watch the hummingbirds come close to the sliding glass doors. Shimmering, they poke their whole red selves into the flowers. I watch them, wrapping a hunk of hair between my fingers. Twirl and twirl it—winding it around my finger until it becomes a thick lump of hairiness, an animal I pat over and over. Sometimes I make a clicking noise by putting my tongue to the roof of my mouth. Tick. Tick. Tick. I sit very still behind the cabinet in the kitchen hoping the hummingbirds don't crash into the glass. On the other side of the counter my seemingly tall mother is making lunch.

"Stop twisting your hair," she says. "Cut it out with the noise already." Then she forgets me, and I go right back to twirling, but I click more softly.

My mother's jewelry box is cream-colored with dark blue velvet inside, soft on my fingers. I want what's inside. It sparkles, it's green. I hold the ring up to my eye to see if I can see into it. I'm going to wear it outside. I know I'm not allowed, but it's pretty. It is loose on my finger, rolling around when I turn my hand to look at it. Once I'm in the sunshine it catches the light. I forget about it soon because I'm making mud pies with my friend. We dig and dig in the backyard, and I get pans of water from the bathroom and bring them outside, so we can stir the lumpy dirt into them. Our shirts and our socks get so muddy as we run around the backyard dumping the pans out and starting over. I love the mud on my hands, so thick and cool in the Texas heat.

When I get inside later, I remember the green ring. It's not on my hand. I don't want to tell my mother. I know it will be like that time when I went into her purse and took her lipstick. She told me how wrong it was to take other people's things and dangerous, too, because her purse had a medicine bottle in it. I don't know how my mother knows about the ring, but she does, and she is yanking my arm to pull me back outside in the dusk.

"Where were you playing?" she yells. Then she cries because she can't find it anywhere. I'm looking too. She calls it the "antique emerald ring."

"You're so selfish," she says, "I can't believe you did this. You're going to get us in big trouble."

I've never seen her so angry.

"It's worth so much money and one day it would have been yours. Your grandmother will never forgive you, and we can never ever let her know it's gone." She looks like she wants to hit me, but she doesn't.

"I'm so very angry at you right now for going into my things again."

I'm in the bathroom with Daddy. He's asked me to come in so I can watch him pee in the potty. He stands up to do it and has a long thing that he holds where the pee comes out. He asks if I want to hold it. I do and it's hard, but soft like Tommy's belly at the same time. He seems happy I'm helping him go to the bathroom.

"This is just between us," he says.

I don't tell my mother.

I become fascinated with how Tommy kills things. All over the back patio are the heads or the tails of the chameleons he leaves behind. He's selective, not eating the whole animal, only one half of it, and my mother must sweep up after him before we can play outside. I inspect the pieces of dead lizards in the dustpan with curiosity and satisfaction. It's as if I killed them too. One day, my mother opens the door when the Fuller Brush man stops by, and the cat runs inside between the man's legs and under his suitcase with a live chameleon in his mouth. My mother chases Tommy around and around the table in the kitchen waving a dish towel and laughing, trying to save what is going to die anyway.

My mother's parents, Nonno and Nanna, come to Texas for Thanksgiving. Nonno is my favorite. He sits in a chair on the patio and reads to me and my little sister. I am playing with a toy car at his feet, and he is reading about a toad in a little car calling out goodbye. I don't understand where the toad is going, but I like the way Nonno breathes and says the words slowly like the way adults do when we are supposed to pay attention. I don't make the clicking sound with my tongue then. The stories he tells have a beginning, a middle, and an end. They soothe me as I run my car over the rough cement, small specks gleaming in the sunlight.

Soon my father has lost his job again, and we are back in Connecticut living with his parents whom my sister has named Duck and Moo since she can't pronounce Grandma and Grandpa. Grandfather Moo swings my sister up over his head like a princess, blue cigar smoke enveloping that corner of the room after he puts her down. Grandmother Duck puts us to bed at night. She tells us to get on our "PJs," and my sister and I, laughing, make her say it over and over like a song. "PJs, PJs, PJs."

I sit on the wooden lip of the step on the back stoop, learning how to shell peas from the garden. First, you pull the fine string along the green envelope. They are all there inside, lined up against a lighter green membrane. I can pick them out quickly with my small fingers and put them in the shiny white bowl between Duck's feet. Soon there will be a whole pile of them.

Moo is a tall man with white hair. He and Daddy talk in loud voices sometimes. My mother says he owns the big factory down the road and has lots of money. Unlike us. I heard Moo tell my mother she deserves a mink coat, a car. My mother told me not to tell Daddy he said that. Later that night, she told me how Moo beat Daddy with a board when he was little.

"And your Daddy's sister, Aunt Faye, doesn't like Daddy much. They don't really talk," my mother said.

I pull another string on the pod and watch it unravel.

"Don't drop any peas before you get them to the bowl," Duck says.

A few weeks later, I'll trip off the stoop and land on my knee. It is my first big wounding and my blood drips down the slate pathway—the one that leads down to the vegetable garden at the bottom of the hill.

It is my father who decides I will go to spend the whole summer where Aunt Faye works, Hazelwild Farm Camp in Fredericksburg, Virginia. I am five years old. I'll be gone for eight weeks. My mother helps Melissa put on her shoes while she explains why.

"Daddy thinks you're too tied to my apron strings."

I ask her what "apron strings" mean.

"Missy, go sit with your Daddy in the living room, while I talk to Debbie."

She sits me on her lap facing her. "I don't think he's right, but he thinks it's important for him and me and your sister to be here altogether, just the three of us." She looks away from me, a little sad, "You'll have fun at camp. And this will make your Daddy happy."

I wonder if it is she or Daddy who is mad at me, but I don't ask. I want to get down off her lap.

"They have horses and a big pool," my mother continues. "You won't even miss us. And when you return," she says, "we'll all live in a different house, in New Jersey. You'll like that."

I sit in the back seat of the car while Daddy drives me to camp. It is just the two of us. I've never been away from home alone overnight before. I see the top of his head over the seat, the green hills of Virginia around us, the blue of the sky. I don't like driving with him because he doesn't stop often. He doesn't talk. And it's far.

The first night, we have dinner in the big hall with all the campers. I am seated at a table next to my Aunt Faye and the other adults, with my small legs dangling. I put my head down after I eat. I feel my arm under my cheek and smell my own skin from the spot where it bends by my elbow. As the voices ebb and flow around me in the cricketed night, I fall asleep. I am left behind. Daddy drives home without me.

One night, I wet the bed and stand in the hall crying as I hold the edge of the wet sheet I pulled off the mattress. I have never wet the bed before. Maybe as a baby, I did, but not as a big girl. Aunt Faye yanks off the rest of the sheets and in a wide arm motion, puts them in a bundle and tucks me in again after remaking the bed. I don't remember if she kisses me.

I like to feed the calves in the barn out of the big silver bucket. There is Backwards Day where everyone wears clothing the wrong way, like pajamas instead of daytime clothing and your shirt turned inside out. It's very hot and I swim in a large pool which is far away from the Big House, across a lawn. Every day, arm over arm, I swim toward the pool's end. I don't go in the deep end yet since you need to pass another test to do that, but I'm trying.

At a huge bonfire on the lawn, sparks shoot out across the sky like fireflies, and my aunt helps me stick a marshmallow from a red and blue plastic bag onto the long, sharp stick. My aunt holds it in the flame for me because I am afraid of fire. I like the marshmallow lightly brown, not black and tasting like fire, but syrupy so it runs over my fingers when I try to eat it without burning myself.

Through that summer the phone in the Big House rings and rings, and sometimes it's my mother and Daddy calling. My sister babbles her new words in the background. I can't speak, don't respond except to look at my own hands, nails bitten and smelling like chlorine, trying not to cry as I look around the Big House hallway. My aunt's encouraging horse-like face and her large, knuckled fingers hold the black receiver down to my ear as she whispers to tell them what I've been doing.

I long to say I rode the pony Western style, but I can't describe the way Peanut's nose feels, bristly in my hand trying to find carrots or the round pellets of grain that smell like summer and fields. I can't describe the night sounds I heard sleeping outside under the stars near the blackberry bushes. Camping with the older kids who don't usually talk to me, I heard dark stories about bogeymen and blood and ghosts. And I can't say, this is how to eat a marshmallow: plunge a stick through its heart and put it into the fire. Then, transformed by the slow heat around the edges, wait till it drips and tastes of smoke and the night sky.

Chapter 3 - Drawdown Warning

I haven't worn my charm bracelet for a few years. It rests in a small red bag inside my antique jewelry box. The first charm is the heart I was given by my stepfather when I was four. For later birthdays, my mother gave me the state of Virginia representing my time at camp and a silver Liberty Bell when we moved near Philadelphia. Two charms, a cat and a lucky thirteen horseshoe, hadn't been soldered on because they were given to me in my teens around the time my family fell apart. About twenty years ago, I finally attached them and decided I wanted more. My mother liked this project and together we found: a bicycle, a castle to represent college, a gorilla and a rhino for my years working at the Philadelphia Zoo, a graduate in a cap and gown for my doctorate, a wedding couple, the boot-shaped Italy where we spent our honeymoon, and the house number of the home Marc and I purchased. She added a shell for my love of the beach. Wearing it feels like carrying a tiny book of my life around my wrist.

Sometimes I'll tell my therapy clients that the goal of your life's journey is not to be burdened with steamer trunks, ancient leather suitcases, valises filled with old stuff—endings, hurts, the past, the sound of your mother yelling, and your father leaving. The goal is to sort through, choose what to take, and decide what you must have with you that's useful in dealing with your present life. We can hope it is a manageable amount, no more than a carry-on bag. Or a jangly bracelet of silver memories with a strong clasp.

I'm thinking about this metaphor as I sit in my book lined

office at home with papers spread in front of me on my desk, trying to make sense of my mother's finances. I text my sister: *Can you get me the number for the New Jersey water company and the long-term care insurance?* My mother won't give me numbers or accounts or even names of policies, so my sister and I are puzzling the details out together. My mother is only superficially cooperative with our beginning efforts to help her, and I can't figure out if it's because she's suspicious of me or really doesn't know the information.

"Sure thing," Melissa responds. "I'm sorry I can't make these calls too."

I tell her not to apologize. I need to call because the POA is in my name, but we are a team trying to figure it all out, and that part of it feels good to me since we haven't always been able to work together when it came to my mother. When my sister and I were younger, my mother stuck me with the task of parenting her, a role that, even in the present, sometimes makes it harder for us to be close.

By the eighth text exchange, she responds: *Can it wait till tomorrow? I really need to get some of Mike's college stuff done.* She's getting ready to send her youngest son off to college in a few weeks, at which point, she and my brother-in-law will be empty nesters. Her daughter, Sarah, is finishing up her undergraduate degree in Baltimore. Maddie, midway through her college career, is preparing for a semester abroad. I tell her I understand and will talk to her later.

Several weeks ago, after my mother grudgingly made us signatories on the bank accounts and said I could start paying the bills for her, we agreed she would continue to take money out of her checking account weekly for the things she needs while we get her situation sorted out. I set up online banking and start going through the last year to see what she's paying or not, particularly so we can get her a working telephone. It's frustrating and time consuming because everything I try to do involves multiple phone calls. Nobody will tell me anything until the POA is notarized and faxed to them and that takes a few days or a week. Between clients at work, I spend hours making phone calls, trying to figure out her financial situation and getting my name placed on all the accounts.

There's one mystery check for a municipal violation in Haddonfield. I joke with my sister, "Maybe she was in a bar fight."

I have some fun imagining my mother fighting with me in a bar: She's pulling the cocktail skewer from her martini olive and trying to poke me in the eye.

"Listen," she threatens, "I don't want you to come near me," as she gulps the last dregs of her clear drink and heads for the door, still tasting remnants of gin-soaked olive.

Melissa laughs.

But the next day I find out she had been pulled over for driving without a license or inspection sticker. I go back again to look at her old statements. There are no car insurance payments either. The last time the phone was paid was April and it's late August.

"After seeing the outside of the house and dealing with her bill issues," I tell my sister, "We really need to have her living someplace else by the winter."

"Dream on," she retorts with a grim chuckle.

Next are the missing utility payments. I call the sewer company about the sewer taxes first. My mother owes for two quarters—$179.67 plus interest. I move on to what I think will be a quick call to the water company. It's a thirty minute wait time, I'm told, but bravo for them when I reach a representative in twenty minutes.

"Hold on," says the account rep, "I'm looking it up and the

address is here, but there's been no account holder for so long there's no name or phone number attached to it."

My breathing stops. "Wait," I say. "Does that mean there's no water at the house?"

"I guess so," she responds a little testily.

"Listen, I'm not trying to be difficult here, but that's my mother's house and she's lived there for more than forty years. Are you sure that means there's no water there?" I'm trying to stay calm—okay, maybe there's something wrong with their records or maybe it's the wrong address. After another wait, a similar conversation with the rep's supervisor ensues. It's not a mistake.

At the end of it, I'm crying hard enough that I can't give her the information needed to get the water turned on. "I'll call you back," I choke out as I disconnect her.

What is she doing about drinking water? This is why her infected toes didn't get better, why she smells musty even when wearing the new outfits she always seems to be purchasing. Maybe she's cleaning her clothes someplace else? Who *is* this person? My mother used to wash all her nurse uniforms every day and hang them up in tidy rows in the laundry room. She left for work in white stockings and a crisp white dress. She'd starch her nursing caps and leave them flat on the top of the washer to dry so they'd be stiff and ready to fold.

Panicked and still tearful, I leave a voicemail message for my sister.

"Call me as soon as you get this. There's no water at the house. She has no water!" Just to make sure she gets the point, I text her the same message, only with more exclamations and distressed emoji faces.

There's nothing else to do but keep pressing on. I imagine

wadding up the stress I'm feeling, along with my mother, and stuffing them both into a giant garbage bag. It's not that I actually want my mother dead, I just don't want to be dealing with what is turning out to be an even bigger mess than I expected. I have my own things to do—client session notes to write, dinner to make, plans with friends to coordinate. What else don't we know about?

I dial the number to the electric company to find out if her small payment to them last month kept the power on. They tell me she owes more money, which I pay. *Good, at least the electricity should be on in the house.*

After that, I spend three hours just with Verizon, trying to get her landline phone turned on. Twelve people, a fax, and an email later, I still don't have it resolved, but they tell me I'm apparently getting closer. There is some confusion about whether the Verizon service person needs to get inside the house to reconnect the line—and I know it's going to be a big problem convincing my mother to agree to that. At this point in the conversation, I'm yelling at the representative that the phone was off and turned on before and nobody was inside the house, why can't they just do it again? They tell me to call another number and I slam down the phone.

Melissa finally calls me back after my near-hysterical messages to her about the water situation.

"How do you think she's been going to the bathroom there?" she asks.

"I've got nothing."

We are both quiet for a minute.

Melissa texts Kathy, our "little sister" neighbor. In the past, when we couldn't reach my mother, my sister would contact Kathy who would then leave a note on the front door, or just let my sister know the car had been coming and going so we'd know my mother was okay. Melissa asks her to double check if there are lights on in the house at night. Kathy tells her she's seen lights on only downstairs, never upstairs. She asks my sister if we want her to go look in the front window behind the bushes and take a picture for us of the living room. Melissa and I agree it's a good idea, although we are both worried one of the other neighbors will tell our mother about it. Also, having seen the jungle landscape of my mother's yard, I feel like we are sending Kathy on a suicide mission through thorns and poison ivy. When you are paranoid like my mother, you have enough accurate perceptions about reality to understand what is happening, but you might have distorted insight about the reasons for it. My mother was worried that we were spying on her. Now we've got the neighbors creeping around looking in her windows. At our urging, no less. My sister and I are a little giddy at our boldness.

  Kathy sneaks over when my mother isn't home and manages to push her way through the dense shrubbery and take a picture. She texts it to both of us and I open it at the car dealership while I'm waiting for my car to be serviced. My sister texts me emojis of horrified facial expressions.

  It's a grainy photo taken through the dirty window screen. It feels like the déjà vu I've always experienced, which my mother taught us to believe in. I've already seen this image. The picture reminds me of that piece of art by Marcel Duchamp at The Philadelphia Museum of Art, where you peer through a hole in a fence and see a naked woman splayed on the ground, forbidden and secret. I can't get oriented to what I'm seeing, turning my phone in different directions. Even later when I blow it up on my computer, it doesn't make sense because there are just masses of indistinguishable things blurred by the filthy window. I understand why my mother told me she is no longer using her front door.

Did my sister and I enable this situation? I rationalize that we were adults managing our own day-to-day responsibilities. My psychological distance from my mother allowed me to preserve a relationship with her. It wasn't a close one, but if she kept her exterior together, like the house, it could pass as somewhat normal.

What the hell are we going to do now?

My sister and I decide we will have dinner on Labor Day weekend with my mother and our husbands at my sister's home in Medford, New Jersey, which is about twenty minutes from my mother's house. Afterwards, we will send the men off somewhere and will sit my mother down and talk to her gently. I've written out a page long list of things that I need (account numbers, information about certain policies, and answers about car and homeowner's insurance). Most importantly, we need to know why the water was turned off. Is there a leak? Something that happened inside the house that we need to address? The house is her only real financial asset, and if we are going to help her, we need it to be in good shape for sale or else fixed up so that she can live there with support.

I've also written out a proposal. Marc, who has plumbing experience from his former business rehabbing houses, will go into the house to assess the water situation. We think my mother may be more amenable to one of the husbands doing this rather than us. She often treats our husbands deferentially, showing more respect for them than she does for Melissa and me.

On my way out of my house to get in the car for the fifty minute drive from Havertown, Pennsylvania to my sister's, I walk into a giant spider web that has somehow gotten strung from the bush by the driveway to the car. I'm squirming like a fly trying to unstick my arms. And out of the corner of my eye, to my right and above my head, I see the spider's black outline against the light. She looks the size of a half dollar and she's moving her legs, irritated I've undone her work.

When we pull up to Melissa's house, I look for my mother's car. She always parks a house or two away from my sister's driveway, so Marc and I walk a little way up the wooded street where they live to find it. We peer in the window at the inspection sticker. The green 2000 Camry sags from the weight of what it contains. It is filled to the windows with papers, books, and bags. The driver's seat is like a deep cockpit surrounded by these objects and is the only clear space inside the car. The sticker is dated June 2018, two years from today. I breathe a small sigh of relief that at least we won't have to confront my mother about this issue.

We sit around the large kitchen table and eat grilled fish and salad, my sister and I with large glasses of wine. My niece, Sarah, has stopped by, so there's talk about her job and grad school for her doctorate in psychology and the weather and what everybody has been up to over the holiday weekend. After we've had dessert and cleaned up, with the husbands and Sarah out of the house, Melissa and I sit my mother back down at the kitchen table to discuss our plan.

"Mom," I start, "I really think it's time you think about housing options. You can't afford to stay in Cherry Hill with the taxes." I've discovered the taxes haven't been paid for the year, but I don't mention that part. "I know you want to be independent," I continue, "but since you were in the hospital in January and have been having a little trouble keeping track of the bills, we need to maybe talk about it."

"If this POA is too much for you and is making your anxiety worse," she snaps, facing me with her arms crossed, "then I'll find somebody else to do it."

My sister, who's sitting next to her, rolls her eyes.

"I'm not anxious, Mom. I'm just trying to straighten things out a bit and need your help."

She shifts in her chair, eyes darting around the room as if she's looking for an escape, and sighs.

Melissa chimes in, "Maybe we could find a nice senior apartment where you wouldn't have to deal with all the yard work. Maybe it could be close to Ponzio's and the places you like to go."

"But in order to do that, we really need to figure out the money," I say before my mother can respond. "I could use some help getting together some of the paperwork for these different accounts."

Even though I seem totally neutral and nonreactive, I can feel the sweat start trickling down the back of my neck. "I'm assuming you can pull together some of that for me as I'm sorting things out?"

I turn to my sister who is trying to remain expressionless and ask, "Is it hot in here or what?"

"It is hot in here," my mother agrees. She stands up with her glass to go over to the sink to get more water.

If my mother gets paranoid about things now, it's going to be impossible to help her. I don't know what we'll do. *So yes, Mom, you're right. I am anxious.*

My mother sits back down, a little red in the face. "You don't need to lecture me, Deborah. I brought some of the information and it's in the car."

Her behavior doesn't stem from a lack of understanding. She

stops making eye contact and starts to stand up. It's obvious to me that she's emotionally flooded by her shame and embarrassment.

She returns from her car with a pretty folder decorated with flowers that contains all her tax papers in it for this year, 2016 (the 2015 taxes aren't finished either it seems). She sits down and watches as my sister pours herself more wine after topping off mine.

"Mom, we know about the water issue and that it's been off. I need to know if there's anything that happened that could damage the house." I'm really sweating, despite the air conditioning. "The house is your only real asset."

Her eyes widen, and she colors more. She looks away from me and doesn't respond. Melissa and I are holding our collective breath.

"There's a leak under the tub or the toilet that went down to the kitchen," she says.

"It's okay, I think Marc needs to go in and look," I say. "Wouldn't you rather have somebody who knows you come and check it out instead of a stranger?" I take a sip of wine before I go on. "He'll have to turn off the water main in the house before the water company comes tomorrow to turn on the water to make sure there won't be a flood."

"Don't have the water company come, put them off," she says, her voice rising so she's almost yelling at us. "Put them off, please. And I don't know where the water main is in the house."

I urge her a little more to get Marc in there, but that's the limit, his coming into the house. She's at least listening and trying to cooperate. I back off then and tell her I'll wait to have the water turned on again until we can figure out the water main.

"Let's you and I have breakfast Friday at Ponzio's," my mother says to me, trying to placate me.

"Okay, we can continue to figure out some of this then," I say. "I know it's a lot to think about all at once." Melissa smiles at my mother in a reassuring way.

My mother makes her escape soon after, when our husbands return to the house, hugging them goodbye and yawning, saying she's "exhausted."

When I get home at 11:30 p.m., I call American Water's emergency line and cancel for the next day. I will need to start all over on the account to get it scheduled again. The very nice woman I'm talking to reassures me the account is still in the system, so it'll be easier. I start laughing then. Nothing about dealing with my mother has ever been easy. Why should this be different?

I hang up and my eyes fall on a framed photo—my mother, sister, and I stand in front of the Christmas tree at my sister's house with our arms around each other. We are wearing matching, brightly colored Norwegian sweaters that my mother brought back from her trip to the fjords. Marc took the picture because I found it so hilarious that we were dressed identically, my sister and me hamming it up in another photo he took by sticking our legs out like showgirls. My mother wanted us to have a souvenir of her trip. I kept the sweater, although I don't wear it. And I keep the photographs because we look happy.

Was she happier then? She made that trip after my grandmother died, when she had money and freedom. During the years before that, her boyfriend had taken her to the Bahamas, Mexico, and Jamaica. She visited Hong Kong and then China with her friend, Mrs. Pan. Norway was the archeology cruise, and she also visited Scotland and Denmark. She brought back gifts every time. Things like artwork, silk robes, the sweaters, or jade carvings in jewelry boxes. She loved showing her vacation photos.

I start to think then about what's inside the house that means something to me, items that I wouldn't want to lose or have disappear. There are several albums of photographs, the only ones of my sister and me as children, with my mother's carefully captioned descriptions. There is my childhood furniture. The antique carved cherry four-poster bed that my grandparents found propping up a Model T and brought home to be my mother's bed when she was little. The cherry bureau that went with it. The black cabinet with frog tiles on the front that my parents used as a liquor cabinet. The frogs reminded me of *The Wind in the Willows*, a favorite book. There were books from my childhood that had been passed down from my grandmother to my mother, and then to me. There's artwork like the Tony Auth cartoon about God and evolution that hung over the sofa, which my mother had promised I could have when I had my own home. There's an antique clock from my grandmother's house. An old oil painting in its original gold frame that came from my maternal great-grandmother's house and is rumored to have been painted by her. The landscape is that of the yard behind her Victorian house near Cooperstown, New York. My mother's gold charm bracelet. The antique rings from my grandmother like the one with the rubies and the pearl in the center that looks like a flower. There's a family photo of my maternal grandmother and her siblings with a goat that hung in our rec room.

I haven't seen anything from the house for so long that these objects seem shrouded in mystery. Do they really exist, or are they only in my imagination? But as I've been working on this plan to help my mother, these things are suddenly becoming clearer. They tether themselves to the stories I know so well, giving them weight as I find myself landing into new understanding about my family.

Chapter 4 - What We Hold On To

Clouds scatter across the roofs in Cherry Hill, and the big fluffy puffs move fast toward Philadelphia in the late spring breeze. I'm six years old and we've just moved to the Woodstock Drive house. In the front yard, my mother kneels next to the azalea bushes with a peanut butter jar in her hand. She is catching the slow, black wasps as they come up from a hidden place in the ground. I am crouched on my heels, a bit away from her, a little afraid of what she's catching. She wants to show my sister and me how animals make their homes. She finds birds' nests of woven weeds and grasses. She points out the wasp nest under the eaves of the long porch outside my bedroom. She pulls down a white cocoon from the 'V' in the slender branches of the pussy willow and tells us about the caterpillar liquifying itself into a butterfly. I think my mother knows many things.

"I'm not dressing up like those other Cherry Hill women to go to the grocery store," she says, looking a little mad. She's speaking to me, but more to herself, which is something she does that's a little odd. She bends over to pick up the pruning shears and clips some of the ivy twirling up the front lights by the walkway. "You don't need to put on lipstick to go to the store."

One afternoon, when I come home from Stafford Elementary School, she is sitting on the chaise lounge in the backyard with a book and talking to a mockingbird, or so she says. Different bird calls rise in her throat as if she had soft rumpled feathers. My mother loves this house we live in. She isn't working as a nurse and is, instead, fixing everything up. It was built for the developer of the neighborhood. It's the nicest house, and inside it has a lot of extra closets and the biggest yard we ever had, with woods in the back, and a creek.

"We are never moving again," she tells me, firmly, as she surveys Daddy walking up the sidewalk between the flowers she's already planted.

I have my own room here. I sleep in my mother's childhood antique, four-poster bed under the framed poster of the tapestry of the Unicorn in Captivity. It depicts a small horse with a horn in a pen. My mother had seen the image at the Cloisters in New York City. She wanted me to have it because I like unicorns, especially one in *The Little White Horse*, my favorite book. Early in the morning, I read it, along with the Narnia books stacked in a giant pile on my bedside table. It is the most comforting feeling of all, knowing you have lots of books to hold like anchors.

Some mornings when I don't have school, instead of reading, I get up right when the sun comes up and long before everybody else does. My mother sleeps with Daddy in the bedroom next to my own and she tells me never to come in there in the morning without knocking, so I tiptoe past their door. I like the aloneness when it's bright outside. It reminds me of when I was all alone at Hazelwild Farm Camp, but I don't mind the feeling here. I go to the kitchen. I take a spoon from the drawer and climb up on the kitchen table to eat a spoonful of white sugar, twice. I love it melting down my throat. I open the back door and look for Tommy, all stripes, and green eyes. He sleeps with me sometimes, so then I let us out together. The day glimmers and turns green, and the dew on the grass makes glinting sparks of light. I go outside in my pajamas. It's warm, early summer, and the grass is cold and wet on my feet. The cat appears, and I follow him. We walk past the willow tree, passing under its long branches with the slender silvery leaves. We walk the edge of the hill that leads down into the woods. There is a creek further down and then a dump back over the other side. We stay on the periphery of the lawn, smelling wet earth and the blue hydrangea bush, everything moist and giving off breath in the sun. Tommy rubs my legs, purring and purring, and the sun warms my back like those flowers. I want to open and be consumed by the sky, the air, the purring cat, the long day filled with nothing to worry about. We go to the side of the yard where the roses climb the trellis off the wide porch. Then past the bushes to the steps. On the other side, a huge bay window. From the porch, I can look into my own room, see the four-poster bed with the quilt turned back, and the indentation of where my body lay. There's the washstand with the white pitcher, the little old school desk, the bureau with the three drawers and my penny collection inside. I am the one who is awake in this green world, and I feel, although I don't name it then, joy—a brightness and freedom about what the day might hold. I know my mother will wake up and pour my favorite Cap'n Crunch cereal in a bowl for breakfast. Maybe she will take my sister and me to the library where I can get more books like *The Princess and the Goblin* or *The Secret Garden*. We might even go to that museum in Philadelphia where there is a giant heart you can walk through. The heartbeat is like a watery drum, beating and beating inside my ears, so I can barely hear anything else, but I'm not scared.

In our sunken living room, we keep a terrarium with plastic palm trees in it for turtles, but they have a habit of climbing out, losing themselves slowly under chairs and along the hardwood floors, trailing dust bunnies and bits of cat hair. There aren't many hiding places in this house, and it's clear the turtles can't really escape. I stand near the terrarium and watch my mother. She climbs on a stepstool and reaches up to the top shelf of the hall closet. She pulls out a box and opens it. It's a gun. She shows it to me and tells me that it's Daddy's and that she is putting the bullets for it someplace else in the house, and I don't need to know where they are.

"If anything bad ever happens when we are fighting," she says, "take your sister and run to the neighbor's."

It's close to bedtime, early evening. I'm wearing baby doll pajamas, a sleeveless top with a ruffle on the panties. I wear them with my underwear. Daddy is screaming at me to get in my bed. I don't want to because it's still light outside. Crying, I push past him out of my room, running out of the house because I know my mother is outside sitting on the next-door neighbor's porch. Daddy follows me out the front door and stands on our front porch. He's only wearing his bathrobe which has fallen open to his nakedness underneath which I don't like, and he's still yelling at me. My mother comes right over from the neighbor's, walks me back inside, and puts me in my bed. I listen to make sure she doesn't leave again.

My doll Lisa lives under the bed in the long box she came in, with blankets and a little pillow I made for her. Still, there is a lot of dark space under there where something else might live. I worked out a deal with whatever it is under there. I go to bed and turn toward the wall with the windows. This way the thing can escape through the cracked door into the dimly lit hall without me seeing it. If I face the door, then it can't get out and it hides in the wide inky darkness holding me. Sometimes I have nightmares and yell for my mother. Sometimes she comes and sometimes it's Daddy in his underwear. I don't like it when Daddy comes because it scares me more.

In the daytime, sometimes I am the scary thing. I wait for Missy, pressed up against the right side of her doorway. When she opens it all the way and comes out, I holler, "Boo" and she screams. You'd think she'd know to look, but I guess when you are four you don't always remember. Once I took her Raggedy Ann.

"Annie, Annie," she was gasping with tears rolling down her face.

I felt bad then and I gave it back, but first I gave it an extra tug on the striped leg, so she'd remember who was bigger. Maybe I am trying to teach my sister how it feels to know there is something waiting outside your room.

My second grade school project is to make a map of something. My mother has an idea. In *National Geographic*, they have published the first maps of the ocean floor. It is 1967, and science can see almost everything. Soon we will see the moon up close. Now we are traveling underwater. My mother gets a big box, maybe three feet by three feet, and puts the map on the bottom of it. We take blue clay and begin to shape it to look like the picture on the map. Pressing down, we make deep indentations and then pile up mounds around the "valleys." It's a very big project and cold in the basement, but my mother is really into this, and I don't want to disappoint her. Night after night, we are making a whole world together. And as we do, my mother talks about my "real" father and how someday she hopes that I can meet him because I would like him a lot.

"We will go find him together," she says. He worked with interior decorators and had a "good eye and is artistic like you." She tells me they lived in an apartment in an old house and discovered a bat living there that they chased outside. His sister, she tells me, lives on a lake with her family north of Albany, New York and I went there when I was very little, so I don't remember.

She pauses, "What I'm telling you about your real father, Malcolm, is something that would upset Daddy." Then she pauses and looks at me sadly and says, "We were so young when Malcolm and I got married," and looks down at the clay map, frowning about how much work still must be done on it.

We sculpt for quite a few days. It will look different than anyone else's project and I will feel embarrassed. I am already different than anyone else because I have a secret father. I feel the loneliness of that ocean, its gray empty depths, and the complicated land masses that exist far under.

There is a moment when I am sculpting a mound when she says, "No, not like that," and "I'll do that part," and I shrink back because she knows the right way, and, after all, it's her idea—although my name will be on it.

What did I learn from that project? Names of ocean ranges, elevations, the depths you can't see through the murky waters. My mother's fascination with what's beneath the surface and how she wanted me to understand something bigger than the broken shells, the starfish, and the ugly sea creatures of my imagination. That she needed a map for herself to know what to do and that I would come to understand the otherworldly terrain she was creating.

Nanna and Nonno are coming to visit, driving down from Gloversville, New York to stay for a week. My mother is cleaning everywhere, muttering to herself as she pushes the vacuum noisily from room to room.

"Go clean your room, too," she demands. "It can never be tidy enough for her." Her mouth is tight, and she yanks the cord from the vacuum to plug it into the outlet in the next bedroom.

A few months ago, my mother yelled at me about cleaning up. Her face twisted as she grabbed my toys and books and clothes and threw them all around my bedroom making it messier.

"It's disgusting," she screamed and slammed the door so hard that my picture of the Unicorn in Captivity shook in its frame and almost fell. "Don't come out of there till it's finished," she yelled.

My mother isn't angry now, but she's putting all the ironing she hasn't done into big bags, so Nanna doesn't see it. She lugs these garbage bags into the back basement and pushes them against the walls of the dark fruit cellar. Nanna irons everything when we stay with her, even our underwear. My mother hates to iron.

"She'll never find out about this," my mother says, laughing a little and shoves her bangs from her sweaty forehead. "It'll be our little secret." I'm becoming used to my family's way of making these pacts.

But when I come home from school, Nanna has the ironing board out in the middle of the basement where we play with our toys and dolls. She carefully presses everything in the big bags my mother thought she hid.

"Your mother never keeps up with things," Nanna says.

My mother rolls her eyes when I tell her later.

"Your grandmother probably did that white glove test on the mantle just to make sure I remembered to clean there." Dusting is my task ever since I wrote "dust me" with my finger on the table next to the chair in the master bedroom where we often watch television. My mother didn't think it was funny.

"You're like your grandmother," she smirked, "since you have so much to say about it, you can do it."

My mother is very proud of the new dining room table in the center of the house. It's Danish, I am told, and my mother polishes the beautiful surface regularly. We aren't allowed to use it except for special occasions such as when my grandparents visit. Nanna and I play Scrabble here. She teaches me this: words have points—you can win with them. You can play off another's words and make something. I learn to beat her, but it takes a few years. She is too focused on the words, not on the winning or the score. I see connections between words, how things can run alongside each other but not collide.

I am sitting at the table, writing something, on that paper with the blue lines—grainy paper with dashes and lines, like a code, I squeeze my letters between. *C-A-T,* I write, and Tommy and I are walking again in the backyard under the willow tree and down into the woods. So early in the morning, there is no sound but his purr, orange fur running past my fingers. He walks with me, an escort into the world of black bark and leaves and water. I write *W-A-L-K* and see how the barbed points of the W keep us out like a fence, like the boundaries on the property. I sit at the dining room table and practice this, the words onto the page, the page onto the world.

When I lift the blue-lined paper the words stay on the table. They mar the smooth surface like the ring a stone leaves when it drops into a lake. In the bright light the words glimmer. My mother yells at me for doing this, leaving my trace, ruining the glossy surface.

At night, the low voices of my parents are getting louder like sharp pieces of glass cutting air. I have nightmares about fire, everything engulfed in white heat. I am afraid when my parents go out for dinner that they won't come back. Daddy is angry all the time, I can tell from the way he snaps drawers shut with a mean look on his face. He tells me to be quiet while he watches the football game. In the evening, I imagine smoke hovering over the picture frame of Wyeth's painting, *Christina's World,* hanging over the living room fireplace. My mother told me the girl in the picture has useless legs from an illness. She tries so hard to struggle up the hill toward the faraway house.

Sometimes my sister and I wrestle like small animals, rolling and clawing until one of us is mildly hurt and weeping. My mother was an only child and doesn't understand how it is to be connected through skin and bone like this. She yanks me over to my bedroom and says something about finding something constructive to do until we can play together again. When we do, I wear a brown fringed wool scarf on my head, so I am a princess with long hair. I make my sister play the queen. She is mean to me and orders me around.

My mother says to my "aunt" (who is really her best friend) on the phone in the kitchen, "I can't take all the stress with him and the girls."

My sister and I fight over everything, how I breathe, who gets to play with the troll house, even the wishbone from chicken. We have my mother wash it, cleaning meat from the white, smooth remains until only some beige strands and gristle are left. She holds it by the flat curved top and scrubs it under the faucet. But we must wait for it to dry, to sit on the windowsill in the next morning's light while we ache to split it. And then, perhaps a few nights later, my mother brings it down for us. I didn't think then that we were fighting about sides, about our parents. We'd just wrap our small fingers, mine with the nails bitten, and pull. Pull as if it was the most important thing for one of us to get the bigger part.

Daddy and I are having a pizza eating contest to see who can eat more. I eat four pieces, feeling a little sick, and nobody stops me. He still wins. He high-fives me and then asks me to scratch his back while we watch television in the master bedroom. I don't like touching him since that time in the bathroom, but I don't think about what I feel and do it anyway.

My sister finds some wires from where the phone people were working in the street. She plays with them until Daddy asks her where she found them. My mother comes into my room later.

"He thinks I'm bugging the house," she says. "Don't bring things in like this, ok?"

Daddy is not working, but my mother says she won't move again, that she likes it here and we are staying. I overhear her talking on the phone. There is a question about his hitting a boss. She says something about Valium and how she is hiding it. Some nights we have a babysitter from up the street, so they can go see a doctor together. My mother is sleeping in Missy's room most of the time because my sister has trouble breathing from her allergies, and she says she doesn't want to wake Daddy up. One night he comes home and there is throw up on his shirt. He tells us he feels terrible. I want to go help him.

My mother rolls her eyes and says, "Don't feel bad for him. He was drinking while taking the medicine he needs." My father slams the door to the master bedroom. "He's sick in the head," my mother explains, "and the doctor we see told me we can't do anything about that."

For weeks, he lies in the bed in a big mountain of sheets and doesn't get up in the morning or even after my sister and I come home from school. He has a golf club next to him, and sometimes he smacks it on the bed. Sometimes he opens his eyes when I scurry past him to go to the master bathroom, and I see his hand under the sheets moving back and forth faster and faster between his legs before I get out of the room.

Before Daddy leaves town for three weeks on a business trip for his new job, he buys several bags of hotdogs and buns and no other food for us. My mother cries after he leaves because she doesn't have any money for anything else. After she calms down, she picks up the phone and calls all her friends. She sells the groceries that Daddy bought so we have some cash and can get what we need.

"See," she says, "We'll make it work out."

My mother takes me to see a priest named Father Burke when I'm in third grade. She says it will be good for me to have "a man to talk to, to trust." We aren't Catholic. We used to go to the United Church of Christ in Cherry Hill, where I memorized all the names of the books of the Bible and won a prize. Then Daddy and the minister weren't friends anymore, so we stopped going. My mother said it was because he was always trying to "impress people and be a big deal." Someone in the neighborhood told my mother about Father Burke and that it was free to go see him.

Father Burke wears a green cardigan over his black suit. I like his sing-song Irish accent when he speaks. I press my whole body against the heavy church door to open it and look for him down a dark hallway. At the end, a yellow-lit office, some crayons, big paper. I color corner suns with long spikes onto the white paper. I'd like to close my eyes, but Father asks me gently what I'd like to tell him about myself. I will tell him a story about an alien. I wave a waxy purple crayon as I stop to think. The alien has lots of eyes, all black, all over him. But he's lonely and far from home. His spaceship has left him behind. I stop. Father begins helping me write the story. He makes lines underneath the picture, so I can shape the letters to fit right. It is my first experience of someone just listening to me. I'm scared of him but at the same time, I love him. One of the last times we meet, it's early spring, and I'm talking so little he takes me outside to play. It's still winter, I have my coat on, and I am kicking my brown loafer off, high into the air like a black shadow across the sky. Then, hopping around to get it. He plays, too; the Father, he kicks his shoe off, and we are laughing and laughing in the cold till my mother drives up and takes me home.

I get a cello soon after this. I'm nine and it's a year earlier than my class is supposed to be allowed to have one, but my mother asked if I could play something since my friends were all older and already had instruments. I got what instrument was left. Tuesdays are lesson days, and my mother drives me to school. Our brown house sits at the bottom of the oval of Woodstock Drive and is the farthest house from the red brick Stafford Elementary. Besides, the cello is too heavy and bumps my hip with its sharp womanly bones dressed in a brown cloth sack as if trying to hide itself, its music.

My mother forgets to come one day to pick me up. It's early spring, and the ground is very wet and cold from the dirty snow that had finally melted two days before. I rest the point of the cello stand in the mud trying not to get the cover dirty and look up and down the street for the yellow Volkswagen hatchback. An hour passes. I'm shivering, and two of my friends have walked by with their small instruments while I wait with my big, ungainly one.

Where is my mother? A woman comes out of the house on the corner, "Are you all right, dear?"

I don't tell people anything, especially about being all right or not, which is relative in my family anyway. I lean against my silent friend. "My mother will be here soon," I say.

When my mother finally arrives, Ken is in the car with her. He has a beard and fixes instruments and has been coming to our house sometimes. We get home, and I go in my bedroom. My sister stays outside on the front porch with one of her friends playing some little kid game. I see her from my bedroom window, which overlooks the porch with the climbing rose trellis on the end. My mother is pleased the roses have conformed, have lived up to her pruning and shaping and have, in fact, blossomed. She nags me to practice my scales for a half hour every day and reminds me all the time that I wanted to play an instrument. She hopes I will bloom into a real cello player, since my teacher has told her I have a talent for music. It is quiet in the living room where my mother and Ken are, and I wonder what they are doing. Daddy is away on another business trip, but this is better, I think.

When Daddy is home on some weekends, my mother says, "If you hear him talking on the phone at night, tell me what he says." She knows I can hear his voice from my bedroom. She doesn't sleep with him anymore, instead she goes to bed in the attic guest room. I pretend to be a spy like Emma Peel in *The Avengers*, one of my favorite shows, and lean my head quietly against the wall to listen. I am on my mother's side.

I am sitting at the long brown wooden kitchen table with my feet tucked under the rungs of the chair. My sister is eating next to me. She started out making faces over her juice glass, but soon we are only eating and looking at our food as the argument between my mother and Daddy in the dining room becomes louder. I taste the hamburger in the back of my throat, and my stomach clenches.

Then the sounds of thudding footsteps, something hitting flesh and screaming. My mother yelling, "Get out. Get out!"

My sister starts sobbing then, with her nose running and blue eyes as big as our dinner plates. I yank her arm, pulling her up from the chair, through the back door and down the four cement steps to the driveway.

We run across the street to my best friend Debbie E.'s door, but there's no answer. Maybe I haven't knocked hard enough; the lights are on.

My sister is asking for my mother. "Where's Mommy? I want to go back and get Mommy."

I drag her across Debbie E.'s lawn to the Penente's house, home of Paulie, two years older, who once showed me how to rip the light from a firefly's body. My feet are wet from the early evening damp. I've forgotten my shoes. Mrs. Penente pulls open the door. She's a big woman, to us at least, and her house smells like onions, but they have already finished eating. I ask her to call the police, that something has happened, and I start to cry. I ask to use her bathroom as she picks up the phone. I lock the bathroom door. It's the same house as my own, only turned around on the other side of the street. And Mrs. Penente has lots of fluffy blue rugs and towels and sweet soap. I don't go to the toilet, although I feel sick and sweaty. I pick up the grass I've tracked in from the floor.

Rising on my tiptoes, I peer out the bathroom window down the street toward my house. The police car lights are flashing round and round and my eyes hurt. I am afraid my mother is dead. What if he has killed her? What if I have no mother anymore? Sometimes our babysitter takes us to her Baptist church where they ask if my sister and I have been saved. I listen for God, maybe he can save us. God is bigger than Daddy, as big as the whole world they say. Then I feel calmer, and Mrs. Penente is outside the bathroom door telling me it's all right and my mother will be here soon. My sister is banging on the door calling my name. I come out in my bare feet and shame at Mrs. Penente's stare. Everyone sees what's happening in our family now.

Later that night, my mother gives us each a little piece of Daddy's white Valium pill to help us sleep. She takes one too. The feeling, as we ride in the back of the car to her best friend's house, is like diving under the ocean. I'm falling deeper and deeper until I fly between the blue underwater mountains, the ones my mother and I have made. I drift there. *Where is my bedroom? My backyard?* My hands open, and there's nothing but water and this strange sleep to hold on to. My mother would like for us to forget it all, but I have helped her make the map. I keep what I know.

Chapter 5 - Going In

I'm running late Friday morning to meet my mother for our planned breakfast at Ponzio's to discuss her financial issues. Weaving in and out of traffic on the Schuylkill Expressway on my way to Cherry Hill, the heat is already making the river shimmer under the early morning sky. I'm preoccupied with everything I need to get done today, running down my mental checklist of errands. Marc and I are leaving Sunday for our annual ten days of vacation in Cape Cod. My reverie is interrupted by a call from my mother.

Good thing, I think, *that I finally got her phone hooked up.*

"I'm not sure I can meet you this morning," she says. "I had a little…" She coughs for a minute and then rasps, "car accident yesterday."

"Oh my god," I say, "are you all right?"

"I'm fine. It's not a big deal," she tells me, although when I gently push her, she says her chest is probably a little bruised. "I don't really get what happened," she says. "Maybe I ran the red light. I was heading up Brace Road and suddenly there was another car coming down Kresson."

"Are the other people injured?" I get off at the Ben Franklin Bridge exit trying to pay attention to traffic and subdue my own rising panic.

She coughs again, and I hear newspapers rustling as she shifts in her recliner. "The lady was older than me. She's eighty-four and I think she hurt her hand. I feel terrible for her."

She adds that her car is in the driveway. She drove it around after the accident for "errands." "But it's probably not safe for me to drive anywhere," she admits. "And I'm worried I'll get a ticket if I drive it over to meet you this morning," She pauses, as if debating whether to share something with me, "Well, I did get a ticket for the accident yesterday."

"What for?" I ask.

"I'm not sure. Maybe careless driving or something?" She adds, "I'm worried about the lady's injury."

What is she going to do without a car? How will she drive to a bathroom or get food?

"Mom, please get dressed. I'll be there in twenty minutes and will pick you up to go to Ponzio's to use the bathroom and get breakfast." I mention the bathroom deliberately, so she realizes I'm thinking about the water situation.

She meets me outside the house, where she is talking to her next-door neighbors, Jim and Sandy, who wave at me from the other side of the yard. We've never been formally introduced because they moved in after I stopped going to the house, but I've heard they've helped her out many times with things like snow shoveling.

I wave back from the car as I'm texting my sister, *I'm aware you are busy, but I'm at Mom's house because she had a car accident yesterday and the car is not drivable. She can't stay there. Wtf. Wtf. Wtf. She's probably going to have to stay with you till we get situated.*

Melissa texts back that she can't take her tonight and she'll call after she's done teaching.

As my mother walks over, I get out for a minute so I can look at the front end of her car and take a few pictures. She tries to wave me off, but I pretend I don't see her. I've left the passenger side door open, so she can get in. The front of her Toyota is totally smashed.

She bends gingerly with a sharp intake of breath to climb into the front seat of my car. She smells bad.

"I think it can be fixed," she says to me.

I don't respond immediately as I pull onto the road. "I'm not sure, Mom. We'll have to see what the insurance says about it. It looks pretty wrecked."

I'm glad when we arrive at the diner that she wants to sit at the counter area so fewer people will smell her, and I don't have to sit across from her and see her face when we talk about what happens next.

We sit down, and my mother reaches over and just takes part of the newspaper from a woman who is sitting next to us. She doesn't say hi or ask her permission. The woman abandons her seat, clutching the rest of her paper, a few minutes later. My mother impatiently says she "wants June" to the first waitress who comes to pour our coffee. June, surly and slow, walks over as my mother motions to her and orders "the usual."

I'm suddenly nauseated from the heat, my mother's scent, and general dishevelment. *What now?* I sip the watery coffee. *How did we even get into this situation?* Our avoidance about what has been happening, and our desire to preserve her autonomy has exploded into a full-blown crisis.

My mother gets up to go to the bathroom without saying anything. She looks exhausted. Her clothing is rumpled and her hair greasy, sticking up where she's slept on it. When she comes back, she spends the few minutes we are waiting for our food ignoring me and reading the front page of the paper.

Over my plain bagel and her eggs, I start to formulate an idea.

"I can drop you back home to pack a few things and call the insurance company, but you can't stay in the house with no food, no water, and no car to get around." I figure I'll run some errands while she's doing this and then go back to the house and pick her up. After seeing the dangling headlight and destroyed hood, I think the ancient car is going to be a total loss.

"Or maybe better," I persist, "I can call the insurance for you later and we'll just head back to my house, and you can run errands with me."

She refuses to make eye contact.

"I think you should come stay at our house tonight, and then we'll talk to Melissa and figure out what to do."

She sighs and doesn't say anything either way. It dawns on me then that this could be the opportunity to get inside the house and deal with the water problem. The thought of doing this makes me so anxious; the bagel feels stuck in my throat. I swallow more coffee, thinking about the piles of solidified newspapers and her grimy back door.

I call the car insurance company when we get back to my house and spend the next two hours arranging the body shop appraisal and filing claims for the car and for medical just in case. My mother is enthroned on my living room couch with her book, and I've made her lift her shirt, so I can check the bruising.

"I'm fine," she tells me. "You worry too much."

But I've given her an ice pack to put on her ribs as she rests there, and she seems to be grateful I've suggested that.

"You need to take a shower," I say, and explain to her how ours works. I don't shame her. I don't say, you smell bad. The truth is it makes me want to gag when I get a whiff of her. Twenty-four hours after this moment, I'll understand why she smells this way, and it will make me want to throw up even more.

"Here's a clean towel," I tell her, putting it on the guest bed.

I coordinate a plan with my sister via text and with Marc in whispered conversations later that night in our bedroom after my mother has gone to sleep and won't overhear us. He'll go over to the house first thing in the morning "to unload the car" and try and get inside the house without the key. My mother and I will meet him and Melissa at the house, where I'll ask her for the key before my sister drives her back to Medford. By noon, Marc has already driven to the house loaded up with equipment he might need for the car cleanout: trash bags, a flashlight, and his toolkit.

He texts me that we need the key to get in. *It's bad. Car is going to take a while to empty. Very scary.*

A few minutes later he calls me as I'm leaving our house with my mother. "The back door is locked, and it smells like urine back here," he says.

My mother is looking at me as I'm talking to him.

"He's working on your car," I tell her.

To him, "We're on our way," I say with fake brightness.

When my mother and I get to her house around 2:15 p.m., it's ninety-six degrees, and Marc is bent over, pulling things out of the beat-up car. He's sweating and cursing under his breath. There's a pungent smell of rotting things and mold in the air and piles and piles of books, the expensive exhibit catalogue from the Brandywine Museum of Art she bought herself when we were there four months ago, the novel *The Deep End of the Ocean*, and a photography book featuring cats are just a few of the titles already lined up on one side of the car. He's only emptied the passenger seat. My mother ignores this scene as she gets out of my car. She strides purposefully around the back of the house and comes out a few minutes later with a colorful quilted overnight bag.

"I have three shirts," she says to me.

"Perhaps get a pair of pants, you may be there for a while." I say, a little grimly as I'm looking at the piles around the car. She shakes her head to disagree with me and looks over at my sister's car across the street where Marc, who has taken a break, is wiping his face with a bandana, and leaning by the driver's side window talking to Melissa. The sun is beating down on us and the humidity is smothering.

"I need your house key." I'm standing in front of her, blocking her path to my sister's car, like she's going to run or hit me or scream. But surprisingly she doesn't fight this request at all. Deflating, she fumbles in her bag, and takes a worn and dirty key off her key ring. She hands it to me.

"Marc is going to see the worst hoarder house he's ever seen from his rehabbing days," she states calmly, like she's telling me about the weather.

She starts to step around me as I move aside.

For a moment, I'm frozen in disbelief. *She's worried about Marc's opinion of the house and not mine? Or my sister's? Does she think only Marc is going inside?* It's her fear that I focus on rather than the magnitude of the impending nightmare she's warning me about. I want to make sure, like I always have, that she's okay.

"Mom, it doesn't matter, no one is judging you," which is a lie that I don't judge myself for in the moment as I lean my body down to hug her tiny one. "We love you and it will be all right."

She walks past me and gets into my sister's car, without looking back at her house. My sister waves goodbye at me, and I watch them pull away. Marc has started taking more books out of the car and throwing them on the driveway piles. The initial moment of relief I felt clutching the key collapses into a big mass of terror, the kind you must feel before a major surgery or a decisive military battle. I'm slightly sick to my stomach thinking about what happens next.

"Are you ready to go in?" Marc asks, pulling off his work gloves and grabbing a flashlight.

At Marc's insistence, I put on a long-sleeved shirt I've thrown in the car, so my arms are covered. This way we won't expose ourselves to anything in the house. He does the same as we walk around to the back door. He unlocks it while I hold open the broken storm door. He pushes against it a little with his shoulder since it doesn't seem to move easily. It opens a tiny bit, less than a foot. It's so dark inside, it takes a minute for our eyes to adjust. The smell is terrible, a wave of funk hitting us like a storm cloud. This door opens to the laundry room and there's a washer and laundry sink to the right, and to the left is the water heater and door to the garage. Except you can't see any of those things because everything is covered with stuff. There is no floor, there's kind of a sloping step made of *things*: bags, unidentifiable solidified objects that are about a foot tall. As my eyes get used to the dim light, I see the piles rise up in a kind of wall between the laundry room and the rec room. The rec room is also dark because the heavy orange curtains are closed, letting in only a tiny sliver of outside light.

The wall of things divides the rec room from the stairs that lead up to the rest of the house, but there are no visible stairs now, even though I remember six of them, covered with 1970s burnt-orange carpeting. There are just objects piled up, like a mountain. We climb over books, papers, clothing, and empty plastic shopping bags, our feet sliding and barely able to push forward, up into the kitchen where there is the ceiling leak my mother told us about. Large pieces of wallpaper hang from it. I can reach to touch the ceiling as we stand next to the refrigerator.

It's like we've landed on another planet. There's dirt and cobwebs and something that looks like rust on the top of the fridge. I'm coughing and choking from the stench. We pause to try and take it all in. The sink is filled with dishes and the counters are completely covered with pans and glasses and vases. The stove is heaped with papers and clothing and dirty plates. There are items of clothing in dry cleaning bags hanging from the doorways to the rec room and the dining room at either end of the kitchen. In one of them is the purple silk suit my mother wore to our wedding twenty-two years ago. The big wall clock in the kitchen has stopped at two minutes after twelve. There is an antique kitchen table that is still there, I think. But the stuff on the floor, which is at least three and a half feet high, rises to cover it so there's no demarcation between ground and furniture.

I'm shaking, numb and in shock. I have no words for what I am seeing. Marc doesn't say anything either. I'm here in the present, but at the same time, I'm remembering how it was in the past. I'm seeing ghosts: my mother and sister and me sitting around the living room in front of the Christmas tree, Snoopy on the sofa where she tried to give birth to her kittens before my mother made me carry her to the box in the rec room, my friends coming through the front door to pick me up to go bowling. My positive memories feel like the vaguely familiar garbage I'm standing on.

We crunch over more things to head into the dining room and living room. It's just a huge mass of bags and paper and clothing and garbage and recycling with weird spots of order that contain some of the items I remember. I recognize the antique curio cabinet against the wall under the high windows between the rooms, the glass salts on the little shelf in the living room, and the giant cat watercolor by the front door. In one corner of the living room, there's a puffy blue recliner I remember from my adolescence. I can barely make out its filthy form because it is filled with papers, used tissues, books, and newspapers. It sits half-buried in the mounds of things rising from the floor. Next to the chair is the phone I've hooked up for her. This must be where she's been sleeping.

I'm sobbing, tears running down my face. "Oh my god, oh my god, what the fuck, what the fuck."

My hand covers my mouth as I look around me and try not to get sick. In the dining room, we are standing on more than two feet of things that make a sort of crunching path like we are walking on glass as we move through the dense mess. There are piles that reach as high as four and a half feet near the window. There's no air here. It's stifling, and we haven't habituated to the overwhelming smell. Marc is clambering toward the living room windows to try and open them. My mother's central air is not working, and it's got to be a hundred degrees here.

"This is really incredible," Marc is saying. He has a look on his face that is part sadness, part dismay and something else, maybe revulsion, that I've never seen before as he surveys the landscape. "It's much worse than I thought," he says with his usual understatement and an unusual lack of irony.

The last time I saw this place, I was twenty-six, and now I'm fifty-six. It feels like two worlds have collided in a planetary disaster, and I'm standing in the middle of the rubble. All I can do is sniffle and cry and moan, "I don't understand, I don't understand."

We crunch "upstairs," which is just another hill. At the top, outside the bathroom and across from what used to be my sister's room, are gallon plastic water bottles strewn around on top of the two feet of stuff. There are hundreds of them filled with fluid.

"What is it?" I'm asking.

Marc says tightly, "Urine. I think it's urine."

The bottles spill out from the bathroom—they are blue-tinged, and Marc says maybe she put toilet cleaner in them. There's a different terrible smell assaulting us from the bathroom area and my nose fills up and I'm coughing again to clear my throat.

We go into the bedrooms and my antique bed is in my sister's old room. There are weird little shrines of objects arranged decoratively in the middle of chaos, like a tableau with my niece and nephew's pictures set up neatly on a dirt-encrusted table. *I have to get out, I have to get out.* "I have to get out," I hear myself saying it out loud like I'm breaking a spell.

Marc says calmly, "Let's go outside. Now." We retrace our steps through the house and out the back door into the light.

I'm crying as I lean against the warm metal side of our car, and then he comes over and holds me. I take my phone out of the car and text my sister, *Holy fucking shit. It's going to be condemned. She absolutely cannot go back there.*

It's after 3:30 p.m., and we need to get the car emptied to drive it to the body shop. Marc had been cleaning it out for several hours already. It's laughable really, what meager supplies we've brought with us to start "cleaning up." We only have one pair of gloves for the two of us and no wipes to clean our hands. We work together to finish the job, and the odor in the car seems to get worse as we go. Marc pulls out containers filled with liquified rotting food; banana peels; books covered with black mold from the trunk, which had been leaking for God knows how long. When we are finally done, the stench is like a living passenger.

Marc turns toward me and asks, "Do you think she was sleeping in the car sometimes?"

I start to tear up as I hand him the last two garbage bags

from the box we'd brought with us so he can cover the dirt-covered driver's seat. Choking and trying not to vomit, with his head hanging out of the window as the dirt in the car whirls like a tornado around him, he follows me the mile down the road to the car dealership. We park the car and lock it. He looks a little green. We joke about the adjustor, imagining him opening the door and slamming it shut as he gets a whiff.

"Please," I say to the girl in the office as I hand her the keys and she seals them in an envelope, "just tell the adjustor to total it, I beg you."

Marc starts laughing. The girl looks at me like I've lost my mind.

On the drive back, we talk about what to do next. I tell Marc I can't go inside the house again today. Even starting to think about it makes me panic. Marc decides he should go in and make a video recording. If my mother ever denies what it was like here or her competency comes into question legally, I want this evidence. I also want to show my sister what we've found. There's no way she can have my mother living at her house and help us with clean up. I'm not sure how *I'm* ever going to be able to look at my mother again after seeing this.

As I sit in the car outside, trembling and tearing up again, I visualize what Marc is walking through. I can see him moving from room to room opening all the windows he can reach. I am so grateful for him in this moment. I remember our marriage vows; I don't think we included a hoarding mother when we listed difficult times when we'd be there for each other.

I'm trying to breathe and understand what I've just experienced. In my mind, it looks exactly like the movie of the tsunami aftermath I watched in high school, only with deeper piles of things and more familiar objects. I keep thinking of that news photo of the wave of garbage that circles around the ocean, swirling and getting bigger as more trash, more things get sucked into the tide. It's vast and endless. What's garbage, what had meaning doesn't matter since it's all lost and part of a giant mess.

I pull out my phone and text Melissa again. *We are cancelling our vacation. We need the ten days here. Going in there today was like visiting a disorganized serial killer's lair. Seriously. You don't want to come till we are more shoveled out. You'll never sleep again.*

I recognize that I'm protecting my sister, assuming my old role. But why should both of us be traumatized?

Back at our house, we stand by the back door in the early dusk and place our shoes in bags. Just inside the door, we strip off all our clothes, carry them upstairs in a bundle and throw them directly into the washing machine, starting the load immediately and running it at the highest water temperature. We need these clothes for the next day. We take turns showering. I use very hot water here, too, and I stand under it for a long time, numb.

After eating something, we sit on the sofa together. Marc starts making a list of supplies we will need to get at Lowe's first thing the next morning: "really good" respirator masks, contractor bags, paper towels, disinfectant wipes, gloves that can't be pierced when we wear them, bottles of water, insect repellant, and Lysol. We try and look at the video together, partly because what we saw inside the house already seems totally unreal. But when Marc goes to play it, it isn't on his phone. I joke that it was a Freudian move to "accidentally" delete it.

When we fall into bed, exhausted, I snuggle into his chest and breathe in the clean smell of soap and him. But even that isn't enough. As I drop into that state before full sleep, my stepfather's face suddenly looms before me, and I startle awake with a cry. *Why am I thinking of him?* It seems my family traumas are all linked together and have piled up into this huge mess.

Chapter 6 - Bullies I Love

I sprawl with Florence on her living room floor above Keller Funeral Home. I'm eleven and we met at my new church, Maple Shade United Church of Christ. After youth group, we walk across the street to her house and shoo her two miniature schnauzers away from the big television, so we can watch the Philadelphia Flyers. They are called The Broad Street Bullies because they are underdogs, new to the league, and are known for fighting. Florence has a crush on Bobby Clarke, the toothless center. Football is on all the time at my house when Daddy's home, but I hate football. The first time I saw a hockey game, I fell in love with it. In a hockey game, everything can change in an instant, and winning and losing sometimes only depends on the puck's random bounce or the player's skill at being in the right place at the right time.

Everybody in Florence's family sits and watches—her grandmother on the floral sofa with a crocheted blanket, her father in his recliner, and her mother in the chair with the ottoman. Nobody believes this team will be good enough to win the ultimate reward—the Stanley Cup. But we cheer and yell for them anyway. I am figuring out the rules as I watch the powerful skaters glide back and forth across the blue line, cracking the puck into the net and banging their bodies against the hard boards that surround the ice. They get hurt often. Somebody like Dave Schultz, or "Schultzy" to us fans, will get high-sticked, and he'll get up and punch the player who did it, blood streaming from his face as he glides over to the penalty box. I learn that's sometimes what you do to win a game.

We continue to live on Woodstock Drive in the house my mother says she won't leave. My mother is not allowed to change the locks. And there's no money for that anyway. Daddy comes to see us, and she has no choice but to open the door. Or sometimes he just walks in. She talks about court a lot because she and Daddy are getting a divorce, but there's something very complicated about the separation and visitation, and I may have to remember the night my sister and I ran out of the house so I can tell a judge what happened. My mother is sitting on my bed, very serious.

She says, "You did hear Daddy say he was going to kill me, right?"

I didn't, but I say I did for her.

My grandparents are visiting us and sleeping in my parents' bedroom next to mine. I hear screaming and banging when I open my eyes in the middle of the night. Nanna's voice in the hallway is shrieking at my mother to let her back in as she pounds on the door. The red lights are flashing around and around on my bedroom walls. I can see the lighted truck from my window when I sit up. My mother is sobbing. The front door slams and the ambulance pulls away, slicing through darkness as it disappears with Nanna and my mother in the car behind it. I tiptoe to my door and open it slowly. I creak over the wood floors to the living room.

Mrs. Hoffman, a neighbor, is holding my sister, stroking her hair. "It's okay, it's okay," she murmurs. I'm not sure what will be okay. She says they took my grandfather to the hospital. She says everything will be all right and we should go back to bed down the dark hall and close our eyes.

I try hard to sleep, but after a while, my bedroom door opens, and my mother comes in carrying my sleepy sister. She is crying.

She says, "Nonno died of a heart attack."

I don't understand what this means. Already I have trouble remembering his firm fingers over mine, the poem he sent me in a letter about Sammy Jay in the backyard that had a real bird feather attached to it. Already I sense the secret my mother doesn't say about letting him die, locking the door to keep Nanna out after she ran to call the ambulance, holding on to Nonno. Making sure he didn't suffer. After this, when I think of Nonno dying of a heart attack it feels like a fist clenching. Or I imagine it must be like what I do to my own hand sometimes instead of crying—squeezing and squeezing it shut.

The sky is the color of pewter, and the trees blow their leaves backwards like hair and then scatter them to the black pavement. Hurricane Agnes is coming toward the end of our annual two week beach vacation in 1972 in Cape May, New Jersey with Nanna. It was more fun with Nonno there. We'd surf the waves together and he'd swim in the pool with us. Daddy is taking care of Tommy while we are gone. My mother has left cat food out on the counter, a big pile of cans, two for each day. When we get back to the house, Tommy is nowhere to be found for a day or two. My mother's worried, but he's been gone before. Sometimes he shows up with a torn ear or a cut on his side, but he always comes home. This time, when he does, he's skinny and rubs happily against all of us. Later that week, I find the shiny unopened cans of cat food tossed down the hill into the woods at the back of our house. When I take my mother there to show her what I found, she clenches her jaw and doesn't say a word.

By early December that year we are spending less and less

time at the house, particularly if my mother thinks Daddy may be around. My mother takes us to friends' houses in nearby towns and we play with their children, or I lie on the sofa and read book after book and don't move.

"Take the kids out for a walk in the woods." My mother is standing above me as I read my mystery about a governess who discovers a murderer in the house where she works. "Mrs. Lee and I need a break from her boys. Take your sister too."

I blink at her. I'm almost my full height of five feet, ten inches. I bump into the corners of doors a lot and trip sometimes. I am trying to grow out my hair, and it hangs over my face in front of my thick glasses with dark rims so my eyes, which are squinty to begin with, almost disappear.

My mother gives all of us little bags to collect pinecones and says to me, "Don't come back for a while."

We tromp to the end of the street into the empty green space where there's a path through the trees. A lone bird sings in the early dusk, as the boys and my sister run ahead. Suddenly there's a man, tall and thin, with gray eyes.

"I'm lost," he says. "Could you tell me how to leave the woods?" He's right next to me. He's taller than I am with glasses and one of those green army jackets.

"What's your name?"

I tell him my first name even though I've been told you don't talk to strangers, but it's polite and he's a grownup.

"Where do you live?"

Later I will hear myself repeating this exchange in my head over and over, telling him the name of my town.

My stomach curls tighter as his hand reaches for my arm and pats it. I catch up to my sister and the boys by walking faster as he moves off in a different direction. I smell dying leaves, hear dry crunching underfoot. Then quiet again.

My sister walks with the boys across a wide clearing. Suddenly they all drop down into a small valley and disappear ahead. I'm calling to them. The man is right next to me again. I walk faster. I'm not rude, so I don't scream or run away. I can't hear what he is saying except "pretty, pretty."

I'm trying to speed up more and can't run because the path has gotten steeper. He's behind me, following.

"Let me help," and his hands touch me all over, outside my jacket, under my jacket, and between my legs. I make no sound. I am not there anymore.

I pull away and start to run. I yell out for Missy and the boys again.

"We have to go!"

I see them ahead of me. There is only pounding and tears in my head. I keep my tears inside, so I don't scare the little kids. The man has disappeared into the woods.

I sit in a wing-backed chair in the living room with my mother on one side and Mrs. Lee on the other. I try to tell what happened between sobs while wiping my face with a big wad of Kleenex, but I have lost words for things.

"A man," I choke out. "A man in the woods...."

The policeman, a giant in his uniform, kneels in front of me with a pad. "Honey," he says, "tell me what he looked like." He asks me what the man said to me. He writes things down.

I don't tell him I told the man where I lived. *Why did I tell him where I lived?*

The neighborhood men and the policeman bring the man out of the woods, holding his arms. I'm crying harder. The policeman stands me up at the big bay window in the living room. The man looks up. He can see me. Everyone can see me.

"Is that him?" the policeman asks.

I nod.

We stay at the Lee's a long time, not going home till it's almost bedtime. When we get home, I'm still crying, even when I'm sitting in front of the television in the master bedroom under a blanket. I'm not even sure what I'm watching.

My mother comes in. I'm not small enough anymore to fit on her lap and she doesn't hug me. She seems frustrated. "Listen to me," she says. "You've cried about this enough now, try and forget about it."

So that's what I do.

I hide in the basement, back in that darkest space where my mother used to hide the ironing. I hide there with Debbie E. who has been playing an endless card game of War with me. We also swap fifty-two Nancy Drew books from a big box that my mother found for me at a garage sale and read one or two a day. If I hide, I won't have to see Daddy when he comes to the house. He didn't feed Tommy. I don't know what he might do to me. My mother continues to sleep in the attic, armed with mace and locking her door. He is allowed to come in the house because my sister is really his, and my mother will always give in because of that.

"Debbie," I hear his heavy footsteps come down the stairs. He's standing by the basement door and looking for me. "God damn it," he says.

"I won't hurt you," he is pleading. He comes all the way into the back basement and, sensing the breathing in the fruit cellar darkness, pulls the string on the one light bulb back there. His face, with eyebrows pointed in, and his big body moving quickly make me shrink back.

"We were playing hide and seek," I tell him. "We didn't hear you." I have learned to lie, started to understand that map below the surface of things.

He yells, "Get upstairs!" Debbie E. and I run fast with him following. He realizes I am on my mother's side and don't want to spend time with him.

A year later, the day of the other court hearing, my own, my mother tells me I must wear something that makes me look young. I put on a lime green dress with long sleeves that is a little tight around my chest and has a cloth belt around the waist. My belly slightly rolls over it. I run my finger over the soft velvet of the choker around my neck. My mother has told me we can't tell Daddy anything about this because he is fighting for custody of us. My mother says not to talk about what happened with the man with anyone, even my sister.

The room is small and stuffy, and the judge is sitting at a big desk and has a black robe on. I look away from him and feel my stomach start to rumble like before you get sick. The man is sitting with his lawyer on one side of the room, and he is wearing a suit, so he doesn't look the same except for his glasses. I don't think I can sit still in the chair on the other side of the room, but I make myself. Inside, I curl up tightly like a small animal, so quiet I am almost not breathing. If I could twirl my hair like I used to, I'd do it.

The man's lawyer says, "Look at her, he didn't know how old she was." There's a pause as the judge shuffles some papers. "My client has some mental troubles; he's come back from the war...."

"She's twelve," the prosecutor interrupts. It goes on for a few minutes or a few days, I'm not sure.

Finally, the judge says something about first offense and misdemeanor and a fine of sixty-five dollars, and we all stand up.

After the hearing, Ken pulls up in his car, and I climb in the back seat. My mother gets in the front. She is crying and telling Ken, "That bastard just had to pay a fine," and he's comforting her with his hand on her shoulder and making sympathetic noises and telling her it will be all right, it's over. I'm sitting in the backseat staring at the backs of their heads and picking my finger so that it's bleeding a small red circle on my little girl dress.

In science class we watch a black and white movie. The wave in Japan is huge, rising higher and higher, eating everything in its path. I'm fascinated by the description of how the earthquake happens far below in the ocean floor, making a giant crack splitting the earth. On the surface, a small movement of water, but then, as it approaches something that doesn't move, can't move, like a coastline, it grows enormous. The wave sucks everything out into the depths in what's called a drawdown as all the water pulls back from the shoreline and then vomits all of it up far inland, destroying houses, people, everything in its path. Afterwards, there's just debris. Giant piles of cars and houses and objects that had meaning are just twisted hunks of waste. I imagine the people, rotting and bloated and unable to be found. After I see the movie, I often dream of giant waves that sweep everything away. Sometimes I'm in them. Sometimes I'm on a wall watching the tsunami come toward me, aware I will drown.

We are at Nanna's house in upstate New York, packing for her New Jersey move to live closer to us, since Nonno has died. Debbie E. calls and says her mother really wants to talk to mine. I hand the phone to my mother and after her mouth drops open, I hear her say, "Did you call the police?" It seems my father came with an axe and chopped through the front door.

My mother hangs up the phone and turns to my sister and me. "I guess we won't be going back home for a while," she says with fake cheerfulness.

My sister and I sleep on the pull-out twin beds in the basement of my grandmother's new house in Westmont, New Jersey for almost a year. I watch the basement television and try not to think about my old house which is only fifteen minutes away. I miss the willow tree in the backyard, living across the street from Debbie E. and riding my bike around the neighborhood. Instead of taking the bus, my mother must drop us off at school. I've started reading Nonno's books about Lincoln and the Civil War. Sometimes my sister and I play with the Ouija board trying to summon Nanna's sister who died when she was our age. When Nanna finds out, she yells at us to stop. At night sometimes I cry quietly when nobody can hear, thinking about missing my room and all the familiar objects in our house.

My mother, sister and I finally move out of Nanna's into the split level on 137 Willowbrook Road. Nanna has bought it for us, so we can stay in the good school system. My mother will pay her rent. The house has a family room where the basement would be, with ugly orange carpeting and lots of bookcases. My mother hangs up some antique family photos on the wall, including her favorite, a black and white picture of Nanna, with Nanna's brother and the sister who died when she was young, and a goat. Nanna gets us a big color television for the rec room. I hang out down there and watch old movies and hockey.

Bobby Clarke is one of my favorite players too. When he smiles during a game, his toothless grin is like an overgrown first grader's school photo. When we are down a goal, he and his line will work extra hard to score. I've learned the Canadian national anthem, and I understand playoff standings. My mother isn't seeing Ken anymore and has started dating other men along with working full time as a nurse at a geriatric nursing home. My sister is either at a friend's house or I'm supposed to be watching her, but I don't really care what she is doing when she's upstairs and I'm downstairs. I learn the calls—holding, interference, icing. I am hollering at bad calls and yelling when they are hitting each other,

"Get him, punch him in the throat," I shriek at *my* team, these big men who grind down their opponents and don't take anything that's not fair. Afterwards, I call Florence on the phone and talk about the game. I stand and hold my arms up like I'm at the Spectrum watching with all the other orange clad fans.

I hate school because of Jim and Jay. They follow me down the hall or sit behind me in class and call me "Fat Chipmunk," "Tank," and "Truck." My mother won't let me wear jeans to school like everyone else, so I have dresses or good pants that she says look "nice." I have ugly brown shoes which are all I can find in size ten. It's easier to cough and stay in bed with my books or the lineup of old television shows, like *Bewitched*, *My Favorite Martian*, or *Patty Duke* in the morning and soap operas, like *Young and the Restless* in the afternoon. Sometimes I really am sick, but more often, I just don't want to go to school and deal with those boys. I miss fifty-four days and still get mostly A's.

I quit playing cello because of the private lesson in the room with the male music teacher once a week. I'm afraid when he shuts the door. Sometimes I think about what happened with that man who knows the town where I live. When I walk outside, I look for places to hide in case I see him. After I think about this I try and forget it immediately by thinking about something else. Sometimes that's about my "real" father, Malcolm. *Where does he live? Maybe he has been looking for me?* I'm also scared about what Daddy is going to do next and whether we will have to live with him. I don't want to leave my room.

In addition to reading *Flowers for Algernon*, *Gone with the Wind* and all the James Herriot stories, I'm reading as many science fiction and fantasy books as I can lay my hands on at the library. I've become interested in space aliens that supposedly came to Earth and made things and then left. Erich von Däniken wrote a book about it called *Chariots of the Gods*. My one school friend and locker mate, Fran, and I get chosen for a special independent research project. We don't have to go to our regular social studies class and, instead, spend our class periods in the independent study room meeting with our teacher planning our presentation. We read everything we can about Stonehenge and Easter Island and think about other things the aliens could have created, such as Mayan temples and cave drawings. We go to the Cherry Hill library together and sometimes people mistake us for sisters. She's almost as tall as I am, and we have the same color hair.

I tell Fran that I have a secret biological father because I'm partly adopted. One day after my mother drops us off, Fran helps me look in phone books from New York for the married name of Malcolm's sister, and the area she might still live in. The task is daunting, and we give up after about twenty minutes and go back to debating whether drawings on the Plain of Nazca in Peru have something to do with von Daniken's theory.

I hang out at Fran's house a lot.

"Call me Nuther Mother," her mother says. "You'll be my Nuther Daughter."

Fran takes her older brother's full-head gorilla mask, and we walk to the 7-Eleven store taking turns wearing it as we wave to cars driving by on Kresson Road. I put it on with her breath still hot inside and enter the store nonchalantly to grab sodas and cookies.

The cashier, a boy older than us cracks up, "Yo, monkey girl," he teases. I'm not shy when I wear the mask.

"*Gorilla* girl," I correct him, and Fran laughs because he doesn't understand the difference.

She pats my hairy head. "She's tame, but don't mess with her," and we make monkey sounds before we give him our money and leave.

Daddy is paying some support, but only sometimes, and my mother is spending a lot of time on the phone crying to her lawyer. After a court order, a white princess phone with its own phone number is placed in my bedroom. This is the only phone Daddy is allowed to call us on, and we have specific times we pick it up even if we don't want to talk to him. When he calls, he tells us we are going to Disneyland over spring break. He says we'll visit Aunt Jan in Connecticut and the Pomfret School nearby to see if I like it. I don't respond when he tells me this, but I'm terrified.

We are in my mother's bedroom while she gets ready for work. "Don't worry," my mother says determinedly. "You might have to go see it, but the lawyer says he can't make you go." She's putting on her nursing uniform as she's talking to me. "Besides, there's no way he has the money to pay for that for very long. He'll lose another job." After tying her white shoes, she stands up to adjust her cap, laughing a little bitterly, "Our lawyer says we have his longest running New Jersey divorce case. I don't know how I'm paying for any of this."

Daddy continues to come for visitations, but because there is a restraining order on the Willowbrook Road property, he is only allowed to pick us up at the curb. My sister and I wait for him outside the house, wild with anxiety pulled tightly between us, an invisible thread of feeling that binds us together whenever there is a threat. My eyes notice everything, how the house looks with neatly trimmed bushes, green in the sunlight, the glint in my mother's eye as I change clothes from pants into the blue dress with the white polka dots, my sister's red platform shoes shiny and new that my mother doesn't want her to wear. I block out most of the details of the visitation itself, except the darkened restaurant with the sip or two of Daddy's beer if I ask, my sister saying she'll only go to the bathroom if I go with her. We do end up going to Disneyland with him. Most of the four days there we stick closely with the female guide who takes us to the front of every line. Neither my sister nor I want to stand near Daddy. We fly home by ourselves, my sister sick and crying from a burst ear drum.

He rings the white phone not to talk to us, but to bother my mother. It rings and rings and rings. It won't stop ringing sometimes even when my mother tells us we don't have to pick it up because it's not Daddy's time to call. Sometimes my mother turns the ringer off, but I know it's still ringing. I can hear it softly, in my head, behind my eyes.

One day, we are waiting on the lawn for him outside, and Daddy does not show up. We wait an hour. Then we wait another hour. We finally come inside, and I try and call him on the phone at my mother's request, to find out why, in her words, he "stood us up."

He doesn't answer.

When the phone rings later that night, my mother has us pick it up. He begins arguing with me that it's a misunderstanding and that I should tell my mother that he *will* come tomorrow, and she's in the background saying, "tell him no, that's not what the visitation was, and tell him to talk to his lawyer...."

I feel something crack inside of me, move apart. Suddenly I am seeing black, and I'm screaming at him on the phone, "Why did you not come! Why are you doing this to us? I hate you! Stop yelling at me! Stop it! Stop it!"

I'm crying and yelling at the same time, and I try and slam down the phone once, twice, three times missing the phone cradle as I hear him start screaming back at me before I hang up. I want to pound that phone like the Flyers do when they take a major penalty by punching the jaw of an opponent and pulling the jersey over his head.

I imagine my father like a goalie, like Bernie Parent trying to protect his net, folding, and then dropping down in front. My words will go in. They hit their mark, and this game is won. No more phone calls from him after that.

A week later, a letter arrives:

Dear Debbie and Melissa: You are both individually and as a pair a major source of shame and sorrow to me. Sorrow that you cannot see fit to treat your own father as a human being. Shame that you appear to be no better than the environment in which you exist.

Whatever possesses both of you to lie to me; tell me you are sick when you are not; not to tell me you are going on vacation so that I can proceed to call you weeks on end without answer; and above all whatever possesses you, Debbie, to berate me over a misunderstanding which still saw me travel six hundred miles to take you and your sister out to dinner?

It may well be the responsibility of your mother but still is a matter for your own consciences.

At any rate, it stops and ceases as of now. When either or both of you have a desire to behave towards me as a human being should behave, you both know how to reach me." And then my father signed, in thick black fine-tipped magic marker ink, *Your Loving Daddy*.

Nobody is home yet, and I'm shocked and tearful. I call my mother at work.

"Don't show this to your sister," she instructs me. "You call that lawyer right away while you are crying and ask what this is."

The lawyer, who is the father of one of my classmates, sounds very sad. "I told him," he says kindly, "that he might not want to send that, but your dad insisted."

I don't say anything.

"Listen," he continues, "I don't think this is really about anything you said to him."

But I don't believe that at all. I understand I have made my father go away.

Not long after I make my father leave, I am standing at my locker before going to the bus. I see Jay tearing down the hall toward me. I shift my foot out in front of me and he trips over it. I am not called out (in hockey it's a two-minute minor penalty) because there are too many kids around to determine the perpetrator. I get away with watching him slide across the floor into the feet of our stern history teacher, Mrs. Richards, who hauls him up by the scruff of his neck and gives him detention on the spot.

It's May 19, 1974, and Fran (who is originally from Chicago and only supports Chicago teams) and I have a two dollar bet on who will win the Stanley Cup. It's game six of the Flyers against the Boston Bruins. The Flyers' coach, whose son goes to my school, writes on the blackboard in the team's locker room, "Win together today and we walk together forever." I am watching by myself in the rec room, and the score is 1-0 Philadelphia. The Bruins pull their goalie in a last ditch effort to score, and they can't. And the clock ticks down as I am standing and crying with the 17,000 fans at the Spectrum and the announcer yells, "The Flyers win the Stanley Cup! The Flyers win the Stanley Cup! The Flyers won the Stanley Cup!" The grinning Bobby Clarke carries the silver cup around the ice. Florence will be so excited. And Fran owes me two dollars. My mother, who doesn't understand my love of hockey, or sports at all, doesn't let me go to the parade on Broad Street the next day where two million fans gather to celebrate. Instead, I'm one of just a few students who show up at school, unable to play sick. While sitting in an almost empty classroom reading my book, I realize I need to try and stand up for myself better. My anger makes me stronger. I don't have to be hurt. Sometimes, I think, when you are the underdog and fight like the Broad Street Bullies, you win.

PART II- *FOUND*

Chapter 7 - Building Myself

I'm a sophomore at Cherry Hill High School East and arrive home on the bus before my sister and my mother. I've learned to cook simple things—tuna casserole, cheesesteaks, and eggs, so my mother doesn't have to make dinner. My mother's bedroom has gotten messier since we first moved to this house. Clothing is spewed over the furniture, and she's taken to tossing her books and papers in piles. I move some to sit in the blue wing chair in the corner of the bedroom to keep her company when she gets home from work.

"I told your grandmother when she bought this house there wasn't enough closet space," she says.

We have dinner at Nanna's weekly, usually on Sundays, with my mother and her in an uneasy truce of mutual need. Nanna makes us rice pudding, my great-grandmother's pumpkin cake recipe, and cookies to take home and eat during the week. My mother drives her to the store and her doctor's appointments.

My mother bought some fashionable clothing to go out on dates with her new boyfriend. She's been spending every other Saturday at his house when she's off from work. Sometimes he comes to our house, but my sister hates that because her bedroom is over the rec room where they stay on the pullout sofa bed, and she can hear them having sex through the heating vent.

"When I'm gone, you need to be responsible for your sister and make sure she's home on time," my mother says. My sister is always out with her older boyfriend and her other friends and doesn't listen to me at all. I don't even try to tell my mother that or how I'm worried about my sister and what she's been doing.

"Get out," Melissa yells when I open her bedroom door. She's still angry I took her *Born to Run* album down to the rec room where the other stereo is because I like the song, "Jungleland." I've also been secretly eating her Halloween stash of hidden chocolate. If she's going to be a jerk to me, I'm treating myself to her candy.

"You are supposed to be back by eleven, Mom said so."

"You aren't Mom," Melissa replies. "Don't tell me what to do."

She's become one of the popular kids and thinks I'm just a nerd, which I am because I'm not going out and doing things with my own friends. I'm staying home supposedly taking care of her, but really, it's because I don't have that many friends yet.

My mother dumps the bag containing some fancy bras and a pair of white pants on the floor after she hangs the new shirts up, pushing the other clothing around to make room. From the overstuffed closet, she pulls out a long v-neck dress with a high slit up the side that reveals a pair of matching hot pants underneath. It has an abstract striped sort of pattern; the red, gold, purple, blue, silver, green bleeding into the black background. The dress is sexy, wild. Like something Cher would wear.

She mutters, "I'm never going to wear this, am I?" She runs her hand over the silky polyester fabric. "Well," she says, hanging it up again, "I'm keeping it. You can never be sure when you might have a special occasion need for something like this."

"I like it," I say. "Cool colors."

We laugh together.

She pulls out a mink stole encased in a plastic garment bag and holds it up. It is something Daddy gave her. She rolls her eyes because nobody wears fur anymore. "I'm tired from working all day," she sighs. "I don't feel like doing this," and she shoves it back into the closet and doesn't bother to slide the door shut.

    Several years before, right after we moved into the Willowbrook house, I heard her crying on the phone. Does she tell me later she fears she's pregnant by the married doctor she's involved with after she broke up with Ken, or do I overhear her say that to the person on the line? It turns out she wasn't pregnant, and that story ended when the doctor had a massive heart attack and became the first person to successfully survive not just one heart transplant, but three. When he first had the heart attack, my mother would come home from work every day, begin to cry, and make me call the hospital desk to see if he was still alive.

    After he was home from the hospital, but before the transplants, we would go to see him at his house on the other side of Cherry Hill, the nicer section. He had children who were older than us and two big German Shepherds that pushed their noses into my crotch each time we walked in. Embarrassed, I'd push them away, but they'd come back as if they knew something about me. My mother visited the doctor in the bedroom while his wife fixed me a snack in the kitchen. She took pickles, provolone cheese, and baked beans and stacked them on a wheat cracker. She told me it was a weird thing, but good and I should try it, so I did. We'd sit eating in awkward silence. My sister stayed in the living room filling her pockets with wrapped candy from the little bowl on the table. I knew my mother had been seeing this man, she'd talked about driving with him to Philly in his Jaguar, yet my mother and his wife behaved like friends during these visits. My mother would take big boxes of partly completed Medicare forms home and his wife paid me to fill out the same repetitive information in the little boxes over and over, so the doctor was paid for the patients he'd seen before he got sick.

"We're helping him and his family," my mother explained. "He is always behind on paperwork."

I didn't understand why my mother seemed fine with this strange situation. *They were having an affair and my mother loved him. Why wasn't his wife mad?*

As we were leaving one day, his wife smirked knowingly at my sister and asked sarcastically if she wanted more chocolates. My sister, feeling the shame of taking something she hadn't asked permission for, shook her head no and followed my mother out the door.

It's during my sophomore year that my mother starts seriously purchasing artwork. She takes us to the Rosenfeld Gallery and buys the black and white ink drawing of a cartoon by Tony Auth that ran in the Philadelphia Inquirer. It shows God pointing a finger as he's saying, *let there be evolution, women's rights…* She has it specially framed and hangs it over our sofa in the living room. She buys other things too: a brass kaleidoscope on a little stand with the most beautiful patterns of blue, purple, and red shapes, that converge and disappear as you turn it; a playful wire sculpture of a bicycle with a sail that she carefully places on the top of the antique curio cabinet she's bought for the living room. I love to turn the kaleidoscope, pointing it toward the dining room window to light up the magic inner glass. My mother seems happy finding just the right spots for what she's bought.

"I hate the design of this house," she remarks, standing back to survey the giant watercolor of a black cat in front of multicolored flowers she's hung over the front hall table. "But this helps."

I like the cat, it's like an Egyptian goddess, watching over us.

"Is it straight?" she asks. I enjoy doing these decorating projects with her. She tells me that Malcolm worked with decorators and passed on a few tips to her. "Your grandmother thinks I'm irresponsible with money, but doing this is important. It's good to have real art in the house."

I don't disagree, although we never seem to have enough money for the utilities or that pair of Oshkosh overalls, she's finally given me permission to get so I can fit in with the other girls at school. The child support ended when Daddy disappeared.

"Be quiet," she snaps at my sister and me, and we stop arguing long enough for her to write out checks for the bills at the dining room table.

When my mother comes home in the late afternoon from her job, she complains, "I worked all day and you guys haven't done anything around here at all."

My sister and I do clean the house, usually when we are going to have friends over. We clear my mother's tweezers, nail files, mirror, and nail polish off the coffee table next to her recliner downstairs. We tidy up the papers and bills on the dining room table, so they don't spread like an infection to other surfaces in the room. We vacuum the blue and green carpeting. Sometimes we take turns dusting. We clean the bathrooms. But we've stopped cleaning her messy bedroom. Instead, we shut the door to it like she is the teenager instead of us.

During my junior year, my mother starts collecting people she feels need her help. First, there is the nurse with bleached blond hair she works with who moonlights as a stripper because, my mother tells us, "She's had a hard life and needs more money to support her kid."

Then there's Josh, eighty years old, who lives at the nursing home where my mother works. "He's lonely and doesn't have a family so we can be one for him," my mother explains when she tells us we are going over with cake to celebrate his birthday with him.

There's our next-door neighbor who's going through a divorce and whose three-year-old I babysit. "Her husband wasn't nice to her before he left," my mother reminds me.

All these people need support, but she doesn't bring them home when she's providing it until Mrs. Pan. She moves in with us for about six months.

"Her husband was abusive to her, and she had to leave," my mother explains to my sister and me after she shows Mrs. Pan where to put her suitcase in the rec room and how to work the sofa bed. Mrs. Pan is Chinese and works with my mother. Instead of my mother's uniforms hanging up in the basement laundry room, I come home from school to find a duck hanging upside down that she's preparing for us for dinner. She also cooks us delicious wontons.

My sister and I adapt to the situation, but we joke that my mother picks up strays like other people rescue cats. This is funny to us because a cat did show up not long after we moved in. This happened after we put Tommy to sleep. My mother told us not to feed "Snoopy," as she was called around the neighborhood, and then couldn't resist doing so herself. But Snoopy turned out to be pregnant after she moved in with us, so then we had a cat and four kittens. We kept the runt of the litter, Samantha, which meant we had two cats more than my mother swore she'd have after Tommy died.

I'm writing hunched over the desk Ken made for me before

he and my mother broke up. My feet tuck under the rungs of the antique chair that's a little too short for my tall body. My bedroom is quiet; my sister and mother aren't home. The room is neat and organized the way I like it to be. In my bookcase, I've kept all my favorite childhood books like *The Little Princess*, about a girl who is left to fend for herself when her father dies. She is finally rescued after struggling to survive a mean headmistress and other terrible travails. Eventually, her identity as a rich princess is revealed and she finds her place in the world. I'm working on the journal my cool teacher, who says we can call her Wendy, has asked us to keep for our Women in Literature elective my senior year. My mother has always encouraged us to keep a diary and has given them to us as presents, but this journal is something I've chosen for myself. In the front of the notebook, I write out a quote my mother gave me. It's about how when you are growing up you are surrounded by mirrors reflecting yourself, but when you finally grew up you understood the mirrors were windows looking out onto the world. Wendy's assignment is to write a dialogue where we answer two sides of a question.

"Can somebody like me in a romantic way?" I write in cursive. On the other side of the page, I don't hesitate with my answer, "You are stuck being the girl boys just want to be friends with." I wonder if I will have boyfriends like my mother does and if they will take me out for dinner and on trips. I have a crush on a boy I met in my church friend, Florence's, high school group, who might take me to prom at their school. I like another boy in my art class. Going out with either of them seems like a long shot to me. Although I'm no longer overweight, I am not very confident and say awkward things, like telling a boy that I liked his birthday suit when I meant his three-piece suit. I'm not in any of the popular cliques at Cherry Hill East, but I'm finally included in a group of smart, creative, and quirky friends, so I don't feel my situation is totally hopeless.

Wendy comments afterwards in red ink, "I remember well. Reading your dilemma brings back memories of days gone by." I love that she understands. She's only about six years older than we are and wears jeans and sandals. She's teaching us like we are in college. We read everything from the biblical Garden of Eden story to *I Know Why the Caged Bird Sings* and *The Awakening*.

I write the names of the boys I like. Despite my mother telling us that diaries are private, and she won't read what we write, I don't fully believe that, so I write poems about the sadness of life and oblique references to how things "aren't fair at my house" in case she does look. My mother doesn't like that I am going out with my friends all the time now that they can drive. Fran, or another friend, pick me up and we go to somebody's house, or to the mall, or a movie. We've started going to concerts—Fleetwood Mac, Steve Miller, and Chicago. Although she's younger, my sister didn't have rules about where she went, but somehow, it's different for me. My mother doesn't like "my attitude" and accuses me of being selfish because "all you care about is your social life." She threatens to ground me if I talk back to her. One day she discovers a boy visited after school and she explodes in anger. She turns red and slaps me across my face. My mother had spanked me a few times when I was younger, but she'd never behaved like this, looking at me so full of rage before telling me I was grounded for two weeks. As I write about all of this in my journal, I realize that I'm taking a small bite of apple like Eve did. It scares me, but I love how it tastes.

My dorm room in Heinz Hall at Beaver College outside

Philadelphia is at the other end of the green lawn that stretches up to Grey Towers Castle with the turrets and gargoyles and mirrored ballroom. I'm here because of that castle, which I fell in love with as soon as I saw it at my initial interview. Maybe it was that story about the little princess that did it. But it was the scholarship money that sealed the deal.

"Do you want the blanket on it too?" my mother asks, as she makes up the twin bed with the cat bedsheets, she gave me for a graduation present so I wouldn't miss Samantha. I try not to think about home and what Sam will do when she can't jump up and get under my covers every morning when my mother leaves for work and lets her into my bedroom.

I shake my head no. It's hot in the room even with the louvered window cranked open, catching the early September humidity. I've rearranged the ugly furniture, but I'm waiting for my roommate to get here so we can decide together how to hang the posters and where to put her stereo. My sister, who is about to start her second year in high school, is helping bring in my suitcases and a box of cleaning supplies from the car. She looks like she's been crying, her face blotchy and streaked. We'd started getting along better as I became more social my senior year.

"Who are you going to fight with while I'm gone?" I joke when she comes back in the room. Her tears are really flowing.

"Don't," I tell her. "If you do, I'm going to cry too." I'd forgiven her for digging her nails into my arm during one fight and she'd forgiven me for the time I tried to kick her and broke my toe on the metal leg of her bed. We both ended up crying when that happened and agreed to tell my mother a lie about it.

I'm going to miss her and Nanna and my friends. I'm going to have to start all over again here. I will even miss my mother, who has tried very hard to make this transition easy, getting me new suitcases, some better clothes, and supplies for my room even though our budget is very tight.

"I got you a surprise I thought you'd find funny," my mother says. She pulls out a t-shirt from a bag she is carrying. "Save a Tree, Eat a Beaver" it says on the front next to a giant cartoon of a lecherous beaver with big teeth. My sister snorts. I'm mortified that my mother doesn't understand the slang.

"Aww, thanks Mom," I say, as I take it from her and quickly shove it into my bureau drawer before anyone else can see it.

"You can wear it at orientation," my mother says, "with the other Beavers here." She laughs a little as she puts the cleaning supplies on my closet shelf. I'm embarrassed, but really, all she wants is for me to be happy here.

"Okay then," my mother says with a little tremor in her voice. "Let me go write down the number on the hall phone so we can call you. Do you need anything else?"

I look around at the standard-issue desk with Nonno's manual typewriter, my dictionary and office supplies strewn on it.

"No, I'm good, Mom."

I've been to the bookstore already with my booklist for classes, and my mother was panicking about the cost. I don't want her to worry. I want her and my sister to both leave and to stay longer, as a wave of sadness and fear wash over me at the thought that I am going to be living here.

I turn toward her to give her a hug and she kisses me on the lips, trying not to cry. My sister begins quietly sobbing on the bed. "It'll be all right," I say to them both as if I'm the parent saying goodbye. "I'll see you in a few weeks."

I'm suddenly more worried about my mother being sad and

who will watch out for my sister, than I am about what's ahead for me. I'm sailing away to my new country, but I don't see that place yet, so it feels like there's nothing ahead but endless open water. It's easier in the moment to look back, wave at them, and try to and ignore the queasiness about my new freedom.

Dr. Wertime is the creative writing professor on campus. I screw up my courage during my first semester and make an appointment to visit him in his second-floor office in the English building to ask if I can work with him individually on my poetry over the Winterim term, which takes place between semesters while I'm at home. He's tall and on the younger side, maybe in his late thirties, but I find I can't really make eye contact because I'm so nervous. He asks to see some of my poetry, and I shyly show him my carefully typed collection from high school. Leaning back in his chair, he grabs a pencil and starts to read. He writes all over the onionskin typewritten pages. *VERBS not adjectives and adverbs, rhythms! Economy vs. Stinginess and thinness?*

"Some of these things are clichéd," he says, "but you have made a good start."

He tells me he'd love to work with me and that I need to get the *Norton Modern Poetry Anthology* and just read to see what I like and write three reaction sheets about those poems. In addition, he wants me to write a new poem of my own each week and he will meet with me during Winterim. He marks the paper up some more, adding "Poetry is the art of causing the word to resound behind words." He tells me that's T.S. Eliot.

All through that first Winterim, Dr. Wertime shapes my words. The scratch of his pencil, the mark it makes in my heart. I can't articulate it then, but I feel hope that this is a special flower just for me. That I can come from my place of hiding and alight on it. I'm very careful in the beginning to never ask Dr. Wertime for too much time in case he changes his mind about me.

My mother drives me back and forth to these weekly meetings because we only have one car. At the end of the five weeks, Dr. Wertime gives me the assignment of writing a sonnet and I spend hours trying to come up with something that works. I'm crying at my desk; I'm so frustrated.

My mother comes into my bedroom, "Do you need help?" she asks. I want my work to be mine, but I'm desperate because my meeting with him is the next day. "We could do something funny for it," she says when I describe what I'm trying to do.

For the next hour, she sits at my desk, and I curl up on my bed and we draft a humorous Ogden Nash type poem about how hard it is to write a sonnet. She wants me to tell Dr. Wertime she helped me write it. I don't want to do that, but, laughing, I type it up and include it as the final poem for the project. I share the whole collection of poetry with her when I'm finished because she is a good proofreader and Dr. Wertime is a stickler for that.

In his final evaluation, he writes "…In your journal entries, your drafts and, not least, your final poems, you display all the makings of a fine writer of poetry…Though much work lies ahead, you should delight in what you've done. It's been a pleasure to work with you."

After that first Winterim, I'm no longer traveling at sea. I've docked at the Castle and found (although I don't have the self-awareness or confidence to allow myself to think this then) a writing father. I don't become a princess like my favorite childhood novel, but I have a clear identity: I'm an English major, a writer.

Cheryl is a senior, also an English major, and the editor of the *Beaver News*. She's boyish with small perfect breasts and slim hips. She's shorter than I am and almost always dresses in jeans and pants. She has a man's vest she got in a thrift store that she wears over her t-shirt and has a thin gold necklace that circles her delicate neck. Her short dark hair and dark eyes make her look vaguely exotic. I don't care about her "being gay," I tell her when we talk in the dining hall, or I visit her room in the Castle. We soon become friends, sharing books and music. Sometimes she comes over after she's done her work-study job in the dining hall to visit me while I'm doing one of my work-study jobs, "sitting desk" as a dormitory receptionist. Cheryl tells me I'm a good writer after she reads some of my poetry and essays. She wants me to write for the newspaper and so I start doing that—humorous essays, movie reviews, and editorials.

Cheryl and I are sitting across the street from school at the Howard Johnson's in an orange booth having ice cream one night at the start of the spring semester. I'm suddenly terrified. I twirl my ice cream spoon around and around on the placemat. I know what I want to say. That I like her like that. Like a boy.

"I missed you over break," I manage to choke out. There's a long pause that holds everything I'm suddenly not able to articulate. She smiles.

We are in the newsroom. It's getting later and later. There's a bed for when she's pulling an all-nighter, which she's doing often, juggling work on her English thesis with her editorial job. Everyone has gone back to their rooms because it's after one in the morning and I lie down for a few minutes. Suddenly, she is there too, and we look at each other. Then she is on top of me, and we are kissing and kissing, and she tastes like the cigarettes she is constantly smoking. The next morning when I wake up in my dorm room, I'm paralyzed with anxiety and sick to my stomach thinking about what we did. Nobody here can discover that we've started a relationship and I'm sleeping with her. But I end up telling one friend I trust. A few weeks later, when my roommate and the other women on my hall refuse to shower with me and say terrible things, I think about Anita Bryant waving her anti-dyke signs and screaming rage. *Screw them*, I think, channeling my inner hockey player. *You can't hurt me.* And I go into the bathroom when the other girls are in there anyway.

"You're going over to Cheryl's *again?*" my mother asks.

It's summer and she planned to go spend the night at her boyfriend's house, but she wants me to do my high school job of being home for my sister, who is never here anyway because she's out with her boyfriend. It's infuriating that she doesn't think anything has changed even though I've been away on my own this year.

"Drop me off, please Mom?" I beg. Cheryl's parents conveniently live ten minutes away from us and she has a pool at her house.

My mother sighs and then agrees. She likes Cheryl. I'm terrified of her finding out. I think back to when I was seven and she told me Aunt Faye was a "lesbian" and the way she said it made it seem like an awful thing. Cheryl and I hang out by her pool and sleep over each other's houses whenever we can. I am reading all of Thomas Hardy, which Cheryl has given me because his books are her favorites. We bond over Tess D'Urberville's trauma and tragedy. Cheryl graduated and is Editor-in-Chief of the *Camden News* as her first job. She loves me. She tells me I will be a successful writer.

In the fall, back at college, my new roommate, Lisa, is a transfer student. Lisa went to Ringling Brothers circus school for a while to be a clown but decided it wasn't for her. She rides her unicycle up and down our dorm hall when she's stressed. I tell her about my relationship with Cheryl early on. I'm worried she will hear something around campus after the bullying I endured the previous semester and even though Cheryl's graduated, she'll be visiting me. Lisa says this isn't a problem because she's going home every weekend. It's working out well until she decides to tell her Christian parents about me. They demand she get another roommate immediately and say they are going to tell the school about me.

Lisa says, to my tearful face, "They said they'd call your mother."

I'm terrified about what happens if my mother hears about this from someone other than me. I have supportive friends both at school and at home whom I've told about my relationship.

"If I tell my mother," I say to Cheryl, "maybe it'll just not be such a big deal."

My mother comes up to school once a semester to take me to Dr. Girsh, the allergist who is nearby. There's a Magic Pan restaurant in his building and it's always a treat to eat chicken crepes after the visit instead of going right back to Beaver. I decide I don't want to tell my mother about Cheryl over the phone and instead will do it when she comes to take me to the appointment. I'm thinking it won't really be so bad. *After all*, I tell myself, *you love who you love.* How can my mother have a problem with that?

My mother and I ride over to the office chatting about school and what writer I'm studying. We sit in the waiting room for a while, reading our books and I realize that I can't really talk to her here with the other patients around. Then we wait under the fluorescent lighting of the exam room. I'm feeling like I can't breathe every time I imagine what I'm going to say. My mother looks up from her book, "How's Cheryl doing?" she asks.

I see my chance. "She's good. She likes being Editor-in-Chief of the *Camden News* and wants me to do some writing for them this summer. That way, I'll have better clips than the *Beaver News* and—"

My mother interrupts, "You really need a better job this summer, so you can make more money."

I'm trying to think of something positive that will please her. "Cheryl got me her old job in the dining hall, so I'm making lots more money during the semester working there. It was such a great thing she made sure I got it."

"That is good," my mother agrees.

My chance is slipping away. "Listen, Mom. There's something we need to talk about."

My mother turns her book over on her lap to hold her page. "What?" she asks, shifting a bit uncomfortably in the hard chair.

"So, Cheryl and I are having a relationship," I blurt out. I'm thinking, *there, that sounds good*. "We've been together about nine months. I'm telling you because Lisa's parents found out and they were upset and threatening to call the school and you. I didn't want you to hear it from somebody else. I wanted to tell you." I say the rest of it like I'm taking a giant spoonful of the worst tasting medicine imaginable and doing it fast so I'm choking and swallowing to finish it.

My mother stares at me blankly. There's a ragged pause so deep I can hear the quiet hiss of the light and the murmur of voices in the other exam room. My heart is thumping and there's a roaring in my ears like a bomb has been dropped.

Her eyes narrow as she looks at me, color draining from her face. "You've been sleeping with Cheryl when she stays over?"

"Uh, yeah, well...." I stammer, coloring.

Another pause. "I don't want to hear any more about this," she hisses, and she picks up her book and stares down at it without turning the page.

"Mom, I just wanted to make sure you knew, I didn't want you to be surprised or upset. Lisa is leaving next semester anyway. She wants to be closer to home."

"I *said* I don't want to discuss it."

Another few minutes of silence follows. *Fine*, I think, *be that way*.

Then she looks up from her book, eyes slightly glistening and says, "Cheryl is no longer welcome in our house. I don't want her anywhere near your sister or talking to her anymore."

I am flooded with rage and shame. The anger rises so high, there is no place for it in this small room, so I let it smash into myself. I pick the cuticle on my index finger till it bleeds and I put it in my mouth to try and stop the flow. The silence after this stretches on and on. We say nothing to each other even when the doctor comes in for the exam. We walk out of the office silently. We don't go to the Magic Pan. She drives me back to campus like we've come from a funeral. She doesn't move to kiss or hug me goodbye when she pulls up to my dorm entrance.

"What are you going to tell Missy about why she can't talk to Cheryl?" I finally say when she turns off the engine. My sister and Cheryl have become close.

"I don't know," she replies, not looking at me as she starts up the car.

And with that, I can't get out of the car quickly enough. I slam the passenger door shut as my rage begins to morph into sadness. I watch her drive up the road past the Castle to make sure she's really gone before I start sobbing.

A week later she calls me on the hall phone. Her voice is

tense, "I want you to go see Sandy, a therapist Mrs. Lee sees. I've talked to her about our situation." I don't say anything. "I'll pick you up Thursday after your class and you'll go have an appointment." I don't really want this, even if I do like Mrs. Lee. I certainly don't want to see somebody my mother has already spoken to, but I also need to go home for the summer and holidays. I don't want to piss her off any more than I already have.

"I cried all the way home," my mother continues. "I can't believe you decided to tell me like that.

"Fine," I say, feeling like I want to punch the door of the phone booth as a stand in for her, "I'll go."

"Come on in," Sandy smiles.

She is a little shorter than me and slender, with very kind eyes and blond hair. She's younger than my mother (nineteen years older than me, I find out later). She leads me into her tiny office, and we sit side by side on a little sofa. I like that I don't have to sit across from her because I can look away.

"I realize you might not like that I've seen your mother a few times," she starts, "but this time is your time to talk to me and I'm not going to share anything you say with her."

I don't trust her, not only regarding this promise, but because I think she's going to take my mother's side. She's going to say I'm not being fair to her and that I'm "selfish," which is my mother's favorite word to use with me when I'm not doing what she thinks I should be doing. I just look down at the rug and wait to see what's going to happen next.

I remember the times my mother took my sister and me to "family therapy" during the divorce. We'd all go into the office together and then the psychologist would dismiss my sister and me to speak to my mother alone. We'd hang out in the boring waiting room, reading our books or flipping through old magazines. It suddenly occurs to me that the therapist thought it was my mother who was having some problems that impacted our family. We never went to these sessions for very long.

She continues, "Why don't you tell me how you are seeing things, so I can understand?" I don't want to be rude, so I look up at her and tell her that I'm just coming this one time because my mother made me. I describe how upset I am that my mother is acting this way about Cheryl and that I don't know what to do. As I talk to her, I'm not emotional, even though I'm shaking inside. My anger is protecting me.

I look back down at the floor. There's a long pause then and out of the corner of my eye I see that she's looking at me and thinking. But then she does something totally surprising to me.

"If you come to see me regularly," she says, "I'm not going to see your mother. I'll be your therapist only. I think you and I will work better together. Your mother can find a different therapist if she wants one."

In that first session, by choosing me, she plants a tiny seed of trust. At the end of our meeting, she hands me a multipage form that's titled *Life History*. She says, "You are a writer, so I think you'll find it interesting to work on this."

Afterwards, back at my dorm, I leaf through all the questions before I start writing until I land on the one at the end. "Describe the characteristics of your ideal therapist," it says.

And I start laughing as I write my joking answer, "Someone with all the qualities of Jesus Christ…." Because it feels like it's going to take someone with a lot of power to save me.

I start seeing Sandy weekly or every other week, even when I'm at school. And somehow over the months that follow, I begin to feel like there's an umbilical cord between us that gives me the nourishment I need to help me grow up. Somehow, I've found, or rather my mother has found me, another mother.

I'm taking Abnormal Psychology and not long after I start my own therapy with Sandy, members of the class begin weekly visits to Norristown State Hospital. We each meet individually with an assigned patient for an hour. We are allowed to read their charts so that we can write a paper about our experiences with them. A staff member must unlock the door to let me on the ward.

My patient, Cecilia, is schizophrenic and eyes me warily, but when it's nice we walk around outside and talk. She tells me about the macaroni and cheese she likes and later begins to share about her life, how she loved somebody she met during an earlier hospitalization, what she wants for herself when she leaves. I like her and try and ask questions and listen like Sandy does for me. I guess the plan is to provide the patients with some socialization, but it's like *One Flew Over the Cuckoo's Nest* there. Green tiled floors, muffled TV sounds, the occasional yelling of a patient or frustrated staff. The nurse tells me about a patient who spoke so fast nobody could understand him. They decided to use behavior modification and slow down his speech by using the ubiquitous cigarettes as rewards. As they slowed him down, they realized everything he was saying was a curse word: shit, fuck, cunt, motherfucker. So, they used cigarettes and speeded up his speech again, rewarding him for being unintelligible but at least being part of the community and not triggering other patients. I'm not afraid of the strangeness here. I feel like it's somehow familiar, like home.

My favorite part of these visits are the grounds around the gray hulking buildings. They are indescribably beautiful. We turn off Skippack Pike and wind through what had once been farmland but is now filled with fields of tall wildflowers and birds and butterflies cradling and holding up the dark center of hospital buildings. I feel like crying every time we drive through.

In Dr. Wertime's Creative Writing class, he throws fifteen objects down on the big conference room table in the library classroom where the twelve of us meet. There's a comb, a matchbook, a pencil, and a sock. He says, "Make a story with at least ten of these objects in it." I write about a boy who has gone away to school. His mother picks up his blue sock from underneath the bed and sadly contemplates her loss as she looks at the matchbook with a picture of an airplane on it. I title it "Man's First Flight." Dr. Wertime comments, "…dispassionate yet generous in its treatment of the characters…."

It's in this class that I attempt the first poem about Daddy. I've started dreaming about him. "My father trails behind/He carries a saw as sharp as his smile/and speaks of killing geese./ Come back, he says and bruises my arm/Before I wake/I will lie down in the dirt;/feel the blade blunt against my heart."

No one has heard from Daddy in the six years since he sent that letter. Although, once my sister said she saw him when she was walking home from school. He stopped paying any child support right after the letter and my mother didn't want to pursue him and spend more money on legal fees she couldn't afford.

Nanna helps me pay for a semester abroad in London my junior year because I can't work when I'm over there. In January, before I board the plane, my mother gives me a small silver pin, with an enameled center that depicts a water scene and a card that talks about being brave and enjoying my journey "across the pond." When she does things like this, it's like there is a truce between us. We hug goodbye.

It's late May when I get home from England. I'm jet lagged and having a hard time being back in my bedroom and dealing with my mother telling me when I can have the car and when I can't after months of freedom. I feel like I'm crammed into a tiny place. Cheryl has been busy, and hasn't been able to see me, and I'm panicked about what is happening to us. When I was in England, she didn't write much. When I'd call her from the phone in the red booth (I'd learned how to scam to get free overseas minutes) she was distant.

I drag the phone in my mother's bedroom across the hall into my bedroom. The cord isn't long enough, so I sit on the floor leaning against the door to keep it closed. It's about 10 p.m. and my sister is out, but my mother is home in the living room watching television. She's already in her nightgown, a peach sheer flowing thing that I don't remember seeing before. I'm ignoring her after we'd had some words about my getting a job earlier in the day.

"I've been back here four days," I snap at her. "Can I at least unpack first?"

I call Cheryl and ask her what's happening with us and when we can get together. "I've met someone," she says. "I don't want to hurt you, but I think I want to be with her."

While we are talking, the phone is clicking like someone is picking it up. I open my door a little and shout down the hall, "I'm on the phone, please don't pick it up," and slam my door closed again. *How could she fall in love with someone else?*

The phone clicks again and I yell downstairs a second time. Then I tell Cheryl I need to go because I'm upset, and I can't talk to her.

I hang up and call my friend Barrie to tell her what's happening. I'm crying harder and harder and choking to get the story out.

Suddenly I hear my mother screaming and her footsteps running upstairs. She shoves the door open, and her nightgown billows out below her contorted face. She looks like a deranged barefoot pumpkin.

"Shut up! You won't talk to me that way. Just shut up," she's breathing hard as she shouts. "You'll never talk to me that way again," she's screaming, and she hits me several times with her fists. I've moved away from her and covered my face, but there's nowhere to go in my bedroom.

"Leave me alone," I holler. "I wasn't talking to you. Get out of my room. Get out!"

I've dropped the phone but haven't hung up, so Barrie is still listening. I can hear her saying, "Deb? Deb?"

My mother turns and leaves the room.

I fumble for the phone, "Come get me," I sob.

"I'm on my way," Barrie says.

I stuff several hundred dollars in travelers checks I still have left from my trip into my red backpack and grab a few clothes from the suitcase that's spilled open on my floor. When I see from my window that Barrie has pulled up in her father's sports car, I walk downstairs. My mother is crying softly, curled up on the sofa with some tissues in her fist.

"Where are you going?" she asks. "We need to talk."

"I'm leaving." I fly out into the early summer night, slamming the screen door behind me. *I am never going back to that house*, I tell myself. I open the door of the silver Celica and Barrie pulls away, revving the engine a little to emphasize my escape. At her house, we grab beers and lie in the backyard grass looking up at the sky spinning over the neighborhood, stars barely visible. I'm not sure if the ground beneath me is enough to hold me up, but right then it's the whole world.

I have Advanced Creative Writing and Senior Seminar with Dr. Wertime my final semester, and it feels like I've gone to heaven although I'm working harder than I ever have. My senior thesis is about Moll Flanders and how she's a sociopath who's manipulating the reader.

Our relationship is different. He loans me books from his office wall because he recognizes I will return them. He has told me about his "mentally ill" father and about a daughter who is somewhat older than me but is from his first marriage and who he doesn't see very often.

For my last assignment in Creative Writing, I write a personal essay called "Building Myself." I write: "For writing is really nothing more or less than a finely tuned listening, for myself, for the self in other people and things that through writing, I can become...The poem or story I create is like those caverns in Virginia I visited when I was younger. They were totally different from the outside world yet connected to it. Ah, I thought, that formation of stone looks like a heart or tree. Yet I knew all the while that it was something stranger and more difficult to explain. The hollow spaces of those caves were filled with a beauty that may have imitated the outside world but held a larger meaning too. Anyone looking at the caves must have an awareness of both places. Caves grow from the inside, out. My writing, too, is like this process."

What I can't articulate to Dr. Wertime, or to my mother, who proudly comes to the special ceremony where I'm given Departmental Honors for English, or to my post-Cheryl boyfriend I've been dating most of my senior year who was accepted into dental school, is my fear. What will I do after graduation? I've built myself, but what's next? Where will I live? What will happen to me?

When I was younger, we would go on what my mother gleefully called "Nonno rides" whenever we took the wrong turn during a car ride somewhere. My grandfather was a pharmaceutical salesman who travelled around his territory in upstate New York and didn't like to use roadmaps. My mother said he always turned getting lost into an adventure. On a Nonno ride, we'd just take different routes, not trying to go anywhere in particular, to see whatever interesting places might exist that we didn't know about. But how lost can you really get? There are maps, other people to ask. Still, it was exciting, not scary, to wander. Somehow, we always got where we were supposed to be going eventually.

It's time to go on a Nonno ride, I think as I sit under the tent on the Castle lawn for my graduation ceremony. At the end, I throw my cap high up into the sky and catch it, tearing up as I look at Grey Towers. I'm the first person in my family to graduate college.

My mother walks over with my sister to hug me, "Congratulations," she says beaming. "I'm *so* proud of you."

Chapter 8 - Shit Show

"Squeeze it," Marc says, putting his fingers up to my nose to press the small metal strip in the respirator mask I'm fumbling to get on. It's a white, rigid, cloth-like material with an elastic strap around the back, and when I breathe my own air rises and fogs my glasses.

I'm standing in my mother's driveway, and it's 8:30 a.m. and already eighty-six degrees out. It's Sunday, and the neighborhood is quiet except for the distant sounds of early morning lawn mowing somewhere around the corner. September 11, 2016 will be our first full day in the Hoarder House. Marc takes his mask off, and even though he's only worn it for a few moments while carrying supplies to the back of the house, a deep red groove runs around his neck from the strap.

We've prepared today, covered head to toe. I'm wearing lightweight hiking pants, an athletic wicking top, a long-sleeved camping shirt of Marc's with vents in the back, high socks, and the sneakers that were new a few weeks ago but are already ruined from our first visit inside the house yesterday. I have sprayed and wiped myself down with two different kinds of insect repellant, the nuclear deep woods stuff, even under my pants, because the mosquitos are that bad. We unload boxes of black, forty-two gallon, heavy-duty contractor bags, disinfectant wipes, a can of Lysol, more masks, "for when we sweat through them," Marc explains, and boxes of black nitrile gloves, the kind that are difficult to rip. We have several different brands of hand sanitizer, including a lemon-scented spray, for when we take them off.

We can do this, I think. I take the grubby key I've attached to a lanyard and unlock the back door. Marc pushes it open and as soon as he does, the fetid smell assaults us again like an angry being we've disturbed. *It must be vanquished*, I tell myself. *We've avoided this long enough.*

First, we agree to go through the house and make another video since the last one didn't come out on his phone. In only twenty-four hours, my mental defense is to make what I saw at the house yesterday fuzzy and distant. By doing this, I try to keep the murderous rage I'm feeling toward my mother in the background. In the moment, I'm fantasizing I won't ever have to talk to her at all about what we are doing or what will be happening with her living situation. But I understand that is not reality. I sternly order myself, *That's something for another day, not this one. Focus on this today.*

"Then after we make the video, I'll work to get this door area clear," Marc interrupts my reverie.

"My mother's room is the better of the ones upstairs. Maybe I should start up there and we'll meet in the middle to make a path through the house?"

He turns and grabs the shovel he brought. A serious shovel. The kind with the point that you dig graves with. "That's a plan," he agrees.

I clamber up the first set of stairs from the basement that lead into the kitchen. Walking through, I step on mounds of plastic bags that crown the three-foot layer that is the "floor." I pass through the dining room and living room, trying not to lose my balance on what is essentially a narrow path of packed layers of papers and objects. I don't want to touch any of this filth, but I definitely don't want to face plant onto it. I hear my breathing through the mask like I'm a space explorer. *Unknown universe, not sure of the danger.*

I walk slowly, clutching my box of contractor bags like a talisman or an instrument I'm going to use to sample the environment I've landed in. Dust and dirt float through the air—debris from mice nests and whatever the hell else I'm stirring up as I walk. A miasma of that putrid odor clutches itself around my throat, making me gag even with the mask. I'm working very hard to not trip and break my leg. *If an eighty-two-year-old woman can navigate this, I can too,* I challenge myself. I push up the stairs, then past the gallon plastic jugs of mystery fluid, some of which Marc has already rolled to the sides to make a narrow pathway down the "hall," a pile of debris two feet deep.

The door to my mother's bedroom only opens a little because there's a three-foot pile of clothing behind it, but there's a foot or so of floor right as I step down into the space, where I can see the brown nubby carpeting underneath. Seeing something below the mess, the only spot of floor in the entire house, gives me a fleeting feeling of purpose and drive. *How much can we get done today?*

Other than my crunching steps and the sound of my breathing, more ragged from my climb in, it's quiet except for the occasional bird call from the open window. I start to tear up as I look around. There's the marble-topped bedside table next to the antique bed with the dark wood headboard. On the table is a lamp with a book, an old shoe, some papers, and a roll of toilet paper. Boxes, bags, and old books scatter the floor. There's a jumble of clothing, a mirror and more bags on the bed which still has filthy sheets on it underneath all the things. She hasn't slept here for a long while. Photographs I remember of my great-grandparents and our old babysitter share space with my sister's and my bronzed baby shoes on the uncluttered (well at least compared to everything else) bookshelves next to the bed. An antique chair has her mink stole draped on the back of it, the pelt matted and covered in dust. There's nothing in the open closet but a few hangers and a cheap black nightgown carefully hung in a clear plastic travel bag. The matching marble-topped tall dresser has her sun hat hanging from the little mirror, but the top of the dresser is completely covered—an empty frog plant holder, plastic bags, old cosmetics, jewelry spilling from open boxes, a travel clock stopped at exactly five o'clock, and assorted tissues and papers. I find a card on the dresser with a picture of the Virgin Mary wearing a crown and holding baby Jesus. *Our Lady of the Sacred Heart* is written in script underneath. *She is the hope of the hopeless*, I read. It makes me snort. Every drawer in the dresser yawns open with clothing and other items spilling out. A long braid of fake brown hair drapes over the top of the piles. *So strange*, I think. *Maybe from her dating days.* A dead plant hangs from the ceiling, its leaves still preserved and black.

Something cracks inside me looking at that plant. Red hot, smoldering rage begins to choke out. Suddenly I'm crying and swearing as I reach up by the window and yank at the whole plant, not caring if I pull the hook from the ceiling. It takes me a couple tries to pull the pot down and I almost slip from the mound of papers I'm standing on. I hurl it at the wall as hard as I can, shattering the pot; dirt flies everywhere, covering more dirt and more disgusting dust that forms a thick coating over everything. *What does it even matter?*

"Fuck you," I shout. "Fuck you! How could you do this?"

My voice is muffled by all the things. I'm wondering if the neighbors can hear me, or Marc downstairs, but I don't care. I stand there for a minute and then powered by my rage, open a contractor bag, and start stuffing things in, sniffling as I go. You can't cry in a mask and I'm sure as hell not taking it off in here.

Later, I'll develop a system for this cleaning process, but at the start it's trial and error. I reach down to pick up something, let's say my old favorite overalls from high school (*Really? She even saved our old clothing?*), but the pant legs are tangled up in my mother's white nurse stockings and other pantyhose and a slip with straps that are wrapped around a dry-cleaning bag with the hangers still hooked in the plastic which is also hooked to a belt from a dress that is tangled up with a black dress pump so when I lift the first object, everything else comes up together like spaghetti and can't be disentangled from whatever is connected. It's a trap on this hostile planet.

I yank hard and almost fall back into the dresser, barely catching myself. Fluttering down near one of my old Dr. Scholls wooden sandals by my foot is a pile of cancelled checks, including one for my application to Beaver College dated December 1977. It's then I realize what's in this room is mostly from 1976 or earlier, around the time my sister and I started closing this door. My mother still slept here, but we went in less and less as we spent more time going out into the world to make our lives with friends, apart from her.

I open a carry-on suitcase that's adrift in the center of the room. Inside is a scuba mask and flippers and binoculars from a trip she took with her boyfriend. I fill one contractor bag by stuffing the whole suitcase into it along with some more clothing. None of it is salvageable because it reeks so badly. Then I start a second bag. And a third bag. And a fourth and a fifth. I look around and the landscape looks the same. I'm dragging each bag out into the "hallway," but they are heavy with purses and clothing and papers. I can't get very far with them. It's terribly hot, but I can't take off any of my clothing, I can't get enough air through the mask as I'm exerting myself lifting the bags. The house is creepily quiet. A kind of terror starts to build that makes sweat trickle from my forehead onto my glasses, making it difficult to see. *I'm trapped. I'm totally trapped.* I can't easily escape the room because the bags are blocking the hallway, and the door keeps slowly closing. It's overwhelming and stifling, and I am panicking. I push my way out into the hall, my feet starting to come out from under me as I slide back down the stair hell holding tightly to the banister. *All I need is to hurt myself doing this,* I think. I work my way back toward the rec room. I can hear Marc grunting through his mask as he's thwacking at a pile near the back door and cursing occasionally.

"Can you help me?" My panic causes this to come out more like a wail than a request.

"Yeah, give me a minute." Thunk. It sounds like he's chipping away at something hardened. *Maybe he's finally reached the floor?*

"I need help with the bags." My panic starts to subside as I talk to him. He follows me back up, and I help him push the bags down the hallway. He hauls them over his shoulder all the way downstairs and out the back door. I stumble behind him to the yard, and we walk around to the front of the house.

"This isn't going to work this way," he says, wiping his face after he removes his mask. "Let me think about it while we take a break."

We hang our wet masks on the low branch of a small tree. I take a Sharpie and put my initial on mine. He says we can dry them out and reuse them a few times. In this moment, as I look at him, grungy from physical labor and after twenty-four years of loving him, I still think he's attractive. He's a little taller than me and muscular, the most handsome man I ever dated, the smartest and the youngest, six years my junior.

My friend, Fran, teased me after she first met him, "Were those dimples chiseled into those good looking cheeks?" I can't believe I have a partner who loves me enough to do this dirty work. No matter what we've been through as a couple, he is the one man who has never run away or abandoned me.

A wall of stultifying humidity hits once we are outside, but at least the festering smell of the house isn't as strong. We strip off our gloves, throwing them into another contractor bag. Then we use hand sanitizer and grab our water bottles from the car. It's been an hour and a half or so since we started. Marc opens and sits in a never-used camp chair with the tags still on it that he found inside the laundry room. For some reason, it only smells a little. He takes a second camp chair for me from the back of his car and leaves the hatchback open, so we have some shade to rest in.

Kathy sees us and walks over from her house. "Listen, I've unlocked our garage. Just walk through and use the bathroom anytime. There's room in the extra refrigerator for food, too, if you want to use it."

She looks at the piles of books and things we've removed from my mother's car that we think might be salvageable and that are still sitting along the edge of the driveway from yesterday. "Shall I run to Goodwill for you?" She looks both of us up and down. "I want to help, but you know I'm not going in there, right?" She starts laughing a little in a way that I've always found endearing. Her whole face lights up when she smiles under her wavy brown hair that's a little graying. I can't believe she's in her forties, my "little" neighborhood sister.

"Bless you," I joke, and then we're all laughing. "And no, you are definitely NOT going in there." Marc shakes his head and looks over toward the closed front door while thoughtfully taking another swig of his water.

I reach into our car for paper bags I've brought to put the books in and hand them to her. Clearly, I don't have enough.

"I've got some boxes and bags we can use at my house. And I mean it. I really don't mind helping you guys," she says, sensing my shame about the situation.

"Be careful what you wish for," I say.

Kathy shrugs and doesn't seem disturbed, even though after sitting outside for 24 hours, the books emit a toxic mildewed odor. I momentarily feel sadness for the sorting people at Goodwill, but it passes when I think about what we need to deal with here. There's only so much empathy I can muster.

"Don't worry about it," she smiles as she heads across the street. "I'll be back later."

Marc and I sit for a few more minutes next to the car having the conversation that has been on repeat since yesterday:

Me: "How can she live like this? Who lives like this? I don't understand."

Marc: "I don't know. I don't know how you live like this."

As we talk, he suddenly looks over at the sprawling bush next to where we are sitting and puts his finger to his lips, "Look," he whispers.

Underneath, in a little scooped out indentation sits a large, unmoving, brownish bunny. Eventually, as we sit there quietly, the rabbit turns over on its back, cooling itself in the heat. I wonder if my mother ever noticed it. I imagine her talking to it. Its spot looks lived in.

We go back to surveying the ten bags we've filled that Marc has already lined up next to the house. He shakes his head. "I don't think we can do this in nine days," he says, unwrapping a power bar.

"We need a different plan. We can't get the bags from upstairs till we shovel a path, and we need to be able to open the front door. Then we can bring things out both ways." We are plotting a planetary invasion.

"Okay," I say. "What next?"

"I'll work by the back door and finish clearing it out and you go ahead of me and start up the stairs into the kitchen. I think we'll make more headway if we do it that way."

I start in front of him, outside the laundry room where the stairs go from the rec room to the kitchen. I feel less panicked, and the shaky, tearful feeling that washes over me every time I think of the enormity of what needs to be done is more manageable in Marc's company. He's stopped saying much, but his sighing and the sounds of the shovel make a tiny island of comfort in this sea of chaos.

If I squint my eyes and look at the rec room, it's almost as I remember it—bookshelves lining the wall, the television in the corner—but when I open them and really look, the pictures on the wall are askew and there's an ironing board in the middle of the room with a photo of my sister and my oldest niece, a roll of Christmas wrapping paper and other papers on top of it. There are boxes stacked all around the room and piles of clothing and other jumbled objects. A clothing steamer sits next to an unopened box of bedsheets, that rests next to a new lamp in a box that is surrounded by bags of all sizes from different stores filled with who knows what. There's so much down here that the furniture (if it's still underneath all of this) isn't visible at all.

I'm getting more used to breathing through the mask, and I breathe in the redolent stench I will never get used to—a combination of body odor, mold and other types of putrescent smells that are indistinguishable because they all blend, forming themselves into a thing that follows us everywhere. Even when we leave the house, I'm aware of it, seeping out of the windows and under the still locked garage door like a Hoarder House ghost that has been unleashed by our presence.

Marc hangs a contractor light on the door to the kitchen and shines it down the steps, so I can see things better, although I'm not sure I really want to. I start picking up what's covering the stairs. This mess is different than what's in the bedroom. It's wet and moldy, water seems to have been running from the kitchen somewhere, down the stairs and into the rec room. *For how long?* I think. I pick up sodden spaghetti clothing and more dry-cleaning bags, but here there are things that are just trash as well—food wrappers, empty coffee cups, unopened mail, training notebooks from continuing education she did when she became a nursing director, books in bags, books we got her as presents or that she insisted on buying as souvenirs in recent years when we went to places like the Philadelphia Museum of Art.

As she's had less money and couldn't buy as much for herself, she'd plead for something like an expensive art exhibit catalog, which I'd get her, maybe for Christmas or maybe just because she insisted like a child. *What's the harm?* I'd think, *it makes her happy*. But in the past several years, I'd have a sick feeling in my stomach as I did it. Some part of me knew there was something wrong, something about the compulsive way she asked and clutched it in the shopping bag after it was purchased.

I knew things were worse in this house, yet my sister and I continued to do nothing. *What was there to do?* Was this about living the way she wanted? Or was it about an illness, something that we should have tried to step in and fix. The thought of having to talk to her about this house after being here makes my skin crawl. I can see her screaming at me. I can see her, more likely, just trying to wave away my sister's and my care and concern for her. *Does she think she deserves this? Does she not see how it really is?* Since I was little, I've felt my mother's vulnerability and strangeness. Other people didn't see it. Even my sister didn't because I was the buffer. But denial is impossible here.

I toss the hardcover catalogue of the Hudson River School exhibit I took her to into a contractor bag. It reeks, it's wet, unsalvageable. I start to cry again, but this time the hot rage is like a river, running through me and giving me energy to rip through another pile of books that are still in their Barnes & Noble bags. Here are hundreds and hundreds of dollars she spent on multiple copies of the same book about China or Scotland. There are also unwrapped presents, often with greeting cards for the grandchildren and for my sister and me. The grandchildren gifts are old items they would have liked fifteen years ago.

At a holiday gathering, my mother would arrive bearing a beautifully wrapped present and hand it to me saying, "I got you something else you'd really like too, but I can't find it," laughing. "Oh, it'll turn up," she'd add. Melissa, Ron, Marc, and I would all glance knowingly at each other and chuckle uncomfortably along with her.

Toward the top of the stairs, I reach over and grab a little stack of objects with an unsigned birthday card that was clearly put aside for my sister. Melissa would like these things—a plaque with a funny saying, a book, and a little ornament.

"Look," I say to Marc, turning around and trying not to fall down the stairs I'm precariously standing on. I hold the little stack up for him to view, "All the missing presents have been found!"

He grunts and looks up from his continued chipping away at a hardened pile of something that I can see looks like a torte or lasagna. He stops. Leaning on the shovel he makes the understatement of the day, "This is not fun."

I go back to the task of clearing the steps. After an hour or so and about eight more bags into it, I've made a passable path almost to the kitchen doorway. You can step on a small area of floor up most of the six steps. At the entrance to the kitchen, pushed up against the door like a wave threw them, are piles of photo albums and packages of photographs from her more recent vacations. Finding these like this disturbs me the most, probably because I value photographs and hold carefully to my own. They are the talismans of memory and will be the only thing left of our stories, long after we are gone. Here are two carefully put together albums from the trip she took to Disney with my sister's family. My oldest niece is standing next to Mickey Mouse and waving. There's a picture with my mother and the grandchildren smiling in front of Cinderella's Castle.

The photos are wet and blackened with mold. The album covers are damaged and torn. *Where is the water coming from? Maybe it's under the refrigerator.* Reaching toward the pile by the door, I realize there are probably a hundred envelopes of developed film and negatives from her trips to China scattered everywhere along the wall. Some are wet, all are damaged. I don't throw any out even though they are probably ruined. They meant something to her once, so I don't comprehend how she could leave them like this. *I don't understand at all. Shut up,* I tell myself. *Not here. You can't do this right now.*

I try and set things like this aside as I go, but mostly I'm throwing out a fortune of unopened, defiled things from the bookstore—books, toys, cards, little games, and tchotchkes for around the house. I find a copy of Dante's *Inferno* buried in the pile.

Crouched on the stairs, I ready my assault on the kitchen. All the other things accumulate like a mountain ahead of me, one on the verge of an avalanche. There's nothing to do but to keep going. I pull out a videocassette recorder tape in a case—a course she took (although she never had a VCR): *No Excuses: Existentialism and the Meaning of Life, Part 2*. I laugh, and I pull off my glove and take my phone from my pocket to get a picture of it nestled in wet moldy sweatshirts, papers, and plastic bags.

"Jesus," Marc says," if you load books into these bags, make them lighter, you're killing me." He laughs and heaves one of the eight bags over his shoulder and carries it out through the back door, which can be opened most of the way thanks to his hard work. He's taken the broken glass out of it, so the storm door is just a frame.

At the edge of the kitchen by the stairs, I dig down deeper where there's nothing but black rotted papers and other mess at floor level two and a half feet down. I'm scooping up rotting muck and putting it in the contractor bag. It smells rank. I roughly pick up another bag and it rips open, spilling something wet and foul onto my arm. It takes me a full minute to process my shock. It's shit. It's my mother's shit smeared onto my arm. My mother was shitting in plastic bags in her kitchen. I start shaking and feel pure revulsion start in my gut and scream its way out of my mouth.

"Oh my god," I yell, "Oh my god. Get it off me. What the fuck!"

"Okay, Okay," Marc yells up to me from below, "I'm coming with the wipes."

I'm sobbing, "It's shit, it's shit, it's shit."

"Yes," he says, "I know." He holds my arm and gently cleans it with the damp Lysol wipe. "Outside," he orders.

"What do you mean, you know?" I ask. He looks away for a minute.

"I've been shoveling feces and hardened baby wipes for the

past three hours," he says. "That's what was by the back door. Bags and bags and bags of it. Some broken open and everything hardened to cement. I was hoping it was only there, but I guess it's not."

I want to retch, but I can't. I've always had a strong stomach, but this is an Olympic-sized test. Who lives like this isn't even a question anymore. It's a refrain. *What kind of fucking person does this?*

"Take a break," Marc says. We walk back out to the car, strip off our gloves, and pour on the lemon sanitizer. Marc holds me for a minute, but I'm so numb. I feel like a hardened piece of shit, bringing him into this mess. We are never going to get clean from the giant turd that has been laid on top of us.

The wedding photo - Deborah, her mother, and Howard, 1963

The sales card for the house on Willowbrook Road, 1973

The house on Willowbrook Road, 2016

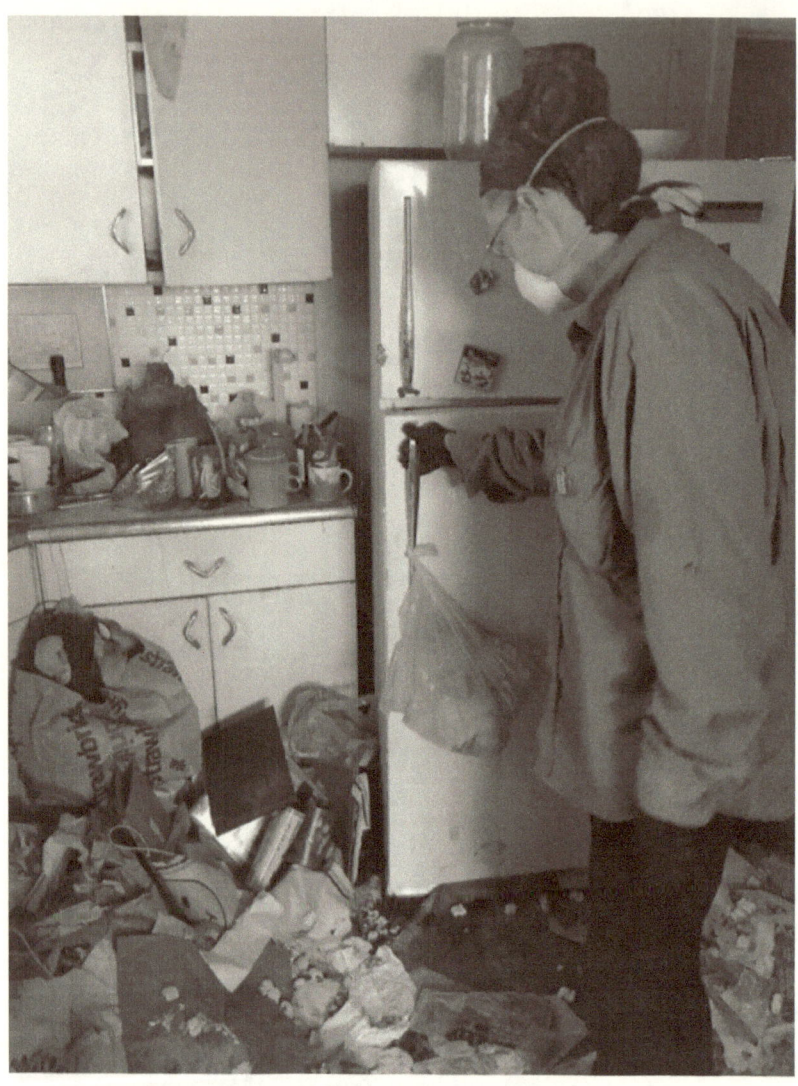

Inspecting the kitchen - Deborah, 2016
Photo Credit: Jacqueline Larma

Deborah's old bedroom and Melissa's childhood bed, 2016
Photo Credit: Jacqueline Larma

The living room, 2016

The sweater photo - Melissa, their mother, and Deborah, 2001

The beach - Deborah's mother and Malcolm, 1955

The first weekend together - Malcolm, Deborah, Andrew, 1995

The Brandywine Museum of Art - Deborah and her mother, 2013

Chapter 9 - The Garden

I'm back at my mother's house after college. It's Christmas and I'm sitting on my old cherry four-poster bed after stashing my books, my journals, my makeshift desk with the file cabinets, my clothes, and extra bedding into my bedroom closet and the garage. I've been away for six months after I graduated from Beaver, living in Delaware in an apartment with Debbie E. and working part time at the Wilmington Convention and Visitors Bureau while attending a full-time doctorate program in English Literature at the University of Delaware. At least that was the original plan, but I hated the program, so I quickly dropped out. I liked the job better, although it was only budgeted until the end of the year.

"I don't expect you to pay room and board unless you're employed," my mother said when we talked over the phone a few weeks before I left Delaware. "You can do chores around the house and take care of your grandmother." She sighed, "My job is demanding, and I'm tired a lot."

I started to cry because I heard, *you won't escape. You'll never escape.*

"Listen," she continued, "it doesn't have to be as bad as the other times you've been home since we're both different."

At this point I made an excuse about having to go, hung up and sobbed. I tried calming down by telling myself, *lots of people have to go home. It doesn't mean they've failed.*

My long legs hang over the edge of my childhood bed here, I'm no taller, but somehow the bed has shrunk. Everything feels small in this house. My mother still works full time at the nursing home, and I generally avoid her when she's around. My sister is off at college.

Most days I spend my time reading when I'm not perusing the help wanted ads for nonprofit public relations jobs. I start reading the French philosopher Bachelard's *Poetics of Space*. In the book, he explores the poetics of intimate spaces, like nests and shells and, particularly, houses. He says these spaces of shelter hold the past and our emotional lives.

I think about memory. *Maybe*, I write in my journal, *when you grow up, your mental space becomes progressively more filled. Time seems shorter. When you are young you have fewer events, so it stretches on endlessly.*

I fill some space with weekly therapy sessions with Sandy, and with thoughts about both Malcolm and Daddy, whom we've been talking about. I am trying to figure out if I should go look for either of them. What would be the purpose for doing that? *I don't seem to have memories of my biological father. I can't find him. All I have is what other people have given me.*

I can look at the pictures in the old photo album in the rec room that show him before he left, playing with me, but I have no memories other than what my mother says about him. "He liked to act in community theatre. He was a good salesman and had a sense of humor."

I can't tell my mother what the real question is. *Why didn't he come looking for me after they divorced?*

I find a part-time gig creating the example paragraphs for an English composition textbook. I write perfect paragraphs about the alcoholic cook in the dining hall at Beaver and how I learned to make pots of coffee in the giant urn early in the morning as part of that job. I write about exploring London and seeing the statue of Peter Pan in Kensington Gardens. I write about my cat Samantha and how when she walks up my chest to greet me in the morning, she drools when she purrs.

It takes three months, but a connection works a miracle and I hear about a job at the Philadelphia Zoo, a place I love. I haven't been there since my Senior Cut Day in high school. Five of us piled into my friend's Mustang and spent the day roaming around the exhibits with my friend Fran telling us about how wolves vocalize to each other and the difference between invertebrates and vertebrates. It was the nerdy kids' alternative to getting drunk at the shore.

When I arrive at the Administration Building, the animal supervisor, Rick, offers to show me around while I wait for my interview. It's a warm day in early March and my coat is open as we walk around the grounds, the flowers just beginning to bud.

"It's America's first zoo," Rick informs me, "even though the Central Park Zoo always tries to claim that honor." He points to the pale, yellow Solitude House built in 1794. "It's empty," Rick explains, "so you can't go inside. But it's the heart of the garden." As we walk, peacocks strut past with raucous cries and tail feathers blooming.

I see some tourists dressed in suits who have apparently never seen squirrels before and watch as they race after them over the lawn with cameras pointing like hunting dogs sensing prey. My fifth birthday party took place at the Houston Zoo. In the childhood album at my mother's house there are photos of me in a green dress with giraffes in the background. There's another with a cake with lions and monkeys on top of it. And one with me riding on the colorful little train that went around the grounds there. I have always loved visiting the Philadelphia Zoo, using my plastic zoo key as a child to operate the boxes that talk about the animals, but now I'm an adult and wondering what it would be like to be part of this place, an insider.

"Want to see something cool?" Rick asks. He's a little seductive, with his blue eyes twinkling at me.

I nod, and he opens a locked gate, so I can enter a large rectangular enclosure. A bobcat approaches me slowly, a little wary of the unfamiliar woman in her best suit who is standing in the middle of her territory. I'm thinking about whether I can run in my new patent leather high heels, but after glancing over at Rick, who is grinning widely at the look on my face, I am reassured.

"Kneel down a little bit," he says. The bobcat comes right up to me like a giant housecat. I gasp as she puts her muddy paws on my black wool skirt, leaving two dirty prints, and leans her face right up toward mine as she lets me touch her head. I can smell her, an intoxicating and slightly nauseating mix of hay and meaty breath.

I am so instantly smitten with her and this place that I'd probably do any job here for free. It feels like that time when I was deciding about college. *This is MY place*, I think. *It's my home.* I'm seeing the zoo as a child does, each sensory detail etched in ink-filled lines. Afterwards, when I try to explain what is special to me here, it's like the print an artist makes from that etching, the details reverse. The peacocks are as difficult to capture as my feelings are about belonging here.

"We got her already tame," Rick explains. After a few minutes of cat communion, he makes a special show of helping me out by holding my arm a little too long as we leave the enclosure. "I wouldn't want you to trip in those beautiful shoes," he jokes and winks at me. "If you get the job," he laughs, "there's lots of other things I can show you."

I am offered the position of Public Relations Manager on my

twenty-third birthday, a few days later.

My office window overlooks the Polar Bear Pool and the African Plains. I swivel my chair to rest my high heels on the window frame behind my desk and watch the animals. The children below press their small hands and noses against the polar bear's enclosure. They scream and jump back as Coldlilocks or Klondike dives into the blue water and smacks a great, white paw against the thick, scratched glass. I can't hear them from here, but the parents are probably reassuring their children that the big bears are just playing. I think to myself, *the polar bears are trying to kill the kids again,* and, in the wild, they would have.

During a typical workday, I'd leave my office in the Administration Building and walk the paths Rick showed me when I interviewed. I'd pass the fake mountains of the African Plains, wander the long walkway that ran around Bird Lake through the heart of the landscape, past Solitude. I'd meander past the groaning tortoises as they laboriously mated in their outdoor exhibit beside the Reptile House, past the flamingos munching flower petals, and by the brown bears wrestling with their peanut butter filled logs. Some days I'd visit the animal nursery (newborns were always good for positive news coverage). Maybe a baby lemur would be playing and would run up one of my arms and down the other, as if I were a firmly planted tree. Or I might stop by to visit the elephants. After these visits, I might smell like a monkey, or the powerful earthy odor of the Elephant House would cling to me. I'd call this my zoo perfume. One of the keepers would sometimes take me inside the elephant enclosure so Petal could greet me by running her bristled gray trunk up and down my coat, leaving a long slimy trail. But I'd always end my errands at my favorite place.

Massa was the world's oldest captive gorilla. His name

was given to him back in the 1930s when white zoo staff weren't concerned about the racist implications. Unfortunately, it was never changed, the excuse being that is how visitors knew him. Home was the Rare Mammal House, alongside the howling chimps and a separate band of gorillas. His exhibit was an older one, tiled like a sixth-grade girls' lavatory. It was decorated with his beloved tire swing, hay and fruits and vegetables for foraging. Captive animals need such things for stimulation. But gorillas are social creatures, and I would find him sitting alone in his exhibit, thoughtfully noshing on a piece of lettuce, watching visitors as they passed by. I thought he had sad eyes.

Sadness was something I was struggling with as well. Despite feeling an immediate deep connection to this place, I spent a lot of time trying not to cry in my office in the first few months. I was terrified I'd be found out as a fraud, the girl who knew nothing. As an English major, I'd slept through biology lectures where I might have gleaned the difference between a phylum and a genus, figuring this would rarely come up in my adult life. Every morning I'd drive to the zoo, tearful and stressing about all the things I had to do and all the things I was certain I'd never understand how to do. My days were filled with calls to reporters, writing news releases, and deciphering how the zoo operated. It felt impossibly hard. I'd often cry on the way home, too. My feared inadequacy was part of my sadness, but there was something else too, a deeper loneliness inside of me.

"There came a time," I tell Sandy, "when the pain was too much—looking back I did things—at the time of the divorce, when Nonno died, but I wasn't all there. I was doing my outward life, but a horrible something was underneath."

"The chasm," Sandy says.

"A lack," I respond. "I really have a very negative view of

the world, secretly, inside," I explain to her, "I believe in all the possibilities, but know that I can't obtain them. Love always leaves and, somehow, it's my fault."

"You don't feel you're worthy of that kind of attention." Sandy says, "from me or anybody. Neurosis," she continues, "is doing the same thing over and over because the problem is in you, it doesn't matter where you deal with it—at home with your mother, at the zoo, anyplace. These things you're feeling aren't real," she insists gently, not taking her eyes off mine.

"So, what do we do about this," I ask, leaning back on the couch away from her, "put a Band-Aid over where my inner earthquake happened, fill it up with cement?" I try and laugh like it's a joke, but I'm afraid.

"No," she says, "We're going to heal it. We need to work on your fathers."

I'm still thinking about this session as I visit Massa, standing outside his enclosure as he watches me eat a sandwich. I find being near him comforting, like when Nonno came to visit when I was a child. He and I would sit in companionable silence together. He'd read me stories, like *Stuart Little*, as I sat on his lap, leaning against his warm chest. Nonno was the safest man I knew.

I'd prop myself against the metal railing in front of the glassed enclosure thinking about the hardships Massa faced in his life. He was silvered a little, with deep-set dark eyes and a jaw that jutted out due to dental problems. And he had his own complicated past. Massa was caught in the wild as an infant in Africa in the 1930s. His mother had most likely been shot. Very sick at the time, Massa was sold by a ship's captain to Gertrude Lintz, a collector of exotic animals who lived in Brooklyn. She nursed him back to health and raised him like a small person. Because it is difficult to tell what sex a baby gorilla is, she thought he was a girl and clothed him in pretty dresses and diapers. She taught him to mop the kitchen floor. One day, she startled him while he was mopping, and he bit her badly. Sixty-five stitches later, he was relocated to the zoo to live in what was then called the Monkey House.

With everyone believing he was a "she," Massa arrived at the zoo to become the bride of a male gorilla, Bamboo. There was a big media "wedding" where the two gorillas were placed in the same enclosure. The living arrangement didn't last long. When it was clear that a mating relationship wasn't going to work out, the two males were separated, and a "divorce" followed. But because he'd been socialized with humans, he couldn't exist in a gorilla band. Massa lived alone ever after. His only family were keepers, and the regular visitors like me. I wondered if, all these years later, he still felt the loss of his animal and human mothers.

So, do you miss your mother? I'd think and imagine him telling me about his story and what it felt like to be him. To be taken captive and forced to turn into something he wasn't, a little girl with a dress.

"And how do you feel," I'd ask.

And his answer: *Alone. Alone.*

I contemplated his life and told him about mine.

"My boss is insane, and there's way too much work for one person to do." He stared at me with wise eyes and listened as I tried try to figure it out. I could imagine him telling me, *Listen, I've lived here more than fifty years, you can last another month in this job and living at home."*

No one knows how long gorillas live in the wild. In my official news releases, Massa's longevity was attributed to "zoo cake," a weighty mix of cornmeal, eggs, ground vegetables, lard, molasses, salt, baking soda, and sometimes meat (depending on the species), which the Philadelphia Zoo had created as a healthy diet for captive animals. The reality was that he had a uniquely Philadelphian taste for Tastykakes, particularly Krimpets, and for Kool-Aid, which his keepers secretly gave him as a treat in a big bowl.

Since primates are dangerously susceptible to human diseases, I was given a yearly tuberculosis vaccine. After that clearance, I could go behind the scenes in his keeper area, too, where the staff could interact with and monitor the animals as they tended to them. Before reaching Massa's two enclosures, I'd have to dodge the poop-throwing chimps and the orangutans wearing empty Pampers boxes as hats to amuse themselves, finally arriving several doors down a small hallway. Here there was no glass between us. He'd come closer to sit and look at me, sometimes holding my hand. Once, I took a documentary filmmaker back there. He observed how Massa came right over to sit near me and put his hand up. He'd watch whatever I was doing. I thought he recognized me from my visits on the other side of the glass.

"Massa responds to you," he said. "Look at him come over and follow you." I love that I am somehow special to our famous gorilla. I love that I am known.

We feed grapes to Massa and some of the other gorillas—including baby Chakka who is a little shy, but still approaches us. There are low rumbles of contentment from the gorillas standing together, Sam and Jess. They are drinking their milk from cups—looking a bit like prisoners. One of the gorilla keepers turns to me, "It almost isn't right. Them being behind bars and that intelligent."

My first big special event was The Great American Teddy Bear Rally. *Bring your teddy bear to the zoo and get a dollar off admission.* There were prizes for the oldest bear, for the best dressed one, for the biggest and smallest. The zoo veterinarian set up a table to check out your teddy bear's health. There were prizes for costumes and all things bear related. My office filled with donated bears from different companies to use as giveaways along with big boxes of ribbons for the contest winners.

"I'm coming," my mother tells me one night when I get back home late from work. Preparations for the rally require me to work ten hour days. "I'm going to bring Nonno's bear and dress up."

"Okay," I say. "But I'll be running around and managing all of it, so I probably won't be able to really hang out with you." I am worried about how the event will go and I don't want to have to feel like I need to take care of her too.

"It'll be fine," she says, her voice a little childish. "Frederick Bear and I will enjoy ourselves without you."

"Go say hi to Fran," I tell her. "She'll be wearing the brown bear costume next to the Impala Fountain." I've managed to get my best friend a job during the summer before she returns to grad school, working in my office and wearing costumes for events. "You can hang out there and keep the little kids from hitting her."

My mother arrives in the late morning of the first day of the rally. My walkie-talkie crackles, signaling that the Impala Fountain bear has some news for me. When I walk through the growing crowd of bear-carrying zoo patrons of all ages, Fran waves a brown fur paw at the registration area, and I spot my mother standing in line. She's dressed in white shorts, blue knee socks and a red and blue striped top that matches the roof fabric on a little toy truck she is pulling. Sitting on the truck is my grandfather's bear, Frederick, about two feet tall, dressed in red Oshkosh overalls my mother has bought for him, his antique blue button eyes gleaming in the warm June sunlight. When Nonno and his brother were children and they were angry at each other they would lop off limbs of each other's bears, and when extremely angry, the head. Fredrick is stiff and worn with patches on his arms and legs.

"What the heck is that outfit she's wearing?" Fran asks, voice muffled through the big-eyed bear head.

"See," I say to her, lowering my face so she can see my expression through the eye holes, "this is just my mother being herself," and I make the crazy sign over my head, laughing. Fran chuckles, but it sounds a bit like a growl through the head.

"I'm entering him in the oldest bear category," my mother says gleefully when I catch up to her moments later. "I think he has a good shot at winning." I am touched that she's come and suddenly think about accusations of nepotism if the family bear does win. My walkie-talkie crackles again with news that a television truck has arrived.

"Good luck to you both, Mom," and I fake salute Frederick before heading down the path away from her.

She finds me later that afternoon and waves at me with excitement as she pulls the toy truck behind her. Frederick is now wearing an official contest ribbon, *Favorite Ancient Bear*. At seventy-years-old, he's come in third place. Fran lifts her bear head off and congratulates my mother. There's some other zoo staff around and I introduce her, feeling both embarrassed and impressed by her creativity.

"Your mom is funny," one of the keepers says.

I'm uncertain how to respond in my professional role, but my mother is already on to her next project. She looks over at the veterinarian who is pretending to listen with a stethoscope as he talks to a child about her stuffed bear's pulse rate.

"I think next year when you do this," she says excitedly, "I should come in my full nurse uniform getup and help him at the Bear Health Clinic."

Fran starts laughing and says it's a great idea, and I nod. My mother *is* funny, she has so much playfulness and joy, like a child sometimes, but there's something just a bit off about how she moves through the world.

After six months of saving my money, I'm able to afford my own apartment and my mother helps me gather up extra pots and pans and things I will need to furnish it. I'm trying not to be too obviously happy about this change in front of her.

I have become so much a part of the zoo community that I participate with the "animal people"—keepers and Animal Department heads—in the rhino birth watch, and spend the night at the Penrose Lab, an old brick building that houses the zoo hospital, waiting for the baby to be born. I watched the live video feed of the mother rhino restlessly moving around her exhibit trying to get comfortable. I stayed up all night, but the rhino did not go into labor while I was there. There was always sex and mating at the zoo: kangaroos humping each other in their outside pen, the chimpanzees going at it behind the glass. Animals know what they must do: move toward each other. And that's what happens when I first see John, a marketing consultant who travelled and consulted for nonprofits. I sat through strategy meetings with him discussing zoo attendance and publicity. I started noticing him lingering near my office. So, when he finally wandered through my doorway wearing his expensive suit and easy smile, it seemed natural.

"Dinner?" he said.

I don't realize then that he's living with his fiancé or that he'd asked a friend of mine out just before he'd asked me. All I know is that there is a romantic dinner at The Garden restaurant where I'm introduced to the bloody richness of carpaccio, Langostinos, and the delight of good champagne. There's salad with garlic, and more than one bottle of chardonnay. He encourages me to eat dessert, the mountains of fruit piling up over the pastry and hurling themselves into whipped cream oblivion. Afterward, we walk through Philadelphia's Rittenhouse Square around the fountain and under the stars. He takes my hand in his fourteen-years-older, more adult one, promising something different and new. I'm a little afraid, but so attracted to him, *I'll just have a bite, just a little taste of this. What could be the harm in that?* We talk about the past, about books and writing, and I am in love with him before we share that first kiss, under the lights in the park, our affair beginning from the moment of *Yes, I'll have dinner with you.* And in the weeks that follow, I discover he's supposed to be getting married in four months in Boston, but he doesn't want to, and, besides, we are soulmates and meant to be. I believe him. I believe with all the certainty in my twenty-five-year-old heart that he loves me more than the woman he lives with, and he confirms this by coming to visit me in Philadelphia as often as he can. We stay in nice hotels with wet bars and plush towels. We visit museums and bookstores and more restaurants, and he makes sure I get home to my apartment in a limo after. He flies me back for an overnight trip to be with him in the middle of my vacation halfway across the country, so he can see me and "figure out how to call off the wedding."

  I tell all this to Massa as I sleepwalk through these weeks at the zoo, happy and full of anxious joy at having someone who loves me like this, who wants me so desperately. Who will, I am sure, choose me. And when I stand in front of Massa's enclosure it is as if he can see the green that was hiding inside of me: the fruit, ripened, that has turned golden and drops richly into another's hands.

But then, like a swerving, out of control car, we fall over a precipice. It ends. John marries his fiancé after all, crying and throwing up right before the ceremony, I later learn. After John leaves, not even Massa can comfort me. One day in the dead of winter, I visit the Reptile House basement. It's a very warm room where eggs sit under red and yellow lights waiting for the right time to crack open. I'm aware that some reptiles are very difficult to breed in captivity. The reptile curator has been studying an ecological problem in Guam where non-native snakes were introduced to control rodents. The snakes then overran the vegetation and birds on the island because they had no natural predators. I picture a lush place, then denuded with gray houses and blowing dust. It's quiet there because all the native birds, the birds that used to sing in the light, have been devoured by a predator they did not expect. The system is unbalanced because of a clever but bad idea to fix a problem. There was nothing to contain the true nature of the snakes. It's so hot in the room, I become lightheaded thinking about all this, and it's as if something is breaking. My own fragile shell, maybe, since John left. There's nothing growing inside, only emptiness and a sterile sadness at my yellow center. But John left me one gift I didn't appreciate till much later. When I cry after he leaves, I finally recognize that this is familiar pain. It's not just about John.

My mother is worried about me. I can tell because she calls me more often, although she hasn't heard any details about my love life. She's seated in my living room while I'm hammering together Ikea bookshelves. Sade plays over and over on the stereo. *Is it a crime,* she sings, *Is it a crime?*

I say to my mother, "It's like putting a coffin together," pounding the stupid metal pins into the pre-drilled holes.

My mother and I have established an uneasy truce since I've left the house. She plans visits and brings me things I might need for the apartment. She also sometimes comes to the zoo on her day off and has lunch with me. It's all very thoughtful. Until one day I get back to the apartment and she's left a framed poster print from Tom Palomar inside my doorway. It's a gorilla reclining on a fancy sofa. I love it because it reminds me of Massa and it's like he's hanging out in my apartment. I call to thank her, and she tells me when I ask that the landlord let her in. *Wait, you came in without me knowing?* I think, *But it's nice...*

"I wanted to surprise you," she says, sensing my agitation. She says this like a disappointed child. It nags at me afterwards.

I call her back awhile later, still uncomfortable, twirling the long cord from the princess phone around my finger as I talk. At first my mother denies having a key to my apartment and then says she doesn't understand why I'm upset; she was only doing something nice for me, but then when I push, she says, "Yeah, I made a copy of the key when you were home in case something happened."

I'm angry then, enraged at this invasion of my privacy, but I try and stay calm. *I can try and talk to her about this,* I think. I say, "I don't want you to come in without permission. I don't come home without telling you...."

And her voice rises to a higher pitch, and she is arguing with me about how I'm not grateful for what she does for me, and she sounds desperate. Then suddenly she is screaming at me about how unreasonable and selfish I'm being.

And then I start to feel my own rage bubble up and it scares me how big it is, like a roaring fire. I shout her down, "I don't want to talk about this with you anymore. I don't want to talk to you."

She starts crying then and making more excuses.

"You will give me back that key," I tell my mother, like she is a bad child, "and you will never do anything like that again." For the first time in my life, I hang up on her.

Each year Massa's birthday was conveniently celebrated on December 30 to encourage public attendance during a holiday week. You'd get into the zoo free if you brought him a birthday card. For his fifty-fourth, I made his "birthday cake" — putting a pint of ice cream, lots of fruit and whipped cream over a large square piece of the zoo cake. Standing high on a ladder that leaned against his enclosure, I hung the crepe paper, some of the cards, and the "Happy Birthday" sign. He sat and watched me all morning, sometimes tapping on the glass between us.

Did Massa remember the woods and greenery? The thick dark forest, the last time he felt the clasp of his mother's arms around him? Did Mrs. Lintz pick him up as an infant, cuddle him as she changed and dressed him? He took a grape from me, his old man hands soft at the palm, with nearly human fingers. After the party was over, the keepers scratched his back through the enclosure, to his great pleasure. He sighed deeply, leaning against the bars with his eyes closed, so the touch would continue.

Later that night the call woke me at 2 a.m. On December 31, 1984, Massa died. The animal supervisor needed the pathologist's help to carry Massa's body out of his enclosure down to Penrose Lab. All that day, the animal supervisor and I handled hundreds of phone calls and media visits. We told Massa's story over and over. It was a slow news day, which meant there was even international coverage of his death.

"We are saddened by this loss of our most beloved resident,"

I said over and over. Repeating his obituary so many times made my own grieving worse.

After his death, I went back to the pathology room where the necropsies were performed. By the time I got there, the big metal table with the upturned sides only held the bloodied instruments of the procedure. His heart and arteries were examined by the zoo's research staff. Parts of his brain were sent to hospital labs for further study. His bones went to an anthropologist who reconstructed the skeletons of prehistoric primates. The pathologist deemed his cause of death to be coronary artery disease. He likely lived far longer than a typical gorilla in the wild, but I couldn't help but think that over time, his heart might have hardened from his solitary existence. I imagined his veins and arteries closing, becoming narrower and narrower till there was only the whisper of life—and then nothing.

After all the media calls, I cried, wondering if Massa had been scared. I thought about my grandfather's heart attack, the ambulance pulling away from our house into the darkness, siren turned on even though he was already gone.

It takes almost five years of therapy before I really cry in front of Sandy, and it happens after John leaves and after Massa dies, and it keeps happening. It suddenly seems that I don't stop crying. "What is wrong with me that they all leave?" I ask her.

She's seated next to me on the sofa, and I still like it better than her looking at me. I can see outside the window to the tops of the buildings. It's a small room, but it doesn't feel confined. I wonder if this is how Massa felt, looking out.

"Nothing is wrong with you," she says, and then I'm sobbing and sobbing snot-nosed tears on my therapist's blue sweater and she is holding me and saying nothing, just being there to help me let all the grief push in like that remembered tsunami sweeping me towards her with what feels like unstoppable pain. She doesn't let me go.

Later, I remember this time in my therapy as when I was looking into a deep chasm, bottomless. But one day the grief lessened, and the earth healed, and trees and vegetation grew where the chasm had been, with ripe hanging apples to eat, and the sun shone down. I bit an apple and had the knowledge that it wasn't my fault people left.

"When you understand those feelings," Sandy says, "then you can make choices."

We speak of love and need in the sessions that follow. "You love me," she tells me, "but you don't need me in the same way anymore."

I start to cry. The image of that chasm fades, it's no longer billowing smoke in the darkness. I see it's closed, sealed up with only the faint line where it had been, so I'd remember it. Sandy tells me I should grieve as I'm doing.

And with her words, a sense of comfort. I envision people patting down the rich, dark earth over that empty space. I'm not by myself anymore.

"What will happen when the chasm opens up again?" I ask.

Sandy says, "You will go down and look, but it won't be like the first time. We'll look together."

And as she continues to talk, I also see—no, feel, and this part is difficult to put into words—how it all fits. Death, and loss are at the very center of life. Dorothy was probably right after Oz. There is no place like home—my therapist's office, Beaver, the zoo, even my mother's house. But home is what you find when you understand yourself. I'm both connected and separate from others. I see how my intensity and ability to experience intimacy aren't hidden the way they were before.

The year after Massa dies, and John is gone and I've told my mother I am living my own life, I find another job at an advertising agency. At the end of my last day at the zoo, I pack up my office and stand at the window looking out into the dark. I can't see the empty exhibits, the trees that had shed the last of their leaves and the peacocks roosting quietly on the closed grounds. My own reflection fills the space in the glass. Beyond me, a few lights cast shadows on the path that leads through the grounds. Mentally, I walk them for the last time. Here was African Plains with the reticulated giraffes, the Solitude House's quiet, the Children's Zoo with the baby goats, the Rare Mammal House with the gorilla family. I remember the baby rhino who only lived a few hours and the mother rhino standing in her dark enclosure, keening afterwards from the loss.

I pick up my box of mementos—pictures of my favorite animals, peacock feathers, a porcupine quill—and carry all of it downstairs and out the path toward the parking lot. Pushing open the heavy iron gate that leads to the outside, I walk away from the Zoological Garden, metal bars clanging shut behind me.

Chapter 10 – When You See Fit

"I want a cat," I cajole my boyfriend of three years before we move in together in the spring of 1988. And while I'm waiting outside the rental townhouse to pick up the keys, a gray kitten with green eyes jumps out of the branches of the maple tree in the front yard, like she's fallen from the sky as a special gift to me.

Kinta moves in with us and becomes my companion as I try to be a weekend twenty-eight-year-old stepmother to seven- and nine-year-old girls. Fred is recently divorced. It's a marriage I had nothing to do with ending, but the girls look at me with sad eyes. The oldest pokes at the cat and then cries when Kinta, after batting her patiently a few times, finally lashes back with sharp claws. Some days I feel like Kinta with them, frustrated and unsure of how to love them well enough, but I feel for them because of my own memories of my mother's boyfriends and how it felt to be loved second. Or to *feel* like you were, whether that was true or not. I try and give them extra attention—special food, activities we can all do together like playing their favorite music. I read them some of my childhood stories, *The Water Babies*, *Charlotte's Web*. After they are tucked in the guest room bed, I fall into the new brass bed Fred and I have purchased together, Kinta sleeping under my right arm with her soft paws touching my face.

Our relationship starts off as a secret office romance during my job at the radio station after the zoo, but somehow, especially once we move in together, he never seems to be able to trust I won't leave him. And the more he worries about that, the more I can't seem to trust myself enough to stay. It starts to feel like when I was separating from my mother, her consuming need for me and my dance to escape it. Fred and I are two sides of the same abandonment coin. In the beginning, we argue sometimes about ways we disappoint each other. Much later those disappointments blossom into failures, and we end with a harvest of hurt and resentment.

But in the early days of our time in the townhouse together, Sandy tells me I'm struggling in this relationship because of the history with Daddy.

"It's time to find him," she counsels me. "It will help you better understand what happens in your relationships."

What are the questions I want answered? Mostly, I want information about what happened the night of the fight between my parents, but I also really want to comprehend how he could have sent that letter and disappeared when I was fourteen. I want to figure out who he is. Therapy and my own experiences have allowed me to examine more critically my mother's ideas about him, but I would like to hear his side of the story, because maybe that will help me contextualize my memories and what occurred in their marriage.

I've started a full-time, sixteen-month graduate program in counseling psychology and am deep into writing a family autobiography for my family therapy class. There's so much I don't know. If I am going to be a therapist, I need to have the courage to confront the denial and secrecy that exist in my own family. Sandy has taught me that.

As it turns out, finding him is not quite as easy as wishing for a kitten, but is easier than I expected. *If I were him, where would I have gone?* I've called his lawyer from the divorce era who kindly gave me his last address and Social Security number. I've called a distant relative who hadn't talked to him in years but said he thought he might be in Texas somewhere. I think, *maybe he went back to where we used to live.* I dial Houston information and the impersonal voice on the other end provides me a number for that last name, no Howard is listed. *Should I call? What will happen?* I both want to do this and don't want to do this.

Fred is supportive. "What do you tell your clients to do?" he asks me. But I feel less courageous when I remember Daddy's rage and his fights with my mother. *What if he doesn't want me to find him?*

"Fine," I tell Fred, picking up the phone again, "I can be brave."

A young girl answers, with a southern accent and, at the same time, a man comes on the line as well.

"Is Howard Derrickson there?"

"Yes," he says.

"The Howard Derrickson who used to live in New Jersey?"

"Yes, who is this?"

I take a deep breath and plunge in, "It's your daughter, Deborah."

There's a pause and then he says, "Not a day has gone by in the last fifteen years that I haven't thought about you and your sister."

I begin to cry. He tells me he looked for my sister when she was in college after being sent a newspaper clipping about her.

"I didn't think you'd come looking for me," he says. "You were so angry."

I ask if he only really wanted me to find him because Melissa was his and I had information about where she was.

He says, "No, I always felt that you were mine too." He goes on to say he needs a few hours to explain, and not over the phone.

"I want to see you both." He instructs me to give his number to my sister. Old suspicions die hard, and I don't give him her address. I do give him mine. He tells me he has another family, and they all know about us—a wife, a stepson, twin boys and the youngest, Ashley, who answered the phone.

"I never stopped loving you, even though I left," he tells me, and goes on to recollect the first time he saw me when I was little, and we drove around to look at Christmas decorations in Omaha. I have no memory of glittering trees and Midwest snow swirling around plump multicolored lights that must have adorned the houses.

"I don't want to hang up," he continues. "You'll call again?"

Afterwards, world tilted, I stand in my kitchen, breathing hard, like I've just touched down, holding the phone in my hand. Who do I call first, my sister or my therapist? He sounds so normal, I think. But that doesn't quite capture it. He sounds reasonable and not scary like the father I remember. Do I feel cheated that he supported another family and not us? But then again, maybe he couldn't have been in contact because that would have meant dealing with my mother. Am I making excuses for him, for his abandonment?

I call my sister first.

"I spent all this money in therapy grieving for him," she is almost yelling at me, "and now you've gone and found him, and I have to go through it all over again. What about Mom?" She gives me a gut punch. My sister's unspoken accusation under her question is true. I have betrayed the parent who was there for us. I needed to do this for myself, and somewhat selfishly assumed it would be healing for my sister too. She's right, I never asked her permission.

I try and reassure her. "He takes his children to soccer practice. He said he wants to talk to both of us. He seemed pretty reasonable…." She listens and then writes down his number, not saying what she plans to do.

"We absolutely can't speak to Mom about any of this," I tell her. We aren't agreeing on much, but on this we need to be one. "Not until we figure out what to do. And what kind of relationship we are having with him, if any." I'm taking charge, my big sister role. My mother has expressed delusions that Daddy has occasionally been stalking around her house and trying to get in. My sister and I have ignored that, but it's clear she's still extremely paranoid about him, even after all these years.

"Oh, my god, no," Melissa says immediately, "We can't tell her." And so just like that, I've created another family secret.

"How does it feel to be this emotional? To just feel?" Sandy asks me the next morning when we talk. Frightening. I am frightened by everything I might have unleashed. I don't have a more specific answer to her question till later that day. *It feels like someone died.*

When I call my stepfather a week later, still weirded out by saying "Daddy," I feel more confused. He tells the story of how Melissa ran away from him when she saw him once during the custody fight. He was in his car and wanted to talk to her when she was walking home from school. He says this is an example of why he left. I'm simultaneously feeling old pity for him and disbelief that he could be so easily hurt by his confused children who were caught in the middle of he and my mother's bitter divorce. I'm an adult and he can't hurt me, but I still find myself shaking.

"I wish I felt that I had my stuff together as well as you seem to," he says, and tells me apologetically that he is a warehouse supervisor. He sounds like a loser when he talks about himself. He's fifty-seven, his second wife, Nancy, who he met he tells me, "… sometime before our break" is forty-one. There's a story of a failing business he'd owned that had "monstrous money losses" and from which he feels he's never fully financially recovered.

"Tell me about your high school years, college years, job

experiences and every detail of your life that I can get you to share with me," he begs.

I respond with superficial highlights from the years of his absence: funny stories about the zoo, about Fred's kids, how I traveled during college, while conspicuously leaving anything out that involves my mother.

The "other" family begins to take shape. He sends photographs from Thanksgiving in his first letter. In one, Ashley perches on his lap, her gangly legs stretched out over his as they both look straight at the camera, not smiling, Daddy's dark-rimmed glasses hiding his eyes.

He is carrying guilt for some things. He writes, "ruining our lives," for example. "I don't like to think about what has probably gone through your heads...."

I feel oddly unmoved by some of these statements. There's something that doesn't ring true about them. It's correct that he did some awful things, but it's more that, what he's saying isn't specific enough to convey that he understands what those things are. There's the leaving, of course, but also the sexual stuff, the ways he treated us growing up. I chalk it up to the newness of our relationship while at the same time maintaining skepticism about what it all means. He keeps talking about Melissa and the way he does it, makes me wonder if he thinks I'm partly the reason, not his conflict with my mother, that made him leave his biological child.

His letters are like love letters, intense and chatty. "I cannot help but feel pride in the way you've turned out and in what you are doing. I also think you are absolutely gorgeous. My father always told me I would feel that way about you. Can you remember anything of him or my mother?" His tone creeps me out a little since I don't know (or maybe don't want to know) what he means by it.

He continues, "I recently read a line in a book which said: *"It's amazing the things we forget and the things we remember."*

Ashley starts sending me a letter every week, ecstatic to have a big sister to call her own. "Send me your picture," she begs after sending me one of her wearing her school uniform, short blond hair, blue shirt, and little red tie. Her face is angled toward the photographer, so I can see the resemblance to my sister. "Yes," she writes me back in pencil on lined notebook paper, "I do like to go to the zoo. I would like to go to the zoo with you."

When I show Melissa the picture, she says, "I hate that I see her in me," she hesitates. "It means he's in me too." My father doesn't apologize for sending my sister and me that letter. Does he even remember he sent it to us? Does it occur to him that it was wrong to use his children in a marital war?

Meantime, my mother and I meet from time to time to visit a new used bookstore or an antique shop. We'll have lunch and go to the Brandywine Museum of Art. I'm seeing my mother as the most prominent piece of my family jigsaw puzzle. What I've understood about who Daddy is has come from her giving me other pieces to fit together as well as my own memories. The pattern that had been created rearranges itself with information from Daddy. The old childhood war between my parents for my loyalty continues to play out in my psyche. Can I have a relationship with both my parents? Am I allowed to love them both?

My sister and I have kept our pact to keep this secret and not tell my mother, but it weighs on both of us. Still, it doesn't outweigh my fear about what she'd do if we told her.

The question I pose to him about what happened to the

marriage generates a whole letter. I wait till I have a break from my graduate classes to read the black fine-tipped pen scrawl on the lined paper he uses at his warehouse job. He often writes me on his breaks there. He claims my mother thought he was rich and that he never misled her about the fact that he didn't have access to his parents' money. After my sister was born, he vaguely explains that he had an extended stay at the VA hospital the summer we stayed with his parents in Connecticut. He believes my mother was done with the marriage after that and she told people he was "extremely mentally ill with paranoid schizophrenia." He believes my mother told my sister and me that he would kill us around the time of the divorce. Then, he says, "When I left, I felt nothing but pain and hurt, but at your mother not at either of you two. Therefore, divorcing you two was not really any issue." I thoughtfully fold the letter back into the envelope. That's not the truth of my own memory or of that letter he sent to us all those years ago.

Six months after that first phone call, and after my graduation with an M.Ed. in counseling, I'm on a plane to Houston to meet my other family. Daddy picks me up from the airport in a beat-up car. He's still a tall man with a short haircut, but more stooped over and thicker than I remember. He seems somehow frailer, with dark hair that hangs in a lock over his forehead. We drive to his house, which is in the neighborhood right near where we lived almost twenty-five years ago. I remember the tidy new houses back then, our backyard with the patio where the chameleons sunned themselves. The houses are smaller than my memory of them, the street is overgrown and unkept, some of the lawns gone to weeds. It's a rental house and it's falling apart: windows rotting, outside paint chipping, smeared dirty walls and room doors that don't fully close.

Nancy looks a little like my mother when she was younger, with short dark hair. She is full of tense energy and intelligence when she speaks. She calls my father Wes, his middle name, and what his father was called. He doesn't use Howard anymore. Nancy gives me a big hug hello.

Waiting for me is fifteen-year-old, blond-haired Zach, who is sullen and somewhat withdrawn in his soccer uniform; twin twelve-year-old Sam and Keith, whom I've brought Batman t-shirts for; and ten-year-old Ashley, who is vibrating with happiness and excitement that I am there and will be sleeping in her room. I've brought the full set of the Narnia Chronicles for her, and she laughs like my sister does, startling me with how she inclines her head with the same tone of voice.

There are several mangy looking, large dogs that everybody yells at as they run out of the house into the dirt yard out back, and then inside, tracking grit all over the old linoleum floors. Nancy and my father tell me they've just decided to start homeschooling the younger kids and Ashley shows me one of her textbooks. I flip through it and read, to my horror, that evolution didn't happen. I feel like I am visiting some other country. I try to be respectful of the cultural norms here and keep my opinions to myself.

I attend one of Ashley's soccer games, trekking across the field in the hot and humid Houston air, thinking about what Daddy would have been like as a parent if he hadn't left. On Sunday, we drive to the big Baptist church. It's like the ones you see on television with several thousand participants, many of whom end up getting saved. There are television monitors in the bathroom, so if you need to go, you won't miss a moment of the pastor telling you about your damnation potential.

My father introduces me to everyone. "This is my oldest daughter," he says proudly. "She's a counselor." He wears a suit. I feel he is trying too hard to impress other people. There is something brittle about him. He's working to impress me too.

In Ashley's room, listening to the sounds of the rest of the family sighing and snoring into the sticky night, I'm wide awake under her posters from the science museum gift shop. On one wall there are stars, planets, and the phases of the moon. On another, dolphins leap through blue waves. My ankles and legs are starting to itch from what will turn out to be dozens of flea bites. I'm flooded with images of my father lying on the couch after we get home from the soccer game, pulling Ashley toward him for a hug or asking her to bring him a glass of water. I find myself closely watching his interactions with her.

I don't like the way he brags about all the soccer and other sport performances of his children, telling me all about how Zach is good enough to get a scholarship to play in college. He reminds me that I should have kept riding horses, "Everybody told me you had talent and a good seat," he says like this is still a point of pride for him. Like he's forgotten taking me to camp when I was five. Like he's forgotten leaving us with no child support money.

It's after our dinner when the kitchen has been cleaned up and my half-siblings are in their rooms that I ask him about the night my mother says he threatened to kill her. His story is that my mother set up the fight to influence the divorce proceedings. He tells me my sister and I were eating dinner with him in the kitchen and then, when he was about to go work out at the health club, she started baiting him.

He responded that he didn't understand what she was talking about and then "when the inquiries with her became more heated

I started to laugh. The more I laughed, the angrier your mother became. Finally, she charged across the room and the noise you heard with Melissa was a chair being knocked over."

He then says that as my sister and I ran out, a neighbor came "in the other door." He felt this was part of my mother's plan, and that "after the arrival of the witness, I left and went to the health club and after working out took a long sauna." He doesn't mention the police coming or that there was at least ten minutes before the neighbor got there.

I let him tell his story. There's some part of me, even in this moment, that fears confrontation with him, so I don't question his version of events.

On the way back to the airport, he tells me the story of how he and Nancy met. She was a former nun who left her order to get married to a former priest. They did missionary work in Africa but her first husband "turned out to be gay," which she discovered when she was pregnant. She returned to America and met my father after Zach was born, and they married when he was around three.

Since I am a counselor, Daddy and Nancy ask my advice about how they should tell Zach about his father's sexual orientation. I am struck how Daddy recreated the scenario he had with my mother and a stepchild except he didn't adopt Zach, who still visits his biological father in D.C.

"I really feel you should talk to his father and let him decide when he wants to share that," I say uncomfortably. I remember my mother always saying my father was entitled. *I'm not your free therapist*, I think, and try not to be impolite as I change the subject to the details of my flight home.

In my own therapy I have tried to create a story that makes sense, put all the different puzzle parts together, but they keep scattering as I gather them up. I tell Sandy later, "I think they were both crazy." But I also feel, over this first year or so as we reconnect, that Daddy wasn't as crazy as my mother had always made him out to be. Or, trying to be generous to my mother, perhaps he's just not as crazy as he had been when they were together.

Six weeks or so after I've scouted the landscape, Melissa also visits him with her soon-to-be fiancé, Ron. Following her trip, Daddy becomes very interested in coming to see us, likely with a future wedding in mind.

I don't respond to his requests for this. I want to continue to protect my mother, which, of course, means saving myself from her wrath and hurt that I have reconnected with him. Yet he can't let visiting go, which feels again like my childhood and adolescence of being caught between them. He keeps bringing up the need to tell my mother about him.

These letters and calls make me question the wisdom of finding him at all. I'm about to begin a five-year doctoral program in clinical psychology, and I've started my own private practice under supervision. I'm trying to think through the best way to deal with all of this. I'm going to be a psychologist. Shouldn't I know what to do?

I remember a story a professor told in one of my classes about his daughter being afraid of the wolves in her room. He went in to talk to her in his best therapist mode and began explaining why she was afraid. She stopped him mid-sentence and said, "Please Daddy, stop talking and check under the bed." I'm tired of all of this and wish someone would just take care of those dark wolves, the lingering secrets under *my* childhood bed.

My sister and I are not the only ones keeping secrets in the family. My mother and grandmother are also hiding something. The year after I find Daddy, Nanna grows frailer, she shrinks to less than five feet tall, her gray pixie haircut highlighting her jutting cheekbones. My mother drives the ten minutes at least once or twice daily to her little house where Nanna still lives alone. My mother checks on her and takes her to the store and to doctor appointments. My mother is irritated by Nanna's one martini a day turning into several, her walking on her own to the liquor store to get more gin. This is new, as Nanna was not the drinker in the family. Nonno was the one who started the martini tradition. Always in control, Nanna ran a tight ship with regimented meals and a cleaning schedule of laundry and housekeeping. She still grows the most beautiful African violets with the fuzzy leaves on a tray table in her front living room window. She does the Sunday *New York Times* crossword puzzle in ink, though, even with my mother's help, not as well as before. My sister and I are aware of the drinking, and that she has Parkinson's like my great-grandfather had. But what we haven't been told is that she has stomach cancer. My mother and Nanna keep this from us like it's shameful in some way. My mother is determined to help my grandmother, even though she is exhausted from both the care she is providing to her and her full-time job as an assistant director of nursing at Medford Leas, a retirement community.

"It's tough with your grandmother," my mother shares sadly, as we are leaving Nanna's one afternoon and getting into our separate cars. "She's terrible to me about everything I'm trying to do for her."

I sympathize, "Nanna can be pretty critical sometimes."

"Sometimes?" my mother laughs sarcastically. "Always. But I promised her she could stay in this house. With her Parkinson's she's shaky and unsteady."

I give my mother a hug. "You're taking good care of her."

My mother decides to take a couple days off from caretaking and go away. Somehow my grandmother falls on the floor and remains there for three days, unable to get up. When my mother returns, she discovers her severely dehydrated and with a bed sore from lying in her own feces.

When my mother calls me, all she will say is that the stench in the house was unbearable and that Nanna's in the hospital. "She has cancer, and it won't be long. I'm trying to get her transferred to Medford Leas, so it's easier for me to nurse her." As is always the case in my family, secrets are revealed in this matter-of-fact fashion.

When I get to the hospital, the staff starts trying to put a feeding tube into my bloated grandmother's stomach. She is supposed to be in hospice care, but I don't know what to do. Nanna looks at me with pleading eyes, shaking her head no, but she's in and out of consciousness and the two nurses ask me to leave the room as they pull the curtains.

"I don't think you are supposed to be doing that," I say. But I'm not sure, so I'm more asking than telling them.

My mother arrives a few minutes later in her full crisp white nursing regalia, complete with nursing pins and cap, which she rarely wears. She looks like a nursing general and somebody who is not only competent, but adept at giving orders.

"What are you doing to her," she roars, pulling open the blue patterned curtain to expose their astonished faces. "She is on hospice, and you pull that tube out immediately or I will call my lawyer." She steps around the staff to stand next to the bed.

I'm amazed by how quickly the staff moves. Almost by magic, there are four nurses in the room and an administrator, and the feeding tube comes out. My mother shakes her head as she looks at me after the room is empty and Nanna has closed her eyes again,

"Sometimes you have to be tough to get things done."

My grandmother is ambulanced to hospice at Medford Leas that afternoon.

It's good that hospice is at the end of the hall on the skilled nursing wing of the facility. Inside the entrance door to the unit, a white-haired woman, wearing a floral housecoat with slippers, says, "I want to go home. I want to go home. I want to go *home*," over and over in a loud singsong voice. I can't fathom how my mother can stand this day in and day out when she's doing her shift here.

"Don't mind her," my mother explains. "She's very demented."

She gently redirects her, by taking her arm and walking her to another room. "Olive, come away from the door." My mother is not officially working, but they are letting her handle a lot of the care for my grandmother.

Nanna's room is quiet and peaceful. In the dim light, her breathing is already rattling as her body shrinks down to the size of a bird. I imagine this happens so her soul can fly up, going past the clear glass greenhouse outside this room at Medford Leas, past houses, past the fields sprouting the last of the sweet corn in late August, past rivers, and roads, up over the highest building in Philadelphia and into the sky. She appears to recognize me as I give her sips of water from the little sponge stick, wetting her lips.

As I sit with her, not speaking, I'm filled with images of her teaching me to play Scrabble, my sister and her and I playing Poker for pennies, her making special desserts for us, or being proud of our grades or accomplishments. She was that grandmother who always asked if you needed a sweater, which in white, Anglo-Saxon, Protestant (WASP) translation means "I love you, so I want to know you are warm and prepared." She was not a cuddly woman, but she loved my sister and me, her only grandchildren. She and my mother, on the other hand, were always in a constant struggle, a fight to control what each of them should be doing or feeling. They were always disappointing each other. I think as I watch my grandmother die, my mother has won their war by outlasting her.

Just outside Cooperstown, New York, we hold a brief graveside service, mist rising over the blue hills. Afterwards, my mother, who has tried to make this burial trip like a vacation, takes us out for a gourmet dinner. We all drink far too much.

"Your grandmother was a piece of work," my mother starts in. "And she said terrible things to me…."

My sister and I exchange looks, quickly changing the subject before the part where she says, "Did I ever tell you about the time…."

I'm sad. I don't want Nanna remembered like that.

On our way home the next day, at my mother's decree, we stop at an antique store she has chosen. She announces, "You girls each need to get a nice antique to remember your grandmother by, pick something out and she will pay for it."

We wander around up and down the aisles, slightly hungover and confused. This is my mother's ritual. She feels it's important to buy things to remind us of people and events. I run my fingers over the dusty tables and chairs in the store and finally settle on a Victorian cherry dresser with a mirror that has old glass, so my reflection appears a bit distorted. I like that it's not quite right and decide I'll use it in my bedroom.

The financial transactions from the estate are murky and happen quickly. My mother decides something different than what Nanna intended and keeps more of the money for herself and allows my sister and Ron to purchase my grandmother's Westmont, New Jersey, house for a fraction of what it would sell for. She makes a great show of explaining how she's split things evenly to me. But even in this, she's taking care of my sister more. As part of her inheritance, my mother owns the Willowbrook house where we grew up.

I'm given money, which I use for a car and to pay my increased living expenses during graduate school since Fred and I broke up not long after the funeral. I take Kinta. He tells me I can't see the girls in person to say goodbye, which breaks my heart.

"You can write them a letter," he says.

In it, I try to make sure they don't feel responsible in any way for what happened between their father and me. I make x's and o's at the bottom of the card. I don't want to do to them what Daddy did to me, even though I'm disappearing too.

There are things that flow into my apartment from Nanna's in the few weeks after we get back from the funeral. The empty mahogany credenza where the photo albums were always kept, but which I fill with the irreplaceable thumbprint goblets Nanna used for holiday dinners, the partial set of her everyday red and white Spode, her books in addition to my grandfather's, some lamps, several antique tables, a bedroom set, and some pictures of relatives in the original 1800 era frames. My mother takes everything that she doesn't give to us—the carefully written genealogies, the photo album encased in a velvet and brass cover that was curated by my great-uncle Sumner, the cherry dining room table, the clock my grandmother always wound just so, and the oil painting from my great-grandmother's house.

She tells us she's storing some of these things in the garage until she can get time to make space and sort her house out. "I've been so tired taking care of your grandmother and working," she explains. "Currently, it's a mess."

My sister and I haven't been inside for the past five years. She no longer invites us to meet at her house. Instead, we get together at my "aunt's" house or a restaurant.

I'm polite, "I'm sure you'll be able to get it done since you aren't running around for Nanna."

That night I dream I'm at my mother's house. *Someone else lives there. I knock on the front door and ask if I can come inside. A woman answers and says, "It's not like you remember it. Things are breaking through the ceiling, moldy things. It can't be fixed. I don't want you to go in."* When I wake, I understand that my unconscious recognizes something is very wrong, but my daytime self continues to ignore how strange the situation is becoming.

Two months later, my sister and I are hanging out drinking margaritas on the back porch of Nanna's old house which my sister has newly repainted and decorated to be quite cozy.

"He's not coming to the wedding, and I don't care what he thinks about it," Melissa says. Ron's leaf blower whines in the background around the yard, cleaning up the first of the golden fall leaves. "Daddy wasn't part of my childhood, and he doesn't get to be part of this."

I nod in agreement. "Besides," I say, "I don't really think Mom can handle one more thing this year."

She agrees.

My mother has been very stressed about her job. There's something about a supervisor there not liking how she's doing things, and my mother seems unusually suspicious that this person may have it out for her somehow. And she's dealing with finalizing my grandmother's estate. She's also been talking about traveling like she's always wanted to. She's planning to accompany Mrs. Pan on a trip to

Hong Kong to see her Chinese family.

My sister informs me one of my mother's ex-boyfriends is coming. "He was the person around for most of my growing up and I don't care if Mom broke up with him a while ago. I want him there."

"It's your wedding," I say and take a sip of my drink.

I think about all the changes happening in our family, the passage of time and my sister and I independent adults—her teaching and marriage, my private practice office, and new apartment. Nanna is gone. Daddy has been found. I briefly wonder, as our talk turns to the details of the wedding, what my mother will do with her life with fewer responsibilities. I flash on the image of Daddy and his Texas family. I think about Malcolm and whether I want to try and find him. *There are still too many secrets in our family.* We want to protect the people we love. But where is the line between protecting others and saving yourself from dealing with their pain and anger? When does a secret become something you shouldn't hold on to?

Chapter 11 – Thirty-Yard Dumpster

I startle awake at 2:30 a.m. from dreaming about things, piles, and piles of things like that frightening scene in *Fantasia* where the brooms come alive. Common household objects turn on me and multiply even in my sleep as my brain struggles to process what I've seen at my mother's house. I roll over and try to go back to sleep, but it's impossible and I toss and turn till the alarm goes off.

We are on the hot and humid highway to New Jersey by 8 a.m. the third day. *A.D.*, I think, *after discovery*. I'm not tired even after my fitful sleep because my adrenaline fuels me. *Nothing like a little acute stress disorder.*

My friend texts, *Carry on, oh yeah, great warriors of the pile!*

"Let's see what's in the garage," Marc says, glancing out the window as he switches lanes, "now that I've got the inside door to it cleared. Maybe it's less bad."

As we pull in front of the house and I see the twenty-five black contractor bags from our ten hours of work yesterday lined up alongside of it, I'm suddenly tearful. "I don't think I can do stuff inside today anyway," I say, somewhat panicked, trying not to have visions of my shit-covered arm. Also, I'm thinking that if we can clean out the garage, we'll have a staging area for ourselves and for the items we are keeping.

We both try the key that opens the back door to see if it will open the garage door as well, but it doesn't work. We still must enter the house to get to the inside garage door. Even with all the windows Marc opened the first day, it doesn't make a dent in the smell. Only the upstairs bathroom is still closed because we can't get past the mountains of plastic bottles and solidified newspapers, clothing, and fecal matter. My mother hasn't had air conditioning in here for who knows how long and probably not heat since the vents were covered. The smell inhabits me like an infection.

After I open the inside garage door from the laundry room, Marc shines his headlamp over the scene as I reach around and fumble for the light switch. I remember it's on the right side along the cement wall. The lightbulb illuminates more piles. *Well, here's what hoarding should look like,* I think. *It should be stored furniture and ice skates and old toys, not gross mountains of trash and shit.* And then, *What the fuck is that?* There are big garbage bags filled with something soft that gives way as I gingerly push my fingers against them. I pull one open with my gloved hand, fearing what might be contained within and breathe a sigh of relief when I find it's just filled with old towels and linens. I push the bags on top of the rusted dryer to the left of the door. In the gloom, I can make out metal shelves on the opposite wall and antique furniture and objects filling the space. Yes, this is more normal, like a disorganized storage unit.

So, like any typical suburban couple living in a parallel hoarding universe, we spend our Monday cleaning out a garage. It takes hours to work our way through the space to the beat-up metal sliding door, but when we do, we roll it up and begin to carry things we find outside.

I text my sister that we have made it through the garage. I don't tell her about discovering her giant childhood Raggedy Ann in a box. Mice have eaten through her neck making it look like her throat has been cut. I throw out Frederick Bear's filthy and moldy toy truck that my mother decorated for him to ride on when they came to the Great American Teddy Bear Rally back when I worked at the zoo. I throw out the moth-eaten florescent cat pillow I needlepointed for my grandmother when I was in high school, stuffing from it dropping over the velvet antique family photo album my grandmother carefully held onto. I pull these things from wet and mildewed paper bags that have been sitting in water that leaked under the garage door. This makes me cry again as each bag is filled with family history and papers, clearly just tossed in the garage by my mother after my grandmother died twenty-four years ago. Much of the furniture, like the antique cherry dining room table, is from Nanna's house as well. Although as we move things around, I see antiques my mother has purchased, some with price tags still on them. A three-hundred-dollar, doll-sized Victorian fainting couch, an ancient beat-up church pew, and two antique white marble-topped dressers are just a few of the items she's bought and stored in here.

"You know," Marc laughs, "to decorate inside when the house is cleaned up."

A painting of a man in a gold oval frame from the turn of the century rests against one of the dressers. When I pick it up, the frame falls apart and the picture comes out. I wonder if it's an unknown and forgotten relative washed ashore in this mess. I'm guessing he'd like to sign up with another family who would take better care of him.

Marc stands in front of the open garage door holding one of the fifteen rusted pruning shears we've uncovered. "We need the biggest dumpster that will fit in the driveway," he says. "We need to schedule them to bring it Friday, and we'll fill it over the weekend. If we have enough stuff, they can take it Monday." He's chuckling a little when he says the part about having enough stuff. He picks up one of the four axes he's found and makes like he's threatening to kill something with it.

"Thinking about taking care of my mom again? That'll do

it," I say, only half joking as I pick up my cell to call the sanitation company. It costs $740, which I put on my credit card since there's not much money in my mother's account until her next Social Security check comes in. I'm told a thirty-yard dumpster should work.

While I'm talking, Marc is looking up at the second-floor bedroom windows.

"If we position it right, we could just lob the upstairs crap into the dumpster," he muses. I have a mental image of the gallon bottles of "mystery fluid" flying through the air and bursting as they land in the metal container.

"Absolutely not," I say, imagining the neighbors' horror. "Are you out of your mind?"

"I think we're both a little out of our minds," he laughs. "Let's see when it gets here."

We're interrupted by my sister texting me at the end of her school day, feeling badly about not being more help. *I'm so sorry, I feel the need to keep repeating that.* Yet even as I reassure her that it's okay, I keep apologizing to Marc about having to do all of this.

He gently says, "Hey, this mess isn't yours or Melissa's. We just have to deal with it."

We arrive home after being at the house for ten hours. We sit on the couch mindlessly watching *Shark Tank* on TV after our showers. My friend has left us a chocolate cake to help us feel better. I cut a giant piece of it to eat for dinner along with a huge glass of wine. I send my sister a picture of my meal and she texts back that we will both need a stint at the Betty Ford Center after this experience. I can't eat; can't focus. I can't even follow the television sharks as they eviscerate some poor entrepreneur's business.

"I don't think we can do this in the next seven days," Marc

says.

"We don't have a choice." Fear chokes my voice. "I can't do it physically without you." I don't have to mention that I can't do it emotionally either.

"I keep smelling that smell," he says, "it's awful."

When we get up from the couch to go to bed, Marc walks past the cat box temporarily located in the corner of the living room. We've had to put it there for our geriatric cat since the basement is too far for her arthritic hips. "Oh my god," he says with no trace of a smile, "we're smelling *cat*, not human urine."

That night I dream. *I'm at physical therapy and need to go to the bathroom, but the toilet bowl is filled with shit that isn't mine. On the grab bar, there are socks and underpants and other clothing with shit on them and I'm trying not to touch anything. Then, all the filthy clothing is falling on me and lands in a big pile on the bathroom floor.* I wake with a start, thinking about the dump we visited as children near my grandparent's house. Objects picked out of the trash were set on a grimy table—the need to save anything worthwhile.

On the fourth day, I'm physically sore from crouching and lifting and the nonstop moving of things. Emotionally, when I'm not feeling driven by adrenaline or rage, I'm raw and tearful. Or, alternatively, I'm feeling like I'm wrapped in a thick, smothering blanket of numb exhaustion. There's no in-between these three states of mind. Numb is almost better. I'm a robot as we get up, get dressed, pack food and water, travel to Cherry Hill, and unlock the back door.

We begin in the living room by throwing out or carting outside for Goodwill, thousands of dollars of books, a file cabinet in a box, unworn clothing with the tags still on, three brand new purses covered with a thin layer of dirt.

"Gee," I say as I open each purse to find papers and lipstick and other items, "I don't understand why my mother can't find her car registration."

Both of us begin howling with laughter and I can't stop until my side aches. Then I start to cry again.

There's an antique rocker with carved wooden heads on the top of it, tipped sideways against a heavy old Bible with metal scrollwork on the front. There's a garment bag, still holding summer clothing from some trip my mother took. And there's trash. Kathy had said there hadn't been trash put outside for the last fifteen years. All that garbage is here, not only her own excrement but containers filled with leftovers like a liquified turkey club sandwich. There are chicken bones, apple cores, empty milk cartons, and a half-eaten jar of peanut butter, all of it just thrown on top of piles.

She's made her life a literal dump. Why is she unable to part with her own trash? "It's like a tsunami," I say, remembering my adolescent fascination, "only contained in my mother's living room." I'm too overwhelmed to try and be in psychologist mode, but I recognize that this behavior is partly about control, a primitive need to hold on to everything related to yourself, even your garbage. According to current thinking, it's also about addiction. My mother couldn't stop herself from shopping and collecting things. *Nothing about this is rational.*

I decide that I will take one nice thing from the house each day we are here. Maybe it's something I remember valuing at one time like the brass kaleidoscope she bought at an art show. Maybe it's something beautiful I can imagine having in my own living room, like the two iridescent blue bud vases I found glowing and intact on a small table half-buried in her dining room. Or maybe it's something that was once beloved in my family because it carried stories and history. These are the kinds of things I want to find and rescue from this disaster.

My job is to salvage—to use the stories people tell me in their therapies and help them understand themselves and others better, the stories I write myself to make meaning out of the joy and wreckage of life. If finding meaning and understanding isn't the goal of what I'm doing, then what is the reason I'm here? I could just hire somebody to shovel all of this into a dumpster. But being an archeologist at this site is about more than preserving what is beautiful and meaningful. It's about saving my mother. It's about understanding my past. It's about all of this not being a gigantic waste.

Today, I decide to take the framed Tony Auth political cartoon. My mother said she would give it to me years ago. Then, in a fit of anger when she felt I was being "selfish" (her code word for "you aren't doing what I want you to") reneged and never brought it to me. It's not lost on me that it's a small bit of revenge to rescue that piece of art first.

As I throw book after book of completed crossword puzzles into a bag near the barely visible blue recliner, I wipe my hand on my soiled white work shirt before retying one of my recently purchased, light blue sneakers which are now a grimy gray.

"When this is all over, I am replacing every piece of the clothing I'm wearing that's been ruined in this shithole and she is going to pay for it with money from her account. Is there anything you'll need to replace?"

"My soul," he says. *I love this man.*

Marc points behind the chair where a wall of garbage is heaped several feet high. "That was the grooming area."

There's the little box of rusty clippers and scissors, also anti-itch cream (tubes and tubes of it everywhere in the room), and full bottles of shampoo. She flossed her teeth and threw the used strands behind the chair, along with baby wipes, and empty containers of yogurt.

"The Chobani period," Marc says.

We find the box with my mother's fake mastectomy boob; more videotapes on Existentialism and Buddhism (the entire house is a study in non-attachment, apparently).

"Look," Marc says hoisting up the smooth body of a teak Buddha that's been buried under piles of old plastic containers from Ponzio's, books, shredded catalogues, and newspapers interspersed with a water shut-off notice from six years ago, family photographs and banana peels. It weighs more than expected and when I reach over to take it from him, I almost drop it. It is probably a foot wide and solid wood. The body of the Buddha is curled up, so its face is hidden in its arms. The whole statue makes a round shape like a giant fist. It radiates sadness.

"What's this one called?" Buddhism is something he's read about in great depth. My mother sometimes likes to talk to him about this shared interest. She buys him books on it for Christmas.

"It's the Weeping Buddha," Marc says. I see that the statue's shoulder is cracked from literally carrying the weight of the Hoarder House on him. "There's different stories about it," he continues. "Some say the Weeping Buddha cries for all the pain and suffering in the world, absorbing and transforming it. Others say that it is in mourning for mistakenly killing his own son in battle. I can't remember all the details."

"I'm taking this home today for you," I say. I tuck the Weeping Buddha under my arm. Am I rescuing the parent who didn't mean to do a terrible thing? Trying to take the unbearable sadness away from this place? I wipe it off and put it on a garbage bag on the back seat of the car. Marc deserves something too.

My sister texts me: *I watched the going in video with my therapist. She cried. I didn't.*

I text back: *Our family, causing therapists to weep for forty years.*

I'm coming tomorrow, she says.

I hate Lysol. I'm allergic to it, but there's no choice. Marc sprays the living room with it for two or three minutes. We wait on the front porch with our masks off for another three minutes, then pull them back up and plunge inside. We've decided we'd rather assault ourselves with toxic fumes than smell the odor in that house. In our tradition that began the first day, our sweaty respirator masks still hang on the branch of the tree out front because we alternate them every few hours with a new dry mask. To distinguish between them, I have drawn faces on each with a Sharpie. Mine has pursed lady lips and I make his have a toothy smile. We take a selfie with them on as we stand next to the seventy contractor bags we've filled with trash.

Having a great vacation! I post on social media, hoping our friends will be amused.

Day Six and I've warned Melissa. "Long pants. And shoes you don't care about."

She says she'll change in the bathroom at school. She teaches second graders. I remember her in second grade. White-blond hair in a bowl cut, blue eyes. She followed me everywhere.

"I'll meet you out front." I don't know why I need to soften this for her, but it's always been like this. I take the rage; she gets the comfort. I protect her. But she's a grownup and neither of us can be protected from this. I believe in some ways she's got the harder job than I do because my mother is living in her house during this. That means Melissa deals every single day with my mother's indirect questions about whether Marc and I are at the house cleaning it out and what is happening with the wrecked Toyota. I can't imagine what it would be like to be in this house and then go home and interact normally with my mother as if everything is fine. And, if having my mother living there isn't enough, a friend of Melissa's moved in temporarily while going through a separation.

"How did this happen?" my sister moans. "I was supposed to be an empty nester when Mike left for school."

I walk her through the back. She's seen the video but really, what can prepare you for the stench?

"Pinch the metal part," I tell her, an expert now on mask wearing.

We start in the laundry room. My sister doesn't say anything, so I fill the thick air by describing what we've done, what we've found and how the garage is working as a staging area and I'm particularly glad we had that idea. But soon I fall silent. Melissa has always had a different relationship with my mother than I've had, so her denial about her and how she behaves has always been stronger than my own. It's been a point of contention between us at times. But in this moment, I'm sure she must see my mother clearly.

She pauses while taking it all in: Marc leaning on his shovel, the half-cleared-out living room, the unbearable stench that never leaves. Her expression is neutral, but I can feel how her shock and sadness mirror my first time here. I wonder how long it'll be before she feels the rage like I do, a giant fissure rumbling in the deep water.

She's looking for a piece of art she made in high school, a

bronze ceramic sun with rays and the center a portrait of her own face. "I want the mold for it," she says.

"I've looked everywhere I thought it might be," I say. "There's still a long way to go."

As we walk through the house, I feel her telescoping away from me. My fury suddenly clenches at my throat when I pick up one of the beautiful art books with the colored plates I remember cherishing when I was young. I throw it in the Goodwill pile because it stinks, body odors clinging to its cover like the dirty clothes it was buried in. It breaks my heart every time I toss another one. Like my own spine is cracking, like my words are being thrown aside and wasted. We love books in my family. We aren't supposed to defile what we love. I don't say any of this to my sister because we don't really talk about our emotions very often. But I desperately don't want to feel alone with the only person in the world who has known my mother almost as long as I have.

Melissa has sharp eyes and somehow finds her face, wrapped in the original newsprint on top of the window air conditioner that's on the floor of my mother's room, pushed against a wall.

She clutches her find like a prize.

"Take it today," I say. "I have other stuff you can get when you come back later."

"How can I bring anything home when she's there?" My sister unwraps the sun and looks at herself.

"A little at a time, I guess," I pause. "Stick it in your garage." I start walking across the hall to my old bedroom.

"I don't know if I can keep living with her after seeing this," my sister says looking around and shaking her head.

"Well," I respond a little too vehemently, "She's certainly never living with me." I stumble over one of the bottles of blue liquid that has rolled back into the path we've made in the hallway. "She's obviously not coming back here." I push it up against the wall with my gloved hand where it sits precariously.

"Maybe we can find her an assisted living place so she's not with either of us." She crunches around in my old bedroom. "Hey," she says, and picks up my antique black dog bank wedged in the corner on the floor, "You should keep this."

I start to tear up. "Where would the money for that come from? The house isn't going to get much."

Melissa stays for a little while and helps shovel some of the living room before she goes back to her house. She's worried my mother won't walk the dog. "I'll be here Saturday and Sunday. Ron will come too."

"Maybe he can help with the bathroom. I think Marc is done," I grimace just thinking about that mammoth task. I walk her out to her car, and we hug each other gently. Two days feels like years away.

The next day, she texts me. *I woke up at 3 a.m. and felt like there was something crawling all over me and I got up and took a shower again.* I can feel her sadness. *I got up this morning and showered one more time. I love you,* she adds. As she leaves for school after her sleepless night, she texts again. *Mom said, "Now that I'm feeling better, it's too bad I can't help you pull weeds from the yard."* She ends with a string of eyeroll emojis.

It could be Day Seven or Day Ten. Time blends together. Days pile up. I find the receipt for my mother's own headstone carving with nothing on it but her name and date of birth. Normally this might be funny or poignant, but it's just one more piece of paper in all this stuff I'm sifting through, *too many things, too much to even take in.* I feel like she's already dead. I certainly wish she were.

Sometimes I want to kill her. I could stab her with the pruning shears and then stuff her in the dumpster, I could tie her up and leave her for the mice to eat, I could set fire to this whole fucking house with her in it.… I chant my sinister plots as I pick up bits of broken glass from shattered picture frames, strip off disgusting bed linens, and pick up used tissues.

The mother I thought I had was a fantasy and she's gone. That mother appreciated art. She traveled and read and had a sense of humor. She told my sister and me to be strong in the world and to work hard. It's hard to reconcile these two mothers—the one who decorates and enjoys nice things and reads and learns things and values antiques. Then there's the other who shits in plastic bags and throws her banana peels on a pile of unwashed clothes that's four feet tall. Sure, I always understood she had vulnerabilities, but it was safer for me not to look too deeply. By doing that I didn't have to deal with her rage, her craziness. Our interactions could stay on the surface. My holding onto the fantasy mother is the same behavior my mother used to deal with the house when I was growing up—focusing on the outside yard and not dealing with the overwhelming things inside. *If she had died at the diner from a heart attack, I could have dealt with this mess, but would never have had to face her again*, I think. There would simply have been the *before* of who we thought or imagined she was and the *after* of this.

People, like my mother's next-door-neighbor, Jim, who stops by and loans us his wheelbarrow, try to be helpful. "Your mother is so sweet," he says. "You have to separate this behavior, this illness, from who she is."

I can't compartmentalize like that. My very much alive, reality mother created and lived in this disgusting chaos. I am expected to still have some kind of relationship with her. *A.D.*, I think again, *after discovery, but not after death.*

I find one of the things I've been looking for—the original picture of my grandmother, her brother, her tragically killed sister, and the goat. When I look at the original goat photo, it's strange how Frances has the crack through her where the photo bends, as if the universe knew she'd be gone. I put it aside to keep.

Inside my old dresser, in a drawer, there's a plastic bag with something in it. I push stuff off a chair and sit down for a minute and unwrap it to find the yellow fabric-covered book I made in high school. I illustrated, in pen and ink and watercolors, a nonsense poem Nonno taught me, and my mother used to recite it when she woke me up mornings. *Awake, awake, the dawn is here! The air is filled with atmosphere....* Because it was wrapped up, it doesn't smell too bad and, unlike most of the things in the house, is basically intact, the cover only a little bent.

On the floor next to the dresser, there's the wedding album from 1963; all the pictures carefully labeled with my mother's tiny, rounded script. *Married July 5, Mead Chapel, Omaha, Nebraska* under the picture of my mother in her little pillbox hat and my stepfather with his floral boutonniere. I flip through the book. There's space at the end to write information about anniversaries and the last entry was their second: *Dinner at home with Missy. We called Virginia to talk to Debbie at camp. I gave Howard just the sort of attaché case he wanted.* I pick up a scrap of paper that has fallen like a feather from a pile of papers which reads: *The palest ink is better than the best memory, Old Chinese Proverb.* In the middle drawer, stuffed in the bottom of a box are old love letters she saved from her high school boyfriend, which I don't examine here. Instead, I place them in the "to be gone through later pile" I'm bringing back to my house.

With a few exceptions, I turn down most of the well-meaning and generous offers to help. One friend whose help I do accept is Jackie's, the senior photo editor of a major news organization. "Would you come take pictures?"

Every night I write in my journal what I've done here and what I've seen, but I haven't taken many pictures. I'm aware that later, when I'm able to slow down, I'll want an actual record of what this was like because my own memory will be fragmented, won't be able to hold all the details. Jackie's covered wars in the Mideast and all kinds of natural disasters. I figure she won't be fazed by what she'll witness here. I also trust she won't judge my mother or us. I still feel the urge to protect my mother from other people, I don't want them gaping at the traffic accident of her life. At the same time, I'm both judging her hoarding behavior and our crime of not helping her sooner. It's shame and guilt, a toxic mess.

When Jackie arrives at the house, we are in full swing for the day, lugging items to the giant blue thirty-yard dumpster. She pulls her camera from the car. "You can wander wherever, but let me show you around first," I say, stepping over the boxes of items piled on the front lawn that are going to Goodwill.

She doesn't change expression once she's inside the house, and I understand she's in work mode. I wish I could see everything like she's seeing it.

"Wow," she says and not much else when I take her into the worst of the three bedrooms. This is where we are focusing today. She takes pictures of the swirling mass of stuff on the bed.

My childhood friend, Debbie E. has come up from Delaware to help for the day and Jackie takes pictures of the thousands of pennies scattered on the floor in the dining room that Debbie E. has been carefully collecting. I've told her to take them for herself. Jackie takes a picture of the dirty ear swabs lined up on the frame of a picture that's on top of a shelf. There are hundreds of them with their yellowed tops. She shoots other pictures as well, but I've gone back to work after the first few minutes, leaving her on her own. *You go contemplate my old troll doll in his sailor suit in the middle of the bedroom floor*, I think, as Marc and I carefully shovel and pick apart the layered piles that remind me a little of bakery tortes in their density. I hold open the contractor bag for him and sift through each scoop finding photographs, tax records from six years ago, and, when we reach the floor, a beautiful pearl and ruby ring my mother used to wear.

As I'm digging, dirty sweat pouring off me, I start to tell my sister, who's working in the same room, all the ways I've been imagining killing my mother, like one of the frightening stories I told her when we were little.

Finally, my sister has had enough. "Stop it," she commands. "You're scaring me."

After a while, Jackie puts her cameras back in her car. "It's so sad for her," she says to me, opening another black plastic bag as she joins us in the cleanup for a little while. I didn't want judgment, but I also didn't want compassion. Not for my mother. I want compassion for me. Jackie is recognizing my mother's illness and how fragile she is. But I can't let my anger go because without it I won't be able to function in this hellish house.

"I've seen a lot of things," she muses, watching me sip from my water bottle outside the garage as she prepares to leave. "I covered Katrina." She pauses and surveys the piles in the dumpster and then looks at me. "This house destruction is worse than Katrina." I hug her, too numb to cry at that point.

That night, when I'm home and looking at her photographs, I'm stunned at how she has made a strange beauty of the scenes. There, in black and white, is my sister's old wrought-iron bed filled with the swirled mass of filthy bedding, newspapers, books, and old peanut butter cracker wrappings. Somehow Jackie has caught the weight of my mother's body where it indented the messy piles, leaving only her ghostly imprint. There, in color, are the solidified newspapers by the back door, seen up close and morphed into abstract artwork from the way the rain and weather have carved them solid, their texture like canyons. She captures me, amidst the trash in the kitchen, about to open the door to the fridge when we finally reach it. I'm joking about what we'll find, but Jackie has caught what's below my humor, the reverberation of my exhaustion, my face partly turned away from her camera as I ready myself for some other horrible surprise. And, from my old bedroom window, a shot of the half-filled thirty-yard dumpster in the driveway below, ripped lace from the soiled curtains framing the view.

What has to happen to bury your own life? To care so little for yourself that you disappear and don't hold onto anything by holding onto everything? I try and work it out over and over again, but I'm not really able to. Then it comes to me. In each photograph, Jackie has captured what I've been trying to understand. This is my mother's creation.

At 4 p.m. when I arrive at my sister's, my mother is sitting on the couch with her book next to the dog, Cody, and has CNN running in the background. Matthew, a category four hurricane, is about to slam into Florida. They are running the path in red to show where it will move up the coast. There's something appropriate about this. My sister goes upstairs to change out of her school clothing and then we sit on opposite sofas with my mother seated on the middle, so we form a U. My mother looks a little rumpled, her color doesn't seem good, and she is heavier than when I last saw her only a few weeks ago. I'm guessing since she's not in the house climbing over the trash, she's getting less exercise. Or maybe the stress of wondering what we are doing in her house has caused her to be depressed. But she looks alert. I notice the places on her arms that had been picked at and inflamed before, now appear to be healed. *Having running water has probably helped with that.*

"You got $3,000 for the car, but there's no money for another one and I'm cancelling your auto insurance," I tell her.

She's distressed by this, so I don't pull out the fact that she drove for six months without insurance and probably for at least that long without a license and registration.

"The court date is in a few weeks, and I'll be taking you," I tell her I'm sorry about the situation and I understand it's upsetting. But I'm like the weatherperson, just reading the script.

She gets up to find her calendar book to write down the court date, and I look over at the silent figures on the television screen warning of disaster. It feels like the map of the coming storm gets bigger whenever I turn my back. With a deep breath I say, "We are going to take you next week to look at several assisted living places that you can afford with your budget."

"I don't understand why I need that," she confronts me. "Why can't I do independent living instead, like we talked about?"

"First, it's not possible without your having a car, and second, there's a long waiting list even if we could work it out."

"But I don't think I need assisted living," she retorts. I can feel my anger start to flare and I stare at her for a minute. This isn't the argument I expected. I thought she'd want to go back to the house. In a way, she's surrendering to moving elsewhere, which is a logical choice.

"Mom, you don't cook, you don't do laundry, and you don't clean," It takes everything in me to not bring up the house. I flashback to the kitchen filled with moldy glasses and pans with old, solidified food, the buried washing machine, the miles of mouse nests. Instead of engaging, I get up and pour myself a glass of wine, sitting back down to face her again after taking a big swig of it.

My sister, feeling bad and sensing my struggle, jumps in. "We can get you Uber maybe and we want you to go somewhere where you can keep your treasures."

I shoot her a look. *Really? Treasures? Like that $400 antique baby crib she stuck in her garage to warp with the weather.* The slow burn of my rage starts to heat up.

"I hope you found those drinking glasses with the chicken and egg pattern," she says to me, sensing the smoke.

"Those aren't there." I'm thinking maybe I have the skills to be an assassin with my calmly focused killer stare.

She looks at me suspiciously. She doesn't remember what she has in that house and what she doesn't.

"I also want my watch necklace."

"I found that," I smile. "I'll bring that over to you."

"And the Villanova sweatshirt," she keeps going, "I had five pairs of pants," she moans. "They were fine." She's getting a little teary-eyed as she glares at me, arms crossed over her chest as she gears up for this argument.

"No," I say sharply, "they weren't. They smelled and were wet and had mouse crap on them. It's a disaster, except FEMA isn't coming. Your car paid for the dumpsters, and you owe both of your sons-in-law big thanks."

I don't say, *You, fucking bitch, you have traumatized me so badly with this I will never get over it.* "It was very painful to have lost all the books that were in the house," I manage to add.

My mother's face looks like she'd rather escape to a hurricane shelter than keep talking to me. She bends over to pet Cody and then sits up and looks back at the television and pretends to be watching the giant arrow of disaster as it arcs over the East Coast. She's trying to collect herself. My sister and I exchange glances, *time's about up*.

My mother says, a little belligerently, "Did you find Aunt Helen's Chinese dragon vase in the office? That's worth a lot of money. I hope you didn't get rid of it. I loved that vase when I was a child. She always said I could have it when she died."

I'm confused for a minute until I realize the hellhole that used to be my bedroom is where she's referring to. "Yes, I found that, in the *office*." It's crapped up and cracked from lack of care. It was a gorgeous piece of ceramic, but it's doubtful it's worth anything because it's been so damaged. *Like everything else in that fucking house*, I think.

"And the painting from your great-grandma's that was in the living room? You didn't do anything with that, right?"

I nod my head affirmatively and suddenly feel exhausted. *Is she going to go through EVERY object to make sure it's okay?*

"Things just got away from me after your grandmother died. I just took everything and dumped it all in the garage and never looked at it."

My sister and I try not to look surprised by her comment. It seems she's taking responsibility for some part of the mess.

"Yeah, I found those papers and photographs." I'm done talking, flashing back to the moldy genealogy books my grandmother had carefully preserved, which my mother threw on the damp garage floor.

Despite my sister's offer of dinner, I elect to head home at peak traffic time instead of staying any longer. *It beats being here*, I think.

"Ok," I say, "I'm heading out," and I get up.

My mother doesn't move to hug me or say goodbye. She stares fixedly at the television.

My sister says, "Mom, Debbie's leaving."

Then my mother stands up and faces me from the other side of the sofa. "Thanks for taking care of this," she says.

It's so grudgingly stated and minimized (like I've done an errand for her by swinging by the pharmacy to pick something up) that my sister gets pissed and interjects, "Deb has spent hours on these things for you."

My mother impatiently waves her comment off with her hand like it's an annoying insect and says, "I know it's a lot...."

So, I guess the responsibility ends there, I think, *you are incredible, Mom.*

Afterwards, I drive home still stunned by some of her responses. Although really, why am I surprised by her minimizing what was happening in the house? To live there she had to dissociate how bad it really was. So, given her reality, her reaction about what we are doing makes a perverse sense.

I open my back door, shoving aside a half dozen paper and plastic bags filled with important documentation, letters, paperwork, and old photographs we've salvaged so far. I dread sorting them. I pull out one of my mother's journals, feeling a little bad about snooping. *Like I'm invading her secrets*, I think, rolling my eyes. It falls open to her tight script, shakier than the wedding album: *January 19, 1992. Herewith a beginning. Last year was the year of rest, this year the year of healing. So, I need to get my life organized before retirement. I dread the thought of dependence on my children.... Hopefully the children should, by then, have room to take some of the beloved possessions which won't fit my eventually reduced circumstances.*

I flip through the pages, but the journal ends after only a month. I rummage in the bag and find another journal where she states she is going to write her memories from childhood, the story of her life. I flip it open, but it's mostly blank, abandoned after a few pages. The puzzle of my mother isn't going to be pieced together from these things I've found either.

PART III - *KEPT*

Chapter 12 – Family Secrets

Scientists have created a floating gauge in the ocean that is able to detect the difference between a tsunami and an ordinary wave, even if that wave looks smooth and green and swells like any other. With a gauge, they can anticipate when a tsunami is coming to knock down all the buildings and change the very shape of the shoreline, then—receding wave—it changes back into itself to become ordinary water again. I have this kind of gauge too, after Nanna's death in 1990, I feel the sea change happening.

I find myself journaling, even with all the work I'm doing in my doctoral program that I began a year before she passed away. I decide I want to use a small notebook to start the year off. I write, *I'm feeling like the other one was maybe too big to haul around, and I've been trying to make what I carry (like my calendar) smaller and more compact for myself.* Maybe finding Daddy has made for less need to drag my past around with me. I'm writing about the present and it takes less space. *It's funny,* I journal, *what you can discard over time....*

Early in July 1991, Marc, who's a year ahead of me in our Psy.D. program and six years younger, begins interning at my practicum site. He's smart, blond, and handsome. I'm rebounding from (and still crying about) my relationship of five years with Fred, ending a few months before. Marc is (although I don't know it at the time) breaking up with a woman in his class with whom he's been living for the past year. I joke to myself, *he'll be my summer boy toy.* He admits later that he noticed me in my pink, short skirt, and high heels in the office kitchen the first time he was there.

After a few days, I poke my head into his office when his door is open between clients. "Want to go grab some ice cream?" *What do I have to lose if I flirt?* I think.

And he says, yes, and pretty much from the summer into the fall, we provide the other therapists and office staff with plenty to gossip about as they observe our falling quickly, totally, and completely in love with each other.

A month after we meet, Marc brings a better coffee maker over to my apartment since I don't have one. As he plugs it into the wall, he tells me, "My brother told me when he saw I was bringing this for you, that I was going to marry you." He kisses me, "But I really just want good coffee."

I grab the bag of gourmet beans he's brought with him to use in the grinder he's also gifted me, "But the truth is," I tease him back, "that you're really in this because I have a car."

Not long after Nanna dies, my mother is fired from a job for the first time in her life. From the earliest I can remember, and certainly since the divorce from Daddy, my mother always worked and had good evaluations. She was often promoted. Staff respected her. When we were younger, we'd go hang out in her office at the nursing homes where she was employed, sometimes meeting the residents, sometimes helping with office paperwork when it was appropriate, and sometimes just hanging out reading if she couldn't find childcare when we were too young to leave at home. This firing is a complete and painful shock to her, and she is upset about what happened although tight-lipped about why, indicating only that there were some conflicts with a supervisor that finally came to a head. She finds another position almost immediately but is anxious about doing well there after what happened. She isn't really interacting much with me as she's busy buying my pregnant sister lots of maternity items and is very excited about her first grandchild, who is expected in October.

I call her about an ergonomic desk chair I need for my apartment after herniating a disc in my back several months before. "I need something," I tell her, "so I can study more comfortably for my comprehensive exams and for writing this dissertation."

"I don't have money," she tells me. "And I still need to pay taxes. I'm sorry I can't help you with that."

"Well, another time. Keep me in mind," I say. "You did offer to get me some office stuff when I needed it," I can't help but add.

Then she says, "Detectives in Albany are expensive."

"What?"

"I'm going to look for Malcolm because you asked about him a while ago and that's going to be expensive to do," she explains.

I'm stunned. "Mom, don't you think this is my decision and my responsibility…"

She interrupts me and says with intensity, "Deborah, you aren't going to do it until it's too late." And I'm not sure whether she means too late for him or for her. It doesn't sound like she's doing this for me. I don't really need another found father to cope with in the middle of my doctoral program. But she hasn't been told about the other one and I'm not sharing that information during our call.

As I think about it after we hang up, I realize it's the same struggle I always seem to have with her. She gives me what she wants, not what I'm asking for or need. Yet in some ways, she's trying to help me, to do a nice thing. It's just that since Cheryl, she can't be in sync with me. Or maybe that's not right, maybe I am no longer able to stretch myself to be in her world and make the interactions work the way they did when we made that map of the ocean floor together.

Later she calls me back to tell me she'll get me the chair because she just realized she'll have a certificate of deposit that will be maturing and can use that money. I tell her I don't really want to hear anything about her search for Malcolm until after my comps are done and that I'm upset she didn't consult me about it.

"I'll see you at your sister's baby shower," she says and hangs up.

In late September, three months after Marc and I first laid eyes on each other, my niece is born six weeks early. Marc's parents are in town visiting and I'm meeting them for the first time. Because they are having dinner in the city, we all end up at the hospital like a family wedding scene in a Shakespeare play—me, my mother, Ron, Melissa, Marc and his parents, and the baby. My mother, enthroned in the chair next to my sister's hospital bed, beams happily about the birth. She's polite and charming when meeting Marc's parents.

I'm increasingly unhappy with my own interactions with her as I've just heard from Fred that she's contacted him to try and have lunch, but he's avoided it because he feels it would be strange. "She wanted to talk about you," he tells me, "and to hear from me what happened."

Newborn Sarah has some health issues and is having trouble latching on for breastfeeding because she's premature. I love this baby like she's my own. I stare through the glass at her tiny face and slightly yellowed complexion. Her jaundice means she must sleep under a light like a little Happy Meal at a fast food place. And she will need to be on a sleep monitor for her breathing when they bring her home. My sister has told me I will get to be her godmother. I want to wave a wand like a fairy godmother, so she will experience only good things and be protected and safe forever. I want my niece to have a different childhood from my own.

My mother has purchased a small photo album, a "grandmother brag book" that she is planning to fill with pictures of Sarah. I understand that Sarah carries, like I do, the baggage of being the first. The seed of love between grandmother and oldest granddaughter, like I had with Nanna, has taken root and I'm curious how it will flower.

After Sarah is born, Daddy tells me he has been diagnosed with Parkinson's disease. I'd noticed his handwritten letters had become shorter and more difficult to read with the sharp angular blue peaks sloping upwards. He tells me he hasn't felt well since April. I don't say this aloud, but I think, *I've just found you and despite all the complications of having you in my life, I don't want to lose you already.*

"I want to come visit and see my first grandchild," he says to me. The implication being that if he doesn't do it soon, he won't be able to. I tell him I'll pass on his request to Melissa.

"Really?" my sister responds angrily. "Really? I just had a baby. Just what I need, Daddy reappearing here." I feel bad. And I don't know if there's a right thing to do in this situation.

Marc and I are eating family dinner, gathered around the table at my sister's home in my grandmother's old house. It's been seven years since we've been inside my mother's house, so this has become the nucleus of the family for weekend get-togethers and holidays. I've held Sarah, smelling that sweet spot at the top of her head, and rocking her till she's finally asleep and can be placed in her crib with the vacuum cleaner running outside her room.

My sister laughingly explains, "They say it's like hearing the sounds inside the uterus." Putting her on top of the running clothes dryer has the same soothing effect. *Maybe,* I think to myself, *it's the ghost of my grandmother in this house, soothing her with cleaning and household tasks.*

I say something during the conversation about what's happening at school for me, and it is like I am invisible—no one responds. My mother doesn't ask Marc much of anything and pretty much ignores him as well.

She says at the end of the meal, "There's a new place we can go for dinner, but it's further away, so Deborah," she turns toward me with a blank expression, "when you are done with all your nonsense, we can go there." The "nonsense" refers to my comprehensive exams coming up.

Marc tells me afterwards, "Your mother seemed like she was totally pissed off at you." He leans over and ruffles my short hair as we get ready to climb into the bed that came from my grandmother's house. "It makes me angry that nobody validates my honey," and then goes on to add, "It's boring that all we talk about is baby stuff." Maybe my mother is still angry about our recent conversation about Malcolm, but it could really be anything she's thinking.

"I don't get it," I tell him with an irritated edge to my voice. "She's a mystery."

What I do grasp is that I have had enough and that something needs to change. I decide I'm going to find a family therapist for us. I am angry at my sister's behavior as she aligns with my mother to treat me like an object. I understand she's just trying get the support she needs from my mother to help with being a new mom. Daddy is pushing to come for a visit and doesn't get that he can't do what he wants, not just because my mother doesn't know about him, but also because my sister and I get to decide when it's right for us.

Mostly, I want to stop being so reactive to my mother's paranoia and, what I finally allow myself to label in my own mind, her mental illness. I've learned that anger is a lazy way of connecting. You are attached but without doing any of the real work of intimacy. I understand she is very fragile, but it can't be my problem anymore to take care of her. It seems my clinical knowledge is useless when it comes to diagnosing her. I fantasize that if I knew what she had, I could be caring yet dispassionate in the way that I can be with my clients when they are acting in ways that make it hard to connect with them. She's often depressed, and we all have anxiety symptoms in my family. Sometimes she seems dissociative, and I'm aware she had some past trauma. She could have borderline personality disorder although at times she has had psychotic symptoms, like when she was delusional about Daddy stalking her or my spying on her in the house. I'm not sure how I'd treat her if I was her therapist.

It is normal, my psychology textbook says, for children to play at running away when they are five or so. This is a developmental test of independence and about whether their parents will still love them if they make their own choices. I have no memory of packing up my things as a child of that age except when I was sent away to camp. Even then I knew there was too much to carry, things that couldn't be folded or shoved into a zippered case, or things that were too big to leave behind: furniture I'd inherited, books, early memories from the house. Leaving home requires that there be a home to be left; a place, an architecture, something more than need, more than an imaginary relationship.

Ann's psychology office overlooks the Philadelphia Museum of Art and has a long, low-slung brown leather couch and two comfortable chairs facing it. Ann sits in one chair. I'm in the other next to her. My mother and my sister sit on the couch across from us. Sarah is sleeping in the car carrier on the floor between them, covered with a little pink blanket. Ann is kind and nurturing, and it quickly becomes apparent that the trouble in the family for everyone is me. My sister and mother pinpoint that the issues in the family began with my mother and me during my adolescence, which is, of course, when Daddy left, and my mother began collecting and bringing home stray people with problems to live with us. None of us (including me) mentions the stray people coincidence. We sit together in her office rigidly looking at each other and not able to say much. It's like a minefield where one wrong step is going to blow off somebody's leg.

In my initial session with her alone, Ann had tried to reframe to me that what I seemed to want from my mother was to "be closer."

I kept fighting with her about this. "No, that's not what I want. I want to be *free* of her."

Ann didn't seem to get it. "Well," she said gently, "let's all talk together and see what happens." Her comment sticks with me, uncomfortable as it is. We attend therapy in different combinations, sometimes just me, sometimes my sister and me, and, as we finally decide to share with my mother about finding Daddy, the three of us.

I find myself depressed in a way I haven't been since college when I saw Sandy. I play Peter Gabriel's song "Digging in the Dirt" over and over in my car on the way to my new internship at Einstein Hospital. *Find the places we got hurt,* Peter and I sing together, *shut your mouth, you know what you are....*

Like when I saw Sandy before, I start dreaming all the time. *My mother is outside her house and trying to dig in the garden where the roses are. She wants to plant things, but the earth is too hard and can't be broken up. She has big, long feces in a bucket and some of them are on the ground. My mother leans over with the small silver trowel, trying to fold them in as fertilizer to grow something.*

During this time, Marc moves into my apartment, and we begin to make a life together by introducing our two cats, Kinta and Fab C (named after a Rorschach score), who warily stalk around each other's space in the daytime, but in the dead of night, howl and hiss and chase each other through the apartment. Given my family history, I'm hoping this isn't a relationship omen.

I tell Ann at an individual session that my boyfriend and I have been talking about getting married and, although this was not a conscious goal when I first called her, I think my underlying reason for being in therapy is to understand these family relationships, not to just protect the well-being of Sarah, but so I don't repeat any of this with my future children. "I just want to be free," I tell her again. And now that she has been treating my family, she understands what I am saying.

My mother's face reddens, and she leans back against the leather couch in Ann's office with her arms crossed. "Has he been up here?" she barks, looking like she's trying not to cry. My sister and I swap glances. This is the earthquake in our family. We are telling her we've found Daddy.

Here comes that tsunami, I think.

"No," my sister and I respond together. "We would never do that to you."

Her eyes narrow. She doesn't believe us, I can tell. I reassure her that he is getting infirm from the Parkinson's and can't do many things without assistance. I don't know if she's afraid of him or not, but I figure the less harmful she perceives him to be, the better.

"Look, it's been several years, and he has a family. He's been okay with us." My mother sits stone-faced, not taking her eyes off me.

"For several years?" she repeats, so that I am clear about the betrayal.

Ann inserts something about how healthy families clear up secrets so everyone can grow and change in their relationships with each other.

"We need you to deal with Melissa and me having some kind of connection with him whether you want us to or not." I'm matter of fact despite feeling like I'm about to throw up. "He is our father and that doesn't mean we love you less."

"Besides," adds my sister, "he lives all the way in Houston so it's not like we're going to really see him at all."

"Our time is up," says Ann. "Let's everybody think about all this, and we'll talk next week."

I picture myself like those people screaming and running away from the wall of water heading toward them. *Why does this have to be so freaking hard?*

Following this session, Marc asks if I can meet him for dinner at our favorite Chinese restaurant, the place of our first real date. "I can't," I manage to choke out, beginning to cry. "That session was horrible. Can we just eat at home?"

Back at the apartment, I throw together some boxed Kraft macaroni and cheese and frozen peas, an old adolescent comfort meal. Afterwards, holding me as we talk, he pulls a ring box from his pocket. He says he already feels married to me, so let's make it official. And it's the best proposal I could wish for because no matter what happens in my family of origin, I have found a true home in him.

"This is the family legacy," Ann says a few sessions later.

"From mother to daughter, the anger and pain from your mother, it's like stone in your heart." She says it repeatedly as if she is hypnotizing my mother. My sister and I are watching my mother go into a trance—she begins to cry. Tries to use words, but Ann is bent towards her—softly talking about her pain, the complicated and sometimes abusive relationship she had with my grandmother, focusing on it, and making my mother pay attention. My eyes fill. I am watching partly to see how a good therapist works with someone by delicately unraveling her defenses. Still, even Ann can't get her there, my mother can't see and continues to talk about how critical, judgmental, and cruel I am to her. In the end, the spell isn't strong enough and she can't let her feelings toward me go. She can't hear that she needs to work on her own pain.

"But," my mother interrupts, "there is something more going on with Deborah than just this." It is the same as it's always been with us. She recounts more distorted stories about how awful I am to her. And she belittles and distrusts my attempts to forge some kind of honest, if limited, relationship.

I am the lucky one, I think to myself sarcastically, *who has been chosen for this role and probably prepared for it all my life*. I feel like I'm an object to her, but one that is invisible, unseen, and not validated. I had to become a therapist myself to carry the pain and a writer to express it. It is, like Ann says, as if my mother is in prison and she needs someone to become her jailer.

And when my mother says in therapy, "We went out to lunch and had a superficial good time discussing the wedding, although I'm not sure who she's inviting...." I know when we do things together, she is watching me, worrying how she will protect herself. I am her difficult mother, the bringer of pain. And the legacy goes on. But I realize I do not have to hold on to the inheritance I am being given.

When we talk after the session, Melissa sighs, "We'll tell all our kids about this when they are old enough to understand the complicated family stories."

I laugh. "Like they'll be able to understand what we're still trying to."

"Nobody's accompanying me down the aisle. I got myself here, I'm walking alone," I joke with Marc when we discuss our wedding, planned for the following year, after I graduate with my doctorate. I have already decided I don't want Daddy to be at the wedding. The compromise I've come up with is for him to visit by himself this summer and stay with both my sister and me for a few days each. My sister grudgingly agrees with this plan. We will tell my mother beforehand, so she can stay away from my sister's house while he's in town.

It turns out the tsunami that carried the Daddy secret into the family did clear out some things. My relationship with my mother improves. Ann was right after all about my being able to be closer to my mother. With my stepfather's existence no longer secret and my having let go of some of the sadness and expectation about our relationship, I'm freer to accept my mother's overtures toward me when she is able to offer them. To my mother's credit, and my happy surprise, she tries to be kinder to me after Ann has reframed this as one way to "help me" with my angry feelings.

My upcoming wedding and having a niece are making me think about eventually having children. If I'm being totally honest with myself, I need to take care of another piece of unfinished business.

"Maybe I need to look for Malcolm," I say to Marc.

There are the obvious reasons for finding him. I need a better health history and he's not getting any younger. My biological father is part of me, and I need to understand why he gave me up. This secret gnaws at me sometimes, especially when I see my brother-in-law hold my niece up high in the air laughing. Sarah is almost the age I was when Malcolm left. At least finding this father won't make my mother angry, although we haven't discussed it again since that time before we went to family therapy.

"Can we get through one father first?" my soon-to-be husband laughs.

Daddy is different when he arrives in August. It's been four years since my visit to Texas. He's trembly and shaky from the Parkinson's and more stooped over. He doesn't talk as much and there's even less expression on his face, so it's hard to read what he's feeling. He spends time at Melissa's first, and while she's tense, she also seems a little happy that he's there. His sister, my Aunt Faye, drives up from Virginia for the day. This is the first time we've seen her in almost twenty years, since the end of the divorce visitations when I was thirteen or so, and we all gather on the porch at my sister's house, awkwardly making Sarah the centerpiece of the conversation. She's crawling around and pulling herself up on the furniture like a small monkey, reaching for different toys and making babbling sounds when she looks at us.

"I'm so enjoying visiting you," Aunt Faye says. She's a slender, short-haired woman whose face is shaped a bit like my sister's. She turns to me, "I often think back on the summers you spent with me. I'm truly sorry that your mother wouldn't let me visit with you for all those years."

Daddy looks at me but doesn't say anything.

"I'm sorry, too," I tell her, "But it's good we can all be here together."

She looks down at Sarah, who is determinedly chewing on a rubber ring. She's teething and drooling uncontrollably. "I was very upset when your mother asked me to not call, write, or come see you. At that time, I felt I had to respect her wishes in the hope that the breakup would not be a bitter fight. The few times your father brought you to visit were pleasant, but I got the feeling that you and Missy were there because you had to be."

I remember my mother's comments when I was younger about Aunt Faye being gay and find I don't really want to bring "unpleasant memories up," as my aunt says.

While Daddy stays at my sister's, he tells them he wants to drive to see his childhood home in Delaware. Melissa and Ron load Sarah into the car and embark on what turns out to be a four-hour-long ordeal down to the southern part of the state where my father stands shakily outside the house contemplating it.

"Sarah is crying, it's unbelievable," my sister tells me afterwards. "He didn't even think about what kind of imposition that would be for us."

"I won't speak for my sister on this," I tell Ann later, "but I think she and I share some similar feelings about Daddy's sense of entitlement." He and my mother both play at being victims at times. He, unlike her, feels the world has treated him poorly. But like my mother, he also recreates history. He becomes grandiose and elaborates about what he's done or pumps up his self image or his children's. Daddy spins a shiny new object out of the past, so I can be impressed by it. My mother tells her revisionist stories to me to protect herself. Both need their defenses against a world they fear will hurt them. I wonder if my mother would take pleasure in the fact that the more time I spend with Daddy, the more I appreciate what she was able to give us growing up.

I'm no longer scared of him, but I do find myself thinking about the sexual abuse, wondering whether his behavior toward me was a pattern. Had anything had ever happened with his daughter? In my work with trauma clients and as I interact with him, I'm understanding more about the effects of this on me.

He sleeps in our apartment on my used floral couch my sister found for me. He expects me to make him food and drive him to places he'd like to go. At night, lying in bed in the other room, I find I can't sleep.

I quietly turn to Marc, as a few tears wet his chest, "I'm thinking about what he did to me as a child." Marc strokes my hair and holds me more tightly. "I don't trust him and I'm not even sure I like him," I whisper, skin crawling.

Marc replies, "It's amazing you turned out the way you did with two parents like you had."

"Maybe I shouldn't have found him," I say.

"But now you know," Marc whispers back, "and that's always better."

Before we drive my father to the airport, we stop by our future wedding venue to show him the site and take some pictures, so he will have them. He turns to me unexpectedly as we pose in front of the window where the ceremony will be held.

"I hope your experience when you find your biological father pleases him as much as your finding me has pleased me," he says hesitantly, Parkinson's causing him to say the words more slowly than he intended.

Touched and surprised by this mention of Malcolm, who in

some way has always been a specter in my relationship with him, I put my arm around his shoulder. "I appreciate that. It means a lot to me."

I've bought us sandwiches to eat in the car on the way to catch his flight, but Daddy, unsteady on his feet, lurches a little and drops most of his on the pavement as we help him out of the car when we arrive at the terminal. I stare down at coleslaw and pastrami scattered on the ground and feel terrible loss. I'm not sure when I will see him again. He may be bedridden with how quickly his disease is progressing. I start to cry when I hand him the rest of my meal, so he has something to eat for the trip. I hug him goodbye. It feels like I'm that adolescent girl he's leaving again.

Thinking about that moment of giving him my stupid sandwich makes me cry harder as we pull out of the parking lot. "It's ridiculous I'm so upset," I sniffle, wiping my nose on one of the takeout napkins.

"Why are you surprised?" Marc says, putting his hand on my knee and speeding up to merge back onto the highway. "Your relationship with him has always been about loss."

That night, apartment empty of my stepfather, I finally sleep. I dream. *I'm supposed to pick up my mother and sister. They want to put all their things in my red Honda Civic and I'm supposed to drive them somewhere. For the first time I say "no." I leave a bunch of stuff scattered in the parking lot behind me—all different kinds of objects from my grandmother's house and my mother's house on Willowbrook Road. My sister's worried that these things won't be there after we leave. My mother keeps yelling at me to stop, she wants to stuff everything into the trunk. I say, "Who cares if it's stolen? We don't need it anyway." Together, we drive away. In my rearview mirror, I can see everything scattered behind me.*

Chapter 13 - Barren

On the front page of the journal from the time where I find my biological father Malcolm, is inscribed "*Xmas, 1993. To Deborah for the recording of her honeymoon in the next year. May the romance of Italy enrich your life with beautiful memories. Love, Mom.*" This is just before she starts calling herself Momdee for the grandchildren, when she is still just the mother of my sister and me.

Several years go by and I've become Dr. Deb and have a new last name and the pages of that journal aren't even filled all the way. I was a writer who wasn't writing then. There was so much to say about things that were happening to me and yet I recorded very little of it. I like to think that during that time, I was speaking things to Marc instead of writing them. But that's not totally true. It was more that living my life was like riding my purple bike from childhood, wheels spinning faster and faster as I raced down a hill toward a place I wanted to go. I wasn't looking at the scenery while becoming a psychologist. It was all about getting to that point. In the little book where my mother kept my elementary school pictures, there was a page that asked what I wanted to be when I grew up. When I was five, she listed: teacher, archeologist (my mother had wanted to be that and had explained what it was), author, and mother. I assume, after my wedding, that the mother part will happen for me, like it's another place I'll easily ride to on that purple bike.

Early June of 1995, there's an entry, a year after my wedding, where I tell my mother I'm going to search for Malcolm. Then there's another one right after that which begins, *in other news, almost too big to even get my head around, I've found Malcolm.*

The reason there's no dramatic tension in writing about this discovery is that by the time I did it, I'd rationalized that it was only about biology. It was about figuring out what health problem might be lurking in my own history as well as potentially that of a child-to-be. Genetic problems, not the problems—psychological, personality—that litter my family like garbage we step around. Malcolm resided at the bottom of that long-ago sculpted sea terrain my mother had helped me make, so heavy and freighted that he and his story were like a sunken ship I'd have to dive into by myself. And for so many years, before the advent of the internet it seemed to be too much work. What was the point?

But maybe there's more to it than that. I am made up of him. Do you lose part of yourself when you leave it behind? This is before I lose pregnancies over and over, beginning to understand even more deeply about grief and loss than I thought possible. How do you leave a living child like he did and not look back?

When I find him, Malcolm asks, why now? And I can only explain by unraveling back through it all. I don't spare anything although I tell my story in my therapist voice. I tell him about Daddy, about college, and my writing, and the zoo. I tell him about my mother and what she's like and what happened to my grandparents. I try to recount what had been important and formative, but how do you tell a big chunk of your own life? He heard it. It seemed like he was proud of me; he even said he liked my then too-short hair.

We are gathered at Glen Lake in New York at Malcolm's sister's house, an A-frame decorated with kitschy sayings and comfortable recliners. There's warm hospitality, plenty of alcohol, and takeout food. My half-brother, Andrew, and cousins I've never met are also there. We all watch an eight-millimeter movie my aunt found of my visit to Albany when I was nine months old. I look with sadness at my young mother as she bounces chubby me up and down in the water next to my cousin, whom I am meeting for the first time and whom I won't see again until this gathering, thirty-four years later.

I look like Malcolm, ruddy complexion, mossy eyes, heavy footsteps, and a humor that is mostly evident when he is not depressed or punishing himself. He has one arm that works. The other, shriveled and child-sized, hangs uselessly at his side from a bad break in the military that wasn't fixed properly. It is as if a child is trying to escape from him—a Siamese twin who has fallen behind and given up the running.

My fundamental early lesson was that people leave and do not return. In my adult life they return but in a different form, metamorphosing from myth to something much smaller, more painful, and less manageable.

Malcolm sips on his second scotch of the afternoon, as we sit by the edge of the still lake, shining in the summer light. He tells me he never signed the adoption papers when they came. He knew my adoption would eventually be approved. That by doing this, he wasn't relinquishing; by doing this my mother was holding on and taking me but he wasn't agreeing to it really. "I thought she was a good mother," he says thoughtfully. "I knew she wasn't right sometimes, but she was good to you."

He's not the only one in his family who held on. His mother, my other Nana, sent gifts to my mother for me the first few years after the divorce.

Back when I was in my first therapy, my mother told me this story, "They were addressed to your old name, after the adoption went through." I realize their behavior wasn't passive-aggressive. How could his mother be aware of my new name, who I was becoming? My mother sent the presents back unopened.

Nana looks at me shrewdly when we first meet, her head tilted in the way that I tilt my own. "I talked to your other grandmother regularly," she says. "For many years we kept up." But Malcolm and my mother didn't know that. Nobody knew. At this first reunion at my aunt's house, Nana hands me an envelope that holds a bunch of United States Savings Bonds. She gave them to all her grandchildren through the years and this is my share. She saved them for me.

Finding Malcolm is like opening a wound long sealed and debriding it. Feeling the ache and bleeding and then relief—there, it's not so bad. He's not a secret father anymore. He's *my* father.

Ron jokes with me when we are all having dinner at my sister's house, "What's up next? Going to go look for your mother's eleventh grade prom date?" We all laugh, but there's an edge. The power of secrets, how something wrong inside can come out and be named for what it is. Loss, here is loss.

My mother, after her four miscarriages, has me, but loses her husband. Or they lose each other. He drinks, claiming it was Nonno's martinis that corrupted him. My mother claims he didn't drink when he was with her. I think it started after, to deal with his sadness and his inability to maintain a relationship with me after the divorce.

"I thought it would be good for you," he says. "I'm sorry it wasn't." He slurs a bit on his fourth Dewar's.

After this visit, when I am trying to get pregnant for the first or the third or the fifth time, I think about how I am made of loss. When I stared into that deep abyss without fear and looked for what was missing, I somehow found the fathers, myself, even. Now, I want to turn loss into something else. I want to make something that is both Marc and me. Marc will be a father. A father who doesn't leave. If I can just hold on.

DNA and our environment, the psychologists say, influence our individual story. They entwine, winding around and around inside us. What part of us blooms from our genetics, and what part is from the people who've nurtured us? Over the first few meetings with my biological father and his family, I find another version of my history. The half I've heard from my mother and the other half I hear from him don't fit together exactly, it's like what I am composed of at my core will always be knotted up somehow. He claims she wanted him to leave. She claims he left her with no car and me, the baby, and no way to get around. I think of scientists trying to decipher those pictures of DNA spirals, unable to read them clearly.

Malcolm sees my mother in me and is really talking to her when whispering his request for forgiveness for his affair after all her miscarriages. My mother tells me as well that she betrayed him with my stepfather. "We were too young. We could have worked it out and should have," she told me long ago when I'd asked. In this part of the story, they agree. I think of my sister whose three children are the only children I have and how they wouldn't exist if this alternate history had happened.

In the end, does forgiveness matter? Our relationships go on anyway whether we have resolved what happened or not.

I tell Malcolm the present is all we have together, and I mean it.

After my longest pregnancy, which ends late in the first trimester, I think about Xaviera at the zoo, the rhino in the Rare Mammal House. How her baby was so sick, barely breathing, how the zoo vets gathered around the silver table in Penrose Lab, trying to save it. An oxygen mask covered the smooth spot on its nose where the horn would eventually be if it got big enough. I remember Xaviera crying in the night as the keepers tried to comfort her. Somehow, she knew her baby was dead even though it wasn't with her. Her keening through the darkness that the elephants, the hippos, and I understood. Instead of fathers leaving me, it's babies, or not even babies really, the idea of babies, the fantasy fathers, all of it falling out of me as if my body can't hold onto something about life.

Another woman at the Community Mental Health Center where I work was going through infertility too. She comes to my office to announce her pregnancy and brings a bluebird—a glass paperweight. Someone gave it to her before they were finally able to conceive. She says, "It's for you, for luck." I hold its cool deep blue in my hand, like a tiny sea, and all I can think about are tears. I put it on my desk, where it perches, listening to the staff complain about the agency and to my client's problems and pain—AIDS, and rape, and sorrow.

I dream. *I'm at my OB-GYN's office and he's doing a pelvic exam.*

"Oh," Dr. Grover says, "this is the issue. You're blocked by something very far back, so far back I can barely see it." He reaches inside me to try and pull it out, but whatever it is stays just out of reach.

Marc asks if I'd feel incomplete without a child. We joke about adopting a highway instead. We have terrible times through this. He doesn't understand my grief. I try and swim up to reach him from the underwater cave I'm hiding in, but the words I'm saying rise past him, hanging between us like incomprehensible air we don't share.

He holds one of the new kittens we got as a hedge against Kinta's eventual demise up to his face. "Does she look like me?" he teases. We are both tired of our lives being only about what we make. Or can't make.

Later, when I give up the idea of being a mother and bequeath the glass bluebird to someone else, I'll wonder if it did help me, magically believing it was absorbing all the suffering.

When Malcolm is lucid for a few minutes in the hospital bed when he is dying of liver cancer in 2018, some twenty-five years after I found him, I say, "There's nothing unfinished between us we need to say, right?"

He looks at me and says, "No, it's good, we're all good," and smiles at me. He's been seeing an imaginary bird flying through the bathroom and keeps pointing it out to me with fascination. He is as sober as he can be on the pain medications.

I tell him I love him, and he says the same.

Two months after he's gone, we bury him with a bottle of his favorite scotch and a small family sendoff. His son, Andrew, forty, and his wife are soon pregnant. Inside, she holds something that will continue my father and Andrew. And it will be part of me, too. A child, flying along on that bicycle, feet pumping as he pretends to soar.

So, both my mother, through my half-sister's children, and my father, through my half-brother's child, will travel on into some future time. Then there's me. I end, except here, in these words on this page.

Chapter 14 – What Remains

It's two weeks after we've first gone into the Hoarder House, and I stand in one corner of the mottled, ripped linoleum floor of the semi-cleared kitchen recollecting the summer before I started high school. I remember how I had grown tired of cleaning up the kitchen after my mother and sister; they would just leave all their dirty plates, mugs, cups, and silverware for me in the sink. One day I decided I wasn't doing it anymore. I would only do my own dishes. How long did it go on? Weeks, at least two or three, maybe more. I can still smell the moldy water in the glasses, the stench of baked-on food floating in the pans sitting on the counters. I'd get myself something to eat and imagine throwing eggs at the yellow walls and watching the yolks run down. Why did I always have to be the responsible person? The person who cleaned up.

How did my strike end? I think I must have just given in. I don't remember if my mother yelled at me. My "aunt" had a talk with me about helping my mother out because she worked so hard. I don't remember feeling guilty about that. Afterwards, I did all those dishes with the music on the radio blaring to irritate my mother sitting in the living room, Joni Mitchell's *Hejira*, James Taylor's *Mud Slide Slim*, their early albums full of sadness, the only acceptable way to give voice to what was under my rage.

I'm numb and witness details within the chaos in a way I couldn't through the cloud of my initial shock. I pluck some black and white pictures of my sister and me from a stack in a ripped box from my mother's photography days with Ken, rescuing her early practice efforts with the camera. There is my pocket watch, a gift from my grandfather, "Moo," on my childhood dresser, its drawers hanging open like gaping mouths with clothes hanging out. During one of my moves, my mother must have taken the watch from me. (*Stole it from me? How did it get back to her house?*) Also on the dresser is a strange tableau of a picture of my mother and Malcolm, a wedding picture of my sister and her husband, and a picture of a woman in full Chinese dress whom I don't recognize. There are seashells everywhere and I've been throwing them out. They've survived billions of years and yet I'm tossing them—these protective houses for sea creatures—in the contractor bags. I yank down the dirty, torn lace curtains and toss them in after them. My college typewriter is sitting in the closet behind old Christmas decorations. Seeing it makes me weirdly happy. I thought that had been lost too.

My sister says my mother doesn't ask about what's happening with the house at all but makes a point of emptying her guest bedroom wastebasket or helping unload the dishwasher. She's mostly spending her days reading or watching television and hanging out with the dog. Melissa wonders if she's ashamed.

"Maybe we should take her to get some new clothing," I say. "It's not like she's getting any of this back," I add as I gesture around the room. "But I can't deal with that or her right now."

"What does she think we are doing over here?" Melissa muses. She's also aggravated anytime my mother asks her to do something for her or complains about what she makes for dinner. "Does she not understand I have a full-time job?"

"Yeah," I respond. "I have a full-time job too, but I'm sure she's not thinking about that."

Ron zips up the white hazmat suit. "Wish me luck," he says dragging the wheelbarrow upstairs to work on the bathroom mountain of refuse and urine bottles that when he carts it away, reveals an entire tub filled with feces. He digs that out with his gloved hands.

The first time in the house, a week earlier, he'd joked "How bad could it be?"

My sister turned to me, "Let him do the bathroom."

As I pass Ron coming down the stairs with the filled wheelbarrow, a vivid memory surfaces from when I was five or so. My mother is sorting the wash in the bathroom and looking at my stained underwear.

"You better make sure you wipe yourself better," she said, "or no man will want you." My face turned fiery back then. I didn't understand what she meant, just the shame of being dirty.

I watch Ron joking with Marc as they both dump the urine bottles into the dumpster together. "I'm going to my happy place," Ron says.

I look through kitchen dishes and start to choke up when I notice, in the "to be thrown out pile" the serving bowl from my grandmother's china set.

Marc says quickly, "Don't pick that up."

When I look at it, I realize that my mother has used it to shit in. *Are there any limits to this craziness?* I think. But the psychologist in me can't help but wonder at the symbolism of defecating on your mother's best china.

Melissa says, "Throw it out."

I put it in a trash bag and tie it up, dried shit and all, to take home and clean. "She told me years ago, she didn't have any of the serving pieces for that set," I say as I head out the front door to put it in my car. In this moment, I hate my mother with every fiber of my being.

My sister sits cross-legged on the lawn packing up some of the full sets of antique glassware we are taking to our homes and a group of three neighbors comes over and asks questions. These aren't close neighbors, but gossipy women from one street over. My anger is white hot, focused.

I stomp across the grass toward them, rip my face mask off and say, harshly, "It's not something we really want to talk about," and grab the box from my sister as I stalk toward the garage.

As I march away, the nagging question explodes, *how?* I think, *how could this happen?* She clearly had some kind of breakdown. I place the box of dust-covered glassware on the garage floor. *Will I ever understand? Was it when I found Daddy? Did she feel that my sister and I abandoned her by doing that? Did she feel too threatened to care for herself?* Some guilty part of me feels it's my fault, that I did it by making her go through family therapy. She was so fragile that she must have cracked. The therapist in me knows I freed my sister and me as much as I could by speaking the truth, by trying to help us all be "normal." A word that seems laughable considering this hell that was her actual life.

Maybe this cleanup is my penance for leaving her. My sister and I were the best things she did, she told me a few months back as this chaos was just starting. Back when I was eleven and we joined that church in Maple Shade, a lady said, "You are named Faith? Then these children must be Hope and Charity."

"You should have seen it." Kathy is laughing when she calls me a few days after the weekend. "First the guy comes with the regular trash truck and pulls around the corner and stops. He gets out and looks at all the bags and picks a few up. Then he throws up his hands, climbs back inside and drives away."

"Oh my god." I'm panicked. "Are the rest of the bags still curbside?" There's another 175 of these giant bags in the backyard waiting for the next pick up the following week. I'm *sure* some of them are more than the fifty-pound limit.

"Wait," Kathy continues. "So then, an hour and a half later, one of those giant highway sanitation trucks shows up, you know, the monster-sized ones, with four big guys. And they take it all." She starts cracking up again.

Even the township of Cherry Hill is probably hating my mother.

I tell my sister that something big was in the attic when I'd been at the house a few days before. It sounded bigger than a squirrel, maybe it was a raccoon. It pooped dog-sized feces. Marc said it was like a scene after a party when he and Ron finally made it all the way up the unfinished stairs—everything paper or fabric shredded into tiny confetti bits. There were the big stuffed tigers given to us by my grandparents; my sister's doll house; my three-foot-tall doll, Lisa, who walked when you lifted her arm and slept under my childhood bed. We found the mouse tree house and the country and city mouse houses that came from FAO Schwarz. The country mouse, that had been my sister's, was missing and Marc told me the animal chewed it up. My city mouse dressed in satin with a fake diamond necklace was still intact. Melissa and I kneel on the front path in front of the Hoarder House as our husbands bring them out and we put them on the concrete sidewalk. We set them up, putting the little furniture in the correct rooms like we used to do in her bedroom when I was eleven and she was seven.

"Remember?" my sister asks. We look at the tidy little houses with their furniture all arranged for a minute, till it's almost unbearable, and then we each pick up our mouse house with all the objects inside and throw it into a plastic contractor bag to go out to the curb.

My sister takes a weekday off from teaching, so she and I can go alone to finish the rec room or, as I'm joking with Melissa, "the wrecked room" before the final weekend push to clear the rest of the house. I finally find the two best childhood albums, which is a relief, but my sister is sad that we haven't found her baby book. These photo albums, wet in places and stuck together, contain carefully captioned history in my mother's tight script next to each photo. This is the curated and chronicled family life up to about the time when her marriage to Daddy started to unravel. My sister and I are starting to divvy up the things we are keeping. My sister wants the small antique sled from my great-grandmother's house even though Ron doesn't really want her to take anything. She puts it aside to bring home later.

A mouse runs under the washing machine while we sort through the papers on the floor and Melissa jokes, "suburban mouse." Another mouse is hiding in the corner next to the dirty wall and that one upsets me. He has a little tail and moves along the wall so he's sitting on the spilled Monopoly game money, chewing the corner of an orange $500 bill. I can imagine my mother feeding and talking to the mouse when she was here.

We throw out board games and puzzles and sheet music to

Godspell. We toss a new toaster oven, iron, curling iron, hand vacuum, dishes. It's all equipment for a life she didn't have. She'd waited so long to have her living situation the way she wanted—fewer responsibilities, no mother to care for, some additional income so her bills were not a struggle and she could travel. Even after this started, she could have lived that life if she'd asked us for help. She could have taken us up on our offers to assist her. I'd try to gently say I knew the house was a "lot to handle" and we could help her clear things out if she wanted. My mother adamantly refused, or she'd look away, changing the subject. She wanted to be independent. Maybe she wanted to be alone. I feel my hatred dissolve into sudden unbearable sadness for my mother, for us—that we are having to shrink her life, distill it to an essence.

My sister pulls out a Partridge Family game and a big plastic flower, a record of *Peter and the Wolf* performed by the orchestra that we used to listen to, and a "World's Best Mother" statue. We make a little tableau of our own in the driveway and take a picture. Then I toss it all. I'm inclined to keep the game, but she talks me out of it.

This was more my sister's childhood house than mine. She was nine when we came there. "It wasn't so bad when we lived here," she says, handing me a pile of papers she's found from the divorce proceedings that I'm keeping although I'm not sure why. "This house could have been nice."

I tear down the orange curtains, the original orange rug on the moldy floor, the bathroom wallpaper with the 1960s floral print that hangs half off the wall.

"I got her that statue for Mother's Day one year." Melissa continues, leaning on the shovel and looking at me with sadness, "I believed it then."

Doing normal things when I am not at my mother's house

feels like coming back from a hostile alien planet. I can't unsee what I've seen. I can't unknow what I now know. I want to isolate myself. I'm overstimulated by everything. I try to read the trashiest novel I can lay my hands on just to see if I can concentrate enough to do it. I'm not able to.

My own house feels serene, with some antique furniture and oriental rugs, comfortable chairs, and books neatly shelved. At home in it, I am grieving my mother's life. I like the beautiful objects in my house. There's the Indonesian dragon candelabra Marc and I bought at the quirky store in Cape Cod, the framed photograph of a scene on Lincoln Drive near the Schuylkill River taken by my photographer friend, the illustration of a Victorian house that is the trunk of a giant tree that used to hang in my mother's house from her art gallery shopping years that she gave me when we moved here, and the antique cherry coffee table that was Nanna's. I could go on. I have so many things that mean something to me. I've brought home my mother's black, wooden, funky frog cabinet with the decorative brass hinges and lock. It bothered me that the antique key never turned up for it until I realized my mother had used it long ago when she created a key holder for my house. An advance gift to me in a way. By taking some of her things that I have loved too, they are resurrected. I don't have children who will inherit these objects with all the stories and memories they represent. My sister's children will take what they want when I'm gone, but whatever meaning I've figured out from saving all this won't matter in the end to them.

I have always found seeing patients, helping others make things better in their lives, to be a good distraction when things were bad for me, but currently, it feels like a burden. I'm pushing a giant boulder uphill every hour, and I have trouble focusing on the content of each session. I love my work, but I find my mind wanders and skitters to images of the house in the present and how I remember it from my adolescence. In a flash, I'm tossing old pots and pans into the dumpster, and then I'm seventeen, practicing parallel parking between two trash cans in front of the house, while my mother stands in the street and directs me—*turn the wheel, no, the other direction*—and Kathy and some of the neighbors watch me hit the cans time after time. Or I'm fifteen, arguing with my sister, as I drop a jar of applesauce from the refrigerator on my foot and we clean up the mess together. And then I'm thinking about how small that bedroom seemed with all our old toys strewn around like a murder scene when we were digging out.

In addition to working and finishing the cleanup, there are endless tasks I'm trying to remember to do: *don't forget to put through POA's and the paperwork for the insurance and various accounts, I need the property form for taxes, where do I find a lawyer, we need an auction house to take the things that are worth money that we aren't keeping and....*My brain runs on and on and I can't stop, even though I'm exhausted.

I find, with the help of an agency, an assisted living facility in Cherry Hill, about ten minutes from my sister and a straight shot over the bridge from Philly for me. The plan is that Melissa will be able to take her shopping, run errands for her, and continue to have her weekly for dinner while I manage all the finances and medical appointments and take her with me for a monthly hair salon appointment.

My sister and I look at the place without my mother, sharing with the staff the hoarding issue. They reassure us they've dealt with situations like this before and tell a story about a resident who took sugar packets. My sister and I start to laugh and then my sister starts to cry and leaves the room. I tell the facility director that housekeeping is not optional for my mother and that unlike what cleaning choices they might allow other residents, they will need to clean my mother's room weekly.

A few days later, after taking her to breakfast at Ponzio's, we bring my mother back for the facility assessment and to set up the contract. She is livid about this, feeling ambushed by our decision despite our discussion about it being necessary. Her face is flushed and she's barely cooperative.

When she and the nurse return from meeting, the nurse says to my sister and me, "Your mom sounds like she was a great nurse and can handle her own medications, I think."

My mother glares at me with "I told you so" eyes and a sneer, which convey she doesn't need assisted living, and that independent living would be *fine*.

Marc's managed to persuade a house-flipping investor to buy the house for $90,000, which will leave us with $87,000 after I pay the back taxes she owed. This is my mother's only asset, besides a few annuities that are almost gone.

My sister informs me, when my mother is in the bathroom, that I will need to take her to my house for a weekend before she is supposed to move in since she is going to be away and doesn't want her to stay alone at her place.

"I'm not doing it," I hiss at her as my mother crosses the room toward us. "We are getting her in there earlier. We'll pay extra if we need to."

After the meeting at assisted living (and arranging her to go a week earlier than planned), we take some routine paperwork to her doctor who has learned about my mother's situation. I've sent him a letter describing her car accident and the state of the house. She has no idea I've been in contact with him, and I've asked him not to tell her. I can feel rage radiating off her as we sit side by side in plastic chairs in the exam room, waiting for the doctor and not speaking. Unlike the other waiting at the doctor's office, where I told her the secret of Cheryl when I was in college, this time it's my mother worried about her own secrets.

"I hope," my mother starts, "that you didn't throw out that green notebook right next to the chair in the living room because I never had time to copy all the information out of it."

I don't say anything. I'm trying to breathe because all I want to do is take her by her neck and slam her head into the exam table. I want to watch it crack like those eggs I fantasized throwing at the wall in eighth grade when I went on strike with the dishes.

When I don't respond, she gets more provocative. She says, "And that book I got, I think it was in the kitchen, for all of us to write down our travel experiences."

After a long pause and several deep breaths, "I'm sorry, Mom, that you've lost so many things. We did the best we could." I'm staring straight ahead when I say this and I'm sure she hears the tension in my voice although I'm being as neutral as possible. What's funnier to me is that I did find the address book along with some of the other items I'd intuited she'd want, but I hadn't planned to give them to her until she was settled. Still, she behaves as if it's a normal house and she can tell me where everything is. *What kind of denial do you have to be in to think I could find any one item in that mess? How can she behave like that shit show was fine?*

From the corner of my eye, I can see her getting a little teary as the doctor opens the door, shaking my mother's hand first and avoiding my gaze as I quickly hand him the forms to complete and excuse myself as I escape to the waiting area.

When I reach the auction lady on my phone, I'm standing in my mother's garage putting different colored stickies on each object: yellow for my house, green for my mother's studio apartment, purple for my sister's house, orange to sell. She's not surprised when I explain our situation to her. "You don't want to take anything that reminds you of how traumatic this was."

Suddenly it hits me that I don't have to carry what my mother expects or wants or needs me to, that I'm not burdened by her things and that I have a choice in the matter. I think, *I don't have to take from her anything I don't want anymore and that goes for her treatment of me.*

Because my mother needs to fill out more assisted living paperwork, I head over to my sister's house to see her after arranging for the final cleanout with the auction people. All my mother wants to do is continue talking about things she wants to bring with her.

She wants a statue that was on top of the frog bar that my sister was supposed to bring to her and didn't.

I tell her I'll bring her back glasses for the room.

"Don't bother," she says, "I can use paper cups. But I want the painting behind my chair in the living room."

When I press her, she can't describe it to me. It is gone, probably to Goodwill or into one of the dumpsters. It was filthy, a reproduction of some Chinese flowers. *Oh, the one,* I want to say, *you used to throw your dental floss at?*

I talk to her like an unruly kid I'm trying to do psychological testing with, "Just one more page, Mom, just sign this." I tell her about the money for the house and what the plan is for the upcoming settlement. I make a list of the art she's asking about.

"I want the Auth cartoon."

"You were going to give that to me," I say, "but then you got angry about something and told me I couldn't have it." *And you then left it to molder in the Hoarding House*, I think.

She says, "I like it. I want to hang it in my room." Her list of objects she wants for her room grows too long. I don't argue when she asks, "If it fits in the curio cabinet, I can take it, right?" I flashback to the day before when my sister and I emptied the curio cabinet and found a half-eaten cookie, crumbs tumbling everywhere on the floor.

"There's new bedding," she says, "in the living room."

"The mice ate it."

"Those cushions on my wicker chair are okay. Did you keep them? We can use them," she looks hopeful.

"No, we threw them out."

As I'm leaving, she says quietly, "Thank you, I know I've been a full-time job," and then immediately tries to change the subject.

I interrupt as I turn from the doorway, "I appreciate your saying that and it *has* been a very full-time job to do all of this." We have a momentary truce. It won't last, but it makes for a little respite as I head out to do six more things for her and the house before driving back to my home.

It's a warm day and I'm standing in my old bedroom. The late October sun is streaming in with that end-of-fall kind of light. The sky is a blue so deep you want to fall into it. The bush at the bottom of the driveway where the rabbit was staying those first few days of the cleanup is a beautiful scarlet red. All the animals—the chipmunks in the garage, the raccoon in the attic, the mice, whose giant nest I pull out of the antique camera I'm sending to my artist friend—have left the empty house. I can hear the sounds outdoors.

Kathy comes from across the street, and I say, "Do you want to see?"

I walk her through, and she comments on how we all have our own little gold door knockers on each of our bedroom doors. I remember my mother putting them up after we moved in, so we'd all make sure to respect each other's privacy if we wanted to enter someone else's space. I don't remember ever using them. As Kathy and I walk through the house, I realize I've righted it.

It will be fine, I think to myself. *It's like a spirit, this energy of the house that held my family. Maybe I've healed something by airing it out. It's not scary to be in here anymore.*

I tell Kathy I'll see her in a few days and leave to pick up my mother's key to her room 333 at the assisted living facility where her new life will begin. Our new life, where we don't worry about her all the time.

In July, when I stood by her broken back door, I had no idea I'd make good on my promise to get her out of here by the winter. And in seven excruciating weeks, I made her life habitable again. *What she does with this change is up to her*, I think. At the assisted living facility at 6 p.m. on a Saturday night, a few of the women are clustered by the door. It must get boring there too. *But maybe she'll make some new friends, find a new hobby she'll like.*

My sister says, "I'm going to repaint her rocker before we move her in next week."

I'm laughing. "Really? Knock yourself out."

I drive away in the early evening singing "Respect" loudly in my car and turn toward my own life. Back into my own space, my own world, trying to feel more like myself again. I make Marc get us ice cream. I have a beer and some pizza. I'm hoping this is okay, that I'm okay.

I'm away all weekend with Fran and Cher, another of my oldest girlfriends, in North Carolina for a trip that was planned months before. We kayak in the bay weaving through tall reeds and sit on the sundrenched porch watching birds in the marsh. At night, we go out for big restaurant dinners with wine and shared desserts. It's fun, but I'm not myself. I'm not okay.

The nightmares start Saturday night as soon as I've had a day of relaxation. *I'm driving up to my mother's house. Kathy is there with the other neighbors. I see the front door is open and realize that I will never be going back there again. When I go up to the door and look in, there's only darkness. It's black and terrifying, like looking into a deep cave. I can't see anything inside. Then I am in my car pulled up in the driveway and I'm trying to wipe shit off myself, and I have toilet paper in my hands. Don't come near me. Don't come near me, I tell Kathy from the car window.* I wake up crying and feeling shame that isn't my own.

But after four days, I'm home and it's Monday and time to move my mother into the assisted living apartment. I'm planning to hang out a bit, maybe have a quick lunch with her before heading up to my office. I enter my sister's house and my mother refuses to look at me. She has a box of things ready to go and a small bag of clothing. There's the urn from her Aunt Helen sitting on the table next to the bag.

She says, "It's too bad there's a big crack inside or it would be worth something."

On the fifteen-minute drive there, she asks again about her lotus lamp. I say to her, "It's gone." This is becoming my mantra with her. She's ramping up.

"Why would you get rid of that?"

Something snaps in that moment, and I say very clearly and

firmly, "I never want to talk about the cleanup of that house again, unless" I turn toward her in the car, "you *want* me to talk about it?"

And then she is suddenly screaming at me, "Enough, Deborah. Enough!" She looks like she'd hit me if she could. It's a primitive animal cry—surprisingly guttural in intensity for such a little woman—and I don't say anything, feeling my own heart beating faster from the shock of adrenaline.

When I do speak, she starts screaming again.

"Look, this is hard," I say, "and I was just trying to make things nice for you."

She continues yelling, "I don't want to talk about it!"

I don't say another word. When we arrive, I ask her if she wants me to carry the box.

"No," she snaps.

We go up to the room and she opens the door with the key I've given her. The yellow room with the big window is beautiful. My sister has made a nice home for her with throw pillows and matching bedding. She has set up the curio cabinet with most of my mother's favorite things. She's cleaned and hung the pictures we've found at the house. She's washed the wicker rocker and put pillows on it. I want to cry because it's so loving and kind of Melissa.

"Where's the Auth?" my mother demands. "Bring that back." Then she tosses her sweater on the bed, and in that small movement is a fractal of the hoarding house behavior. It makes a swirl on the bed like a whirlpool, reminding me of Jackie's photograph. I can hardly stand to see it and flashback to the smells in that back room, my old room, the worst of the bedrooms.

When we go into the health office there's a little description of my mother stuck on the wall for new residents, which I wrote when I filled out her application—just saying it was time to move because of an unsafe environment. My mother doesn't notice it. Before I leave her, I say, "I'll pick you up at 7:45 a.m. on Thursday for your court date about the accident."

"How will I wake up?" she says.

"I can call you if you can charge your phone," and ask her what time she wants to be called.

"Seven," she responds, like a petulant child.

I say goodbye to her—she doesn't hug or kiss me.

As I'm leaving, she says to me, "We're just different people." Like that explains all of this. Maybe it does.

I run into the marketing person for the assisted living facility on my way out. She reassures me it'll be fine, and I thank her and get in my car and drive away, shaking with unexpressed feeling. I recognize this as abuse. It's always been abuse. And I don't have to take it anymore.

It occurs to me as I head home that my mother can't bear me because I am the reminder of all the things she has lost. And maybe, in fact, this has always been true, even before I made her leave her house—my biological father, all the other miscarriages, even that first home on Woodstock Drive.

As a kind of truce (and because I need her to sign the real estate paperwork), a few days later I offer to run some errands with her. My mother smells better and she is wearing a little lapel pin. We go to the dollar store, and she replaces things she feels she needs and tells me how she'd been going to the Episcopal thrift shop next to the facility. She wants makeup (which she hasn't worn in years) at Ulta. We go to Barnes & Noble last because she wants crosswords. In the house were piles of completed crossword puzzle books strewn on top of the clothing, as if keeping her mind in that chaos was very important to her. Like an addict, she compulsively buys two books and a magazine.

The girl says to her while she's checking out, "You want a shopping bag, right?"

The memory of those bags of shit is suddenly vivid as I quickly step outside to catch my breath. She takes a free pen at the UPS store when we get the real estate POA notarized.

I drive to my sister's afterwards and she and I drink wine and divide up the good jewelry we aren't giving her back—the diamond cocktail ring shaped like a nautilus; the stick pin that was appraised by a jeweler for $1,000, which my sister pulled off a sweater in one of the clothing piles; the pearl and ruby ring I found at the bottom of the living room floor after shoveling three feet of trash off it.

Afterwards, I go check on the house. The only things there are a ladder, a brass lamp, a box of garbage bags, and the weird sculpture of the man with the clock for a head running between black and white that used to hang in the laundry room. The auction people even took the chime off the front porch. They cleaned it all out. The emptiness echoes.

I find one small shell on the kitchen shelf that I pocket. Settlement is next week, but I want to say my goodbyes now to the grubby, streaked walls and the stairs dotted with carpet tacking holding small pieces of the blue and green rug. The smell is still there. I take a few more pictures of things, like REDRUM which Ron wrote on the sink mirror at some point during his bathroom cleanup. As I walk through the laundry room, I spot a block of wood on the floor. I flip it over with my foot. It says, "Let it."

As I pull out of the driveway for the last time I see, not even four feet away from me, a hawk. I stop. He's killed a squirrel and is eviscerating it, one claw on the carcass as he pulls the intestines out like spaghetti. He's more than twelve inches tall and looks right at me while he continues eating. Two mockingbirds dive-bomb him for a few minutes, trying to get him to move, but he's focused only on the kill. I'm happy it's not the little brown bunny who slept near us that first terrible day we were at the house. That would have made me cry. I don't think I could bear witnessing the ending of that sweet rabbit. Even now, it comforts me to think of it resting in the shadow of the leafy bush which turns such a beautiful scarlet in autumn.

Chapter 15 – At The Center

A few weeks later my mother is tucked into her studio apartment, or as she has taken to calling it when she speaks to my sister, "my prison." She is angry they won't let her go out for a walk in the nearby neighborhood because she'd have to navigate along a major road.

"They lock the doors at night," she moans. "I just want to be able to go where I want to."

After everything she's put us through, I'm having trouble feeling empathetic. Part of me feels like she belongs in prison. *Or maybe Norristown State Hospital from back in my college days.*

I stop by my sister's house to drop off some old photographs of her family I'd salvaged from the mass of photos marooned at the Hoarding House. "Do you want them for yourself? Or to make a new album for Mom?" I ask her.

Melissa rolls her eyes and puts the brown paper bags in her garage. "I haven't even cleaned the other stuff I took yet," she sighs.

I've sorted through all the jewelry. My mother's gold charm bracelet is missing. I apologize to my sister that I didn't find it when I was cleaning out the house. I'm afraid it may have been thrown out.

"I took it," my sister sheepishly tells me. "I think it was after college when I stayed there, before finally moving out."

I tell her I understand and not to feel bad about it. Maybe it's like the books I went in and rescued when I got my first apartment during my zoo days. I also took some photographs from the good albums back then, tugging them out of the little black corners that held them to the page, leaving a faded window where they'd been. We both hightailed it out of that house as soon as we could, trying not to look back at what we were leaving. Yet, we paused long enough to take little tokens from our childhood, objects we treasured that reminded us of home and of our mother, things we loved and feared would become lost memories when we were no longer there. We must have sensed the tsunami coming.

Later, Melissa texts pictures of the bracelet. Tiny gold baby shoes that represent my sister. A charm of a little girl who looks like one from a storybook, wearing a dress and socks, her hand out like she is starting to wave. That is probably me. A gold heart that says Faith and Daddy and on the reverse a pearl glowing like an embryo, my sister in the beginning. And a charm that has my mother's nursing degree etched into it. I don't recall the last time I saw her wear the bracelet. Maybe when I was a child when we all dressed up for Easter. Maybe before Howard left. Unlike my own bracelet, my mother's is sparse, unfilled. I am wondering about the never-added charms, trying to understand what the missing pieces represent.

I finally decide to go into the plastic bins that hold some of what I've saved from the cleanout. I told myself the reason I had to be the one to sort through all the papers and photographs in that mess was because I wanted to save the family history, salvage any documentation my mother might need for her current life like her old taxes, or divorce paperwork that turned out to be useful for getting dates she might need for her future Medicaid application. But the truth is, I'm still trying to understand my family. Sandy used to tell me that therapy is never done. I am reminded of Paul Valery's quote that a poem is never finished, only abandoned. You circle back when you are ready to work again, always the same themes coming up. You spiral around it like a moon, viewing Earth from different angles and hoping to better understand what lies at the center of your universe. In my case, my mother.

The boxes are stacked up in the corner of my writing room. There are also brown paper bags and some cardboard boxes, filled with stacks and stacks of photographs and papers. When I sit at my desk, my back is to them, these boxes and bags that tower almost to adult height. It's like a being is sharing my space. I resent its intrusion into my organized life, but I haven't felt strong enough to revisit what I managed to save. I feel like I'm too shell-shocked to trigger the memories again. I continue to have the occasional nightmare and struggle with my focus at times, another thing I've kept from the experience.

When I open the lid after all this time, there is the smell of mouse feces. The anti-mildew packets I haphazardly tossed in during the cleanup have somehow melted and left a greasy mix of water and brown goo over the very things I'm trying to save. The photographs of people and places who look familiar and yet feel almost like strangers from someone else's past are covered.

"Oh my god," I shriek. "What have I done?" And call out for Marc to come help me. I'm almost wild with grief.

Marc helps me sift the things that have been damaged, from the things that have not, moving them from box to box. Then he takes each plastic bin to clean in our laundry room sink. He says from the other room, "So, are we done with your mother yet?"

"Apparently not," I respond laughing a little after my initial freak out, fanning out the photographs to dry across unfolded newspapers covering my office floor.

"We'll never be done," I choke out, and he comes back in the room, stepping around the large wet stack of divorce papers. He puts the clean container on the floor and reaches over to give me a hug.

A quote falls out of the undamaged papers I'm holding in my hand. Like me, my mother collected sayings, but unlike me, because I keep mine organized neatly in books. A few lines she's copied from her favorite T.S. Eliot poem about how, at the end of exploration, we arrive back where we started and know the place for the first time.

And then I start laughing again. *Thanks, Mom, right?*

Because I damaged it, I take apart my mother's album of her pilgrimage back to her childhood home after Nanna died. She was my age then. Was it after this trip that she fully broke down? My grandmother's death changed everything for her. She was free but she and Nanna were so tied together in their relationship that maybe my grandmother haunted her. It was clear from the mess in the house that the hoarding became totally disorganized around that time. Prior to that there were things piled everywhere, but some kind of organization existed. After that came the chaos of not even throwing out trash. *Why?* Maybe it happened after she got fired from Medford Leas, the nursing home where she worked, where Nanna died. Maybe she felt more alone with no one to care for anymore.

Mixed up in the loose photographs I've dumped into a cardboard box are familiar people and places, yet they feel almost like strangers from some other person's past. I find a photo of Nanna and her best friend with their dolls in 1925. It's faded. They are ghosts. There is a photo from April 1971 of my grandparents in Florida that was taken five months before Nonno died. The picture is snapped from a distance, and they stand under palm trees, dressed up in out-to-dinner clothes. I haven't thought about them for a long time. And there is a studio portrait of my mother when she was four or so, her hair in a little braid, holding a stuffed cat.

There are other parts of history I salvage from the paper

mess. There are black and white photos from her nursing school years. When we were younger she'd tell us sometimes about boys she dated, the wealthy one with the car; her high school boyfriend, Red, who went into the military. One damaged picture, white spots blooming where the photo itself has pulled away from the paper, shows him, I think, wearing a sailor uniform. And there's a picture of her sitting on a wall with an unrecognizable handsome boy and I wonder if he's the rich one.

There's a mystery about how she met Malcolm. I don't remember her ever telling me. I find only three pictures of them together that must be from my grandmother's collection of photographs. I don't recall seeing them before. In one, Malcolm kneels in front of my grandparents with my mother off to the side holding a cat on a leash. I'm guessing that's Hop Along, who liked to sleep in the bathroom sink. It's funny how she told me more stories about that cat than my father. The second photo shows them standing next to a car, my mother smiling at the camera and my father looking down at her adoringly. The third photo looks like it was taken after their wedding, my father looking so much like me, his round face and squinty eyes, the long shape of his chin. I can see my half-brother in him too, his dark hair and crooked grin. My mother is wearing a light-colored dress with short sleeves. A corsage blooms over her breasts and a little hat with a veil covers her light-brown hair. She is squinting into the light like she is having trouble seeing something far off. They stand tilted toward each other in front of a backdrop of bushes that could be anywhere, swirling leaves in the wind. She is much tinier than he is and leans into him, maybe against the eventual storm. Their hands are tightly clasped together as if that will be enough. My mother looks so young in her early twenties. Her smile, the way she stands, foreshadows my sister, my nieces. Yet, I have her cheekbones, her full lips.

My mother is still mentally sharp, but stories of her past have always been untrustworthy, revisionist. She makes creative nonfiction of her life. I look more closely at that album she made of places from her childhood and it's mostly factual—photos of the house, other places she knew like her school and downtown Gloversville are accompanied by straightforward descriptions. The buildings are solid as she recreates her past.

What is murkier is the emotional experience of her connection with my grandmother in that place. Sometimes Nanna was "so nasty to her." Other times my mother tells familiar stories but changes the meaning of the incident, or who was at fault. Sometimes she tells me about how my grandmother would say something negative about me and describes how she would defend me. Other times, she protects Nanna and explains she wasn't a well woman. I suspect my grandmother didn't understand my mother much of the time. My mother used to say she was closest to and most like her father, and that drove Nanna nuts. My grandmother wanted my mother to be responsible in the same ways she was—with money, with making herself respectable by other people's standards. I think, sometimes, my mother hated her because she had to be dependent financially after the divorce, but I don't know that for sure.

Growing up, my mother told me I was just like my grandmother—critical and angry. I'm "perfectionistic" like she was, and too "compulsive with my cleaning." The opposite of love is indifference. My mother is never neutral about Nanna. She was bursting with rage at her sometimes, complaining to us when we were adolescents about how difficult she was, yet practically killing herself caring for her when Nanna was shakily infirm from Parkinson's and stomach cancer. They were like those people tied together in a one-legged race, unsupported without the other, unable to finish if they untie.

And yet, in the papers I salvaged from the house, her love for her mother is apparent. I find a draft of an autobiography on lined notebook paper my mother started writing at Thanksgiving, 1982. It was after I'd graduated college. I'd left home that summer before my senior year and didn't come back home after graduation, house sitting for the summer and then moving to Delaware. My sister was also gone for her second year in college. My mother begins: *The Buddhists divided life into a three staged progression from Desire to Form to Formlessness. Perhaps therefore one muses in attempts to orient the self between the latter periods.*

She goes on to talk about how it had been forty-five years since she'd lived in Gloversville, writing:

Many of my early memories invoke scenes of my constant illnesses. There were long days in bed fearing nightfall—which brought vomiting or nightmares. There were the unverbalized feelings about "being different" resulting from continued school absences. Food smells gave me nausea, waistbands hurt and no one else seemed to be that way. But mother brought stacks of books and read to me, and Daddy came up to my room right after he arrived home from work. I remember the delirium of high fevers which seemed unending. I was carried or supported down the hall to the bathroom unable to comprehend the reason for such effort. It was as if I were pulled from a nether world of formless intrusive shapes looming in foggy dreams. There was that calm clear voice cutting through the fearful tides in which I rode with no volition at all. "I'm going to roll you over now—let me sponge you—you'll be better soon." Were those the words? I don't recall exactly. But the reality and trust in loving hands is with me yet, and long have I known the effort and hours behind these memories. Surely your grandmother had fine training in bedside nursing care.

But the increasing care and anxiety for one you love is a task of untold dimension. No Mother's Day card will ever tell—nor do my poor words.

She's writing this to me. She wants to offer her memories as a *continuing gift—perhaps some small part of what follows will have value.* But I don't find much else that she wrote. She started another journal again with these descriptions of the trauma of her early illnesses and my grandmother's care of her, but it seems by then, the last one in 1992 after her trip to Gloversville, she loses her words. Or maybe she literally begins to block herself in and pull the house around her like one of those hermit crab shells, not allowing anything out, making herself a prisoner there. Her garbage, things she buys, create a barrier to the outside world. The books that will never be read, newspapers, pennies, and unopened presents for the people she loves. At its center, a recliner where my mother sleeps, next to a phone that doesn't work.

It's during this time, after my Nanna's death and after retiring from another nursing home job, that my mother begins volunteering. I remember her sitting in a little shared office in the basement of the Cherry Hill library. She brings my nieces and nephew there like it's her home, and when I meet her for lunch, I bang on the thick back doors of the library so she can let me in to meet her. She fixes the broken books there. Saving what needs repair, a nurse if you will, of words. She has a cart she's made up of things. The books to be repaired, her tools: threads and scissors and glue. She carefully sews the pages back in that have been ripped from the art books, gently massaging their broken spines, and wiping away the grime from the older ones so they can be reshelved, given back to people who want them, who hopefully won't hurt them anymore. I imagine her there sometimes late at night, long after the library closes, in the darkness pooling outside the large echoing hallway beyond the room, bent over a wounded book, light from the little lamp shining on her hands that take the needle back and forth on the pages. She gets the volunteer of the year award there at some point and doesn't go to the celebratory lunch or tell us about it until it has passed. It's almost like she's ashamed. Eventually, she leaves the library because she gets paranoid and angry about the new director.

Was it then that the situation spiraled downhill more rapidly at the house? She smells worse, seems less healthy. Was it after her two bouts with cancer? First, lobular breast cancer, which is surgically removed, and then she has the other breast taken off to be sure, and it's in there too. And then, after three years of taking the tamoxifen, she gets uterine cancer, a rare side effect from using the drug, and has a hysterectomy. *Did she think she was going to die soon?*

Like a cancer, does history get carried from generation to generation? Is the seed of it about her great-great-grandfather who married the "Indian Princess" and created a scandal? I find a picture of them. She's solid with a weathered face and high cheekbones, not the fantasy I'd pictured of a woman a man would leave his family and children for. I'd been told about his abandonment as a child.

There's a newspaper picture of Nanna, his granddaughter, when her engagement to my grandfather was announced. She's beautiful, with smooth skin and high cheekbones. I used to play dress up in her silk wedding dress, a kind of draped, drop-waisted brown and gold floral art deco print. That marriage survived, but my mother tells stories of their unhappiness, a family of three. My grandfather had affairs. My grandmother had an affair with a doctor. What is true? My grandmother only had one child, my mother. There was some story of her being "burned down there."

When I was younger, my mother told me once about something that happened when she was in eighth grade, a neighbor boy assaulting her or raping her one summer evening when my grandparents weren't home. Afterwards, Nanna disbelieved my mother when she told her. The stories run together like this sloppy history I've managed to salvage.

In the plastic bins, I find the yellowed newspaper article about the accidental death of my grandmother's sister. My great-grandmother lived in a huge black and white Victorian house in West Winfield, New York that was once run as an inn, The Victoria Lodge. We visited her for the last time there when I was fourteen.

Not in a long time [has] the village of Bridgewater had so shocking [an] accident as that which occurred here last Wednesday morning, October 13 when Frances, the twelve-year-old daughter of Sumner and Lydia Russell Wickwire was almost instantly killed in the yards of the Standard Oil Company, just across from the child's home, begins the news story. Frances had taken three-year-old Lydia for a walk to give my great-grandmother *a few minutes rest as she had only recently returned from the hospital and was not able to have the entire care of the little one*, the article continues.

The two children strayed over to the yards and into the barn where they found their father (who is a manager of the oil plant in Bridgewater), all hitched up and just ready to drive the rig up to the gas tank to fill it with gasoline, and childlike, they climbed up on the seat and Frances picked up the reins and wanted to drive the team of mules out to the tank for her father, and in doing so she must have driven a bit too close for the big arm that reaches out from the oil tank, caught the top on the rig and tore it completely off. This frightened the mules and they started to run, and both children were thrown off the seat, little Lydia some distance from the rig and Frances directly in shape [sic] so that the heavy rig ran over the child's chest and shoulder causing her death almost instantly. The child jumped up onto her feet but pitched forward and fell to the ground.

Her father picked her up at once and carried her to her home, but her life was extinct when he reached the home and no doubt the child died in her father's arms.

There is no mention of my great-grandmother standing on the porch witnessing the whole thing. Or where Nanna was at the time. After the accident, to escape the constant reminders of the trauma, the family moved from Bridgewater to the house I remember in West Winfield. After my great-grandmother died, Nanna told me they found the dress Frances was wearing when she died stored in the attic. Bloodied and in a box. My grandmother had one picture of her. The one with the siblings and a goat.

In the bin, I find other history. Nanna wrote "Things I Remember" with her spidery handwriting: *My older sister was killed when I was ten and as Mother had first returned from the hospital, she had a relapse. Everyone had to make a greater effort and with help of friends and neighbors we managed. The Doctor wanted Mother to go away for a while, so we children went to visit an Aunt and Uncle in Rural Grove on a farm. We rode on hayrides on hay wagons, drove cows, and fed chickens. Played in hay mow and corn cribs. Uncle kept bees, so it was considered courageous to help him collect honey.*

That year continued bad as shortly after we returned home, my oldest brother had an infection in his arm, and it had to be amputated. While he was in the hospital, my kid brother had pneumonia.

My grandmother did much of the caregiving after Frances was killed. She graduated high school early, at sixteen, and worked at a private girls' school where she "set silver, glasses and napkins," and since she'd never been to a fine restaurant, wrote, "I was learning too." During the summers she was employed at a private camp for girls, saving all her money from both places to pay for nursing school. The brother who lost his arm had played concert piano, but he couldn't after that and became a photographer. The kid brother, Ray, was a minor league baseball player who was going to the majors when World War II broke out. He drove for a general (supposedly General Patton) in Africa and was never right afterwards. Lydia, who was the baby in the accident had difficult marriages and died of lung cancer when I was an adolescent. There were so many lost dreams my mother must have inherited, so much left behind that she was told somehow to save. Maybe Nanna couldn't love her enough because of the trauma of Frances. But my grandmother tried to take care of my mother and us after the divorce. Every week she'd make something, like rice pudding in the red pan or the best old-fashioned pumpkin cake with raisins. Those recipes lost forever too.

It's a metaphor—to ignore or damage something through neglect, but not to ever let it go. Maybe that was Nanna's relationship with my mother. But after everything with the house, I've started to think about it differently. Maybe she knew how fragile my mother was. When I search through the letters, I find one from Nanna that she sent to me when I lived in London that college semester. It was loving and reasonable. She wasn't a warm woman, but she was very present in her letter and tried to be interactive. My mother ruined all my grandmother's carefully stored photographs and papers she'd lovingly preserved. A hedge against forgetting that washed up wet against the garage door of the house Nanna bought for her.

As I rummage through the bins, I have a thought about why I have such a hard time getting rid of things my mother has given to me. It's like if I throw them out, by extension I'm tossing her and her emotional intentions away. When I was growing up, my mother loved our imaginations, understanding, like a child does, that inanimate objects had feelings and lives. For my mother *everything* had meaning. She was porous in allowing the world to come in and for me it was magical in some ways. As an adult, I also understand it is the essence of paranoia. It's a burden too, this giving and keeping of things. My mother gave me books and taught me to spell, to connect through writing, and value words. And it's only through this ability to make a story that I can try to understand what happened. I make a narrative in which I am not an object for her projections but allowed to be myself and be my mother's daughter. I had to find the fathers because she lost them, she couldn't hold on. In the end, she couldn't hold on to me. Now, I am holding on to her. Because I choose to, because it's my obligation, because I should do this, and because I love her.

    I am the same age my mother was when my grandmother died. I am the same age she was when she took her trip back home to where she grew up and made an album and carefully wrote down her memories. I am still sorting through those boxes in my room. What if all the memories we seem so sure about aren't true? Aren't real? Like a snow globe that can be shaken with the view then obscured, I need to believe the scene stays the same no matter what the artificial weather.

Chapter 16 – A House is Not a Home

When I take the diamond cocktail ring to the jeweler to be appraised, I learn it is the most expensive piece of jewelry I recovered from the house.

"It's worth about $2,300," the jeweler says to me. I ask him how much if I sell it. "Maybe $600," he says, as he looks at how it's sitting on my right-hand ring finger. Shaped like a nautilus made up of tiny diamonds, it's filthy. If I put my hand up near my nose, I can smell the faint funk of the house—fermented body odor and shit and unwashed clothing, rotting food and miles of mice nests and their urine. There's nothing like that cocktail of house horror.

I take it off, contemplating.

"It looks great on you," the jeweler says. "It's unique. You should keep it. I'll fix the prongs and clean it up for a hundred dollars."

I found it on top of my mother's dresser, tossed in a box with a bunch of costume jewelry. I can't remember when she last wore it. Maybe when she went out that night with her best friend to the Latin Casino when I was around nine? I remember their black dresses and done-up hair. *This ring*, I think, *is a reward for sifting through the shit, something beautiful and glowing and worthwhile that will survive it. Something to treasure.* My stepfather gave this to her. He must have loved her once.

"Go ahead and fix it," I tell the jeweler handing it back to him. "I'm keeping this for myself."

I'm having lunch with a friend I haven't seen since *before the Hoarder House hell*, as I've internally nicknamed it. I'm trying to describe what life has been like and my friend is listening, mouth agape, as I share the story. "How come no one knew about the house?" she asks. It's a perfectly reasonable question, one that friends from my childhood, who knew my mother, don't ask. No matter how hard I try and capture the experience when I talk about it, I can't fully convey the horror of what I've encountered.

"We did know," I pause. *We didn't know, really.* What do I say? I've asked myself this question a thousand times since I walked through that laundry room door. I respond that until she faltered—the unpaid phone bill, the increasing physical issues—it was clear it was bad, but she was an autonomous person and refused all our offers of help. And as I'm telling my friend this, I feel shame, the shame of my own failure to help my mother the way she needed.

I remember how, about sixteen years ago when she was very sick with flu, I offered to bring over juice and some other groceries and leave them outside her door. She screamed at me not to. No one went to the house. My nieces, when they were little, thought she lived at the library where she was doing her volunteer job or before that in the nursing home where she worked. She was so organized on the job. She was a very caring and responsible nurse. Things were always clean, files labeled. And yet, everybody knew. Especially her neighbors who saw that she didn't put her trash out for at least fifteen years. They knew she stopped taking her mail from the mailbox. They noticed the drawn curtains, the closed windows. Even one of her oldest friends, Mrs. Lee, recently told me she'd stopped by a few years ago and my mother yelled down from a window that she was busy and didn't come out to see her.

As a psychologist, it's clear that you can't do anything about a mental illness if the person doesn't want help. Autonomy trumps beneficence unless there's a danger to self or others. She was not committable. She didn't want therapy or medication. She chose to hide the secret and it just got bigger and bigger like the mess. Was it derelict to let her live the way she wanted? Was this neglect necessary for me to be able to separate from her? I don't say all of this, of course, to my friend. This is why I feel alone and different. It's my childhood all over again.

My mother's house is being renovated and Kathy sends the pictures.

"They are painting it blue," she says. "The neighbors think that makes it look small. And why black shutters with a brown door?" She asks me as if I have the answer.

It would drive my mother nuts that the colors didn't match. When we were young, she cared how the outside of her houses looked. We did tell her it was being fixed up, but she didn't seem interested.

The rehabbers have stripped the landscape around it. The rose bushes along the side of the Reese's house and the creeping juniper bushes that grew down the hill, which my mother planted because grass would never grow there, have disappeared. The beautiful bush with the leaves that turned scarlet in the fall where the rabbit was sleeping when we were cleaning things out has been pulled up. The big tree she planted near the birdbath is a flat stump. The gnarly tree that hid the front window, which the raccoon climbed up to get into the house, has been cut down along with the poison ivy underneath it. All the trees and grasses where the mice probably sheltered after they fled the house when we cleaned out are gone. The hawk I saw on the last day won't find meals there anymore. The house has been restored to suburbia, no longer the wild place between worlds it inhabited for thirty years.

Kathy looked in the front window again and said they kept the hardwood floors we found underneath the filthy carpeting. They also renovated the kitchen we gutted and opened a side door to it, so that the downstairs became the more open floor plan that today's families want. Soft cream-colored carpeting blanketed the rec room over the concrete floor. There were new windows and wainscoting in the dining room area off the kitchen. The person who buys it next won't have any idea what was there before, the filth, the stacks of objects, the shit in bags, the little knockers on our bedroom doors.

My mother has begun to pile things on the table in her studio apartment. She wants to hold on to all the little things because, in the end, the big things like her relationships, even her children in the way that children do, all leave her. So, what she has left is this: a stuffed cat she makes a basket for from the craft store and asks me to pet when I pick her up to get our hair done.

Kathy calls to tell me there's going to be an open house Sunday for the rehabbed house. I tour through it quickly, admiring the sanded and refinished hardwood floors, fresh white paint, and refurbished bathrooms. I'm disoriented by the changes until I pull open the closet door in the wall of the rec room and realize they've done nothing in there. There's the original brown linoleum and shelves, and when the door opens, the faint whiff of my mother's house emerges and puts me on high alert. The investor's representative asks me what I think.

"You must clean that closet. It still smells like the Hoarder House."

She looks startled for a minute.

I laugh. "You won't sell it if anybody opens that door."

It does sell quickly for $244,000 to a recently divorced man with two young children. The family is like a doppelganger of my divorced mother, sister, and me. The story of the house begins again.

My mother and I drive back to the assisted living facility after our hair appointment. She wants to show me the bird's nest on the back patio inside the porch area. It's supposed to be a decorative birdhouse, not one for actual birds, but she *shhhs* me and we move closer, and I can hear the babies singing inside. My mother has a delighted childlike face, full of wonder. She tells me about finding a blue robin's egg and being surprised by its size. She gestures with her fingers to show me. She hugs me goodbye, and I don't say when I'll see her again. She rejected my Mother's Day offer for the following weekend, and I feel relieved, off the hook, but sad. I'm sorry about how small her world is even though I recognize, as we age, that this can happen.

My mother takes the broken wind chime off the tree. "I've found the missing piece," she explains. "I'm going to take it back up to my room and fix it." She also furtively pulls up a little of the outside ivy to grow in her room. She eyes some of the purple flowers. "I wonder if those would grow inside too?"

Does she forget all the other things she had? Does she long for those objects? Or maybe she grieves them as if they are dead people who've disappeared, except in the memory of the person who knew them. And then, when the person who remembers them is gone, they are like those photographs we used to look through in antique stores we found on our rides with Nonno when I was little.

People without families, with no connection to anything, alone and unclaimed in a box with other lost people.

When we go upstairs to her room, she opens her calendar to write down the date for our next hair appointment and there's a photo stuck in it of Melissa and me at maybe four and eight with our chopped-up hair. "It was the 1960s pixie cut," she says to me. "Remember? We went to a barber in Haddonfield, but he did such a good job with you girls."

I remember hating it there and feeling weird. I wanted long hair like a princess, although at one point before I met Marc, I had a short buzz cut. Why did she take us there and not to a regular salon? She must have squirreled away photographs in some of the books we brought from the house, and these turn up whenever I visit the room, startling me. It's like I'm a child again and she is so powerful she can magically conjure up various things of hers I haven't saved for her. It freaks me out a little.

She brings up topics out of the blue: "Did you see the show on PBS about the astronauts returning? When they came back, the gravity was so hard, one broke his leg. And despite exercising, they'd still lost calcium and had some long-term effects."

She also talks about how the ophthalmologist didn't have eclipse glasses and how outraged she was by that, and then she moves on to how she remembered her sunglasses today and isn't it beautiful out. Then she discusses whether I knew the corona of the sun had a different temperature. Then we are back to the astronauts. Anything to not talk about the house and lost things. The astronauts returned and broke their legs—bones disintegrating under the weight of the world. There are consequences to being in space and returning.

"They are blue flies," Marc explains from our kitchen where he's looking for something to slap them with. "They hatch from maggots." He's looked them up on the internet and read about how they are flesh-eating, cleanup insects. Something has woken them, probably a mouse that has died in our attic. The enormous, creepy creatures stupidly buzz by us in slow circles the way my mind does as I'm trying to deal with my mother's finances and the Medicaid application paperwork. The forms are endless and scare me. She will be running out of money sooner than we think.

Marc has killed a lot of the flies with the slow slap of *The New Yorker* magazine that leaves a trail of fly spooge on the windowpane as the black insect bodies hit the floor.

"Gotcha," Marc crows.

I call him my fly killer and make jokes about his prowess. It's not funny. It's like bad karma has infested us. I have been sick again with another virus. It's like my immune system laid down on the trash heap in the Hoarder House and just gave up on me.

My mother continues to complain to my sister about not being able to go for a real walk and being "institutionalized" at her new home.

She's angry there's no bus trip to Barnes & Noble or the library, only to Walmart. "I don't know how to be useless," she moans. I talk to the person who runs the activities at the assisted living facility about identifying some ways for her to volunteer there.

My sister, who sees her more often than I do, has become more heartless about my mother's comments, and says on the way out to me after we've visited, "Because climbing over mountains of trash was useful," and rolls her eyes.

I don't respond, but I think, *she passed time by surviving. When you are shitting in a plastic bag and wondering if you'll have enough money to keep buying books to get the bags that work from Barnes & Noble, that's one way of coping.*

I'm back at Ann's, the family therapist who saw my sister, mother, and me all those years ago, and later just me for a few sessions when I was dealing with my infertility grief. I'm sitting on the low-slung brown leather couch that shows some worn places where too many people have sat for too much time trying to get better. When I called Ann to make the appointment, I told her it was a lot to explain and that I was sending her some writing about what had happened. I photocopied my journal pages and emailed them to her.

I'd looked around for other therapists before making the call to her, but in the end, I said to Marc, "I may as well just go back. She's familiar with my family dynamics; she's seen my mother and it's exhausting to think about rehashing all of that with somebody new." What I don't say, and he understands, is that I feel like any other therapist wouldn't believe this story about what my mother is like and what we have been through.

"So, then I find out there was no running water," I sigh, tired of hearing myself telling all of this *again* and wondering how I will be able to share everything in the hour I've got. But once I start talking, the story gushes forth. Ann is older, grayer, and she listens with her kind eyes steadily on me. I feel my shoulders start to relax, but still, I can't cry about this. It's as if I'm numb, but also like my anger is the only engine I've got and when I run out of fuel, I'll be a spaceship drifting through the cold dark.

Ann interrupts my confused and pressured narrative in a surprising way, "You have done enough."

I stop midsentence as if I'm hearing a different language.

She repeats my new mantra. "You have done enough."

It's a clanging gong that wakes me up. I stop, shaken, waiting for her to say something after that. *Where's the "but"? What's the next thing I'm supposed to do?* And it's right then, in the space she creates for me, that I finally start to feel I don't have to carry this mess any longer.

It's three years later and my mother's funds from the house and her annuities are running out. Because she's not living in hoarder hell anymore, she's showering regularly and socializing at the assisted living facility. She looks very functional for a woman in her eighties. To qualify for Medicaid, she is required to have problems with the physical activities of daily living that necessitate her current level of care. The physical requirement is in addition to her financial need. I deliberately did not put a lot of information in her chart about why we put her in assisted living because I didn't want staff to shame her or have other people see her differently. That choice is coming back to bite me.

The Medicaid nurse calls me before she sees my mother for her evaluation and I explain the situation to her, offering to provide a letter with documentation about what happened.

"Oh," she says, "I just evaluated a hoarding situation last week." She tells me to go ahead and write the letter. This is how I end up basically composing a psychological report about my own mother, attaching some of Jackie's pictures of the house so she can see what I'm talking about.

Two weeks later, the Medicaid nurse calls me. "She qualified," she says, and stops.

I realize she's debating whether to tell me more.

"If you just met your mother superficially," she continues, "she wouldn't qualify. But I spent two hours with her. She's delightful and I really enjoyed meeting her. She told me all about her grandchildren, the art in the room and her travels. I also read all your materials. It doesn't seem like it could be the same person. I was shocked. Sometimes I talk to my husband about my tough cases, but I couldn't tell him about those pictures because he was eating dinner."

Something is stuck in my throat. It's grief. I *have* done enough.

Once you are on Medicaid, you are required to share a room. My mother will have to move from her studio apartment in assisted living to a one bedroom with another resident on Medicaid. One of them will have the tiny bedroom and one will have the compact living room space.

I tell the facility director to show my mother what's available and let her choose which of these she wants. "I want her to have as much control over this move as she can," I tell her.

My mother is weirdly resigned to it. We've been talking about it for months, but it is finally happening. She tells my sister she wants the grandchildren to come and choose what they want from the room as she will have to downsize and get rid of many of her things. She seems almost calm about it, maybe because she is deciding where her objects will go. It's still a lousy situation and both my sister and I feel bad about it, but there's not another option. In the end, she will be once again living in a space almost as small as that wrecked recliner in her old living room, but there will be a working bathroom, and a walk-in closet to keep her things. It's sad and fitting in the same way.

What have I lost, found, and kept? I've lost some of the patience I used to have. I don't mince words anymore. By doing enough, I have been freed of being responsible for somebody else's mess. I'm only responsible for my own, and that's enough. Sometimes, I regret being harsh with my mother and wish we could have done things differently, the way all the psychological books about hoarding cleanups advise. I feel sad that I was angry. I have gained so much appreciation for the husband who shoveled next to me, who recently built me a sun porch with wide windows where light streams in and comfortable chairs where I sit writing these words. He doesn't see or treat me as something to be torn up or thrown away. And I have finally fully allowed myself to believe that I am to be treasured and kept.

Five months before my mother dies, when I'm driving her back to the assisted living facility from her cardiology appointment, I take the road that goes by the turnoff for both neighborhoods where we used to live. My mother waves her hand imperiously from the passenger side of the car. "Go around the circle," she orders, pointing to the Glenview neighborhood sign where the first house on Woodstock Road was located.

"To our house?" I ask, surprised.

"I want to see both," she says.

In the seven years since everything happened, I've occasionally done the nostalgic drive-by for my growing up houses, but not with her. She'd never asked before.

Our Woodstock Drive house, her favorite, was the one that looked like you could run through the bay window as you came down the street. It's a different color, taupe, instead of the dark brown it was when we lived there. It's more run down. I wonder if she's remembering too.

"It looks small to you," my mother says, "because you were so little then. I wonder if the willow tree is still in the backyard."

"True," I respond as I drive slowly by it. "Almost fifty years ago."

I circle the car over toward Brookfield and onto Willowbrook Road. I weave through the neighborhood as I used to do on my bike, still remembering the route without even thinking about it. I don't say anything until we are in front of it. It's well maintained and freshly painted in better colors than what the house flipper had chosen.

"Your house has been sold three times," I tell her. "Once was to the flipper and then to the divorced dad. Kathy says another family just bought it a few months ago when he moved to someplace bigger." I pause, but she doesn't say anything. I wonder what she's feeling. *Is she sad?*

"They cleaned it up nice," she says finally. "Okay, let's go."

As I'm driving her back, I'm thinking, *They? They cleaned it up?* Part of me wants to laugh.

My mother and I lost so many opportunities to talk about the past. I don't feel I can even bring the old photographs I rescued in the cleanup for her to identify. She's still angry with me about this house. When she is gone, my grief will be complicated because it will end the hope that things between us will ever be better. She's told me a few times that she's grateful and appreciative for everything I do for her. She tells me Nanna never told her that and she wants to make sure I hear it from her. We do laugh together about some things— what my cat is doing, funny travel stories—and it's like those times when I was younger and closer to her. But it's never without the tension of what happened with the Hoarder House. After the drive by, she never mentions the house again.

The day after her eighty-ninth birthday, when my sister and her family have said their goodbyes and stepped out of my mother's ICU room for a minute, I lean over, touching her through the blankets the nurse has carefully wrapped around her. I say that we each did our best and tried in our relationship. I tell her I know that we never meant to hurt each other and that she was as good a mom as she could be to my sister and me and that I was grateful. I tell her what a special grandmother and great-grandmother she has been and how she's important to so many people. I say other things and then I reassure her we will all take care of each other, and she can leave whenever she is ready.

I tell her I love her. Her heart stops at that moment.

I can't help but think, because people die the way they live, that even in this she is protecting my sister and the grandkids, by dying just before they reenter the room. And how, at her end, I am trying to keep her from being alone and afraid. Her brief illness and death are over in less than twenty-four hours.

My eulogy ends with a memory. The summer I was twelve and my sister was eight, Hurricane Agnes begins to blow into Cape May. My mother, sister, Nanna, and I are finishing our annual beach vacation, the first since Nonno died. Standing near the sliding door of our hotel room overlooking the pool, we watch the Montreal Inn sign swing wildly as the sky darkens. But there's no rain yet and my mother says, "Come on, let's go walk on the boardwalk and see it." Nanna is horrified. But my mother is fearless, grabbing our raincoats and yelling at us once we are outdoors to *hurry up* across the street to the wide walkway emptied of people. Below us, there's little beach visible as the tide rises. Black ocean water is churning and foaming with whitecaps. The furious wind strengthens, so we have to reach for each other's hands, a line of three women in bright jackets pushing against the elements as the rain starts to sputter and spit.

My mother pulls off her hood, laughing. "Isn't it fun?" she cries. And my sister and I are laughing too. It will be okay because we are with her. We are excited to be brave girls together on an adventure. We pull each other along in the gathering storm, holding on.

Epilogue – *The Star-filled Dark*

"Looking a little hoarderish," Marc says, grinning when he walks past my home office door on his way to make coffee.

I make a joking sad face at him as I'm piling my journals, more than fifty, all numbered, on the desk that I salvaged from my mother's, the one her old boyfriend made for me. I keep my journals in bins under my old childhood four-poster bed that lives in my guest room. I'm looking for number forty.

I find the draft of what I was looking for, scrawled in black ink. I was imagining what it must have been like to go into space—travel so far away and then come back. How disorienting it would be, how it might feel to go crazy, to feel lost. How it would be to come back home afterwards:

Every night out of the black square of window—the white frame in the glass intersecting it to make a bull's eye—it rises. Now, at the drifting away of summer into the cool air of the changed season, it ascends, pink, a round fruit turning to a dull glow that gradually vanishes into the sky. She watches it from her bedroom, light casting shadows over the street and the car silhouettes and the neighbor walking his dog. The dog with the rough brown coat and the limp. His owner stepping slowly beside him in the evening light.

When she was nine years old, they watched it. The black and white television on the stand in her parent's bedroom. She and her sister on the floor, their heads next to each other on the patchwork pillow, a light blanket tossed over them. Usually, they weren't allowed up after nine. It was after 11 p.m. when their mother shook their shoulders, saying look, look now. The men in the white suits, puffed up and floating across the white landscape shadowed with holes. The flag reflected in the face of the one astronaut's visor. Voices crackle and she dozes through the words: one step, one step, she thinks as her eyelids drop and darkness settles over everything.

In college, she remembers reading about one of the astronauts, Buzz Aldrin, who wrote about coming back. What do you do after you've been to the moon and returned, his interviewer asked. And Buzz had replied something about stepping off a regular curb, feeling the weight of the earth on him, how small and insignificant he was, how even the half-moons of his fingernails tormented him, and he felt he was sinking down, all the way into a deep black crater, falling endlessly.

Splash, and everyone cheered at the sight of the rocket dropping into the water. She watched on the television in school as the boats and the men dragged it out after the scalding heat of reentry and took those men to debrief. They might have been carrying germs or foreign infection. They had been somewhere else where nothing held them, nothing kept them tied to the green lushness of this planet. The men always looked tired, shocked, but she never heard any of the others talk the way Aldrin did about it. Maybe he was weaker, maybe somehow more sensitive. Saw something that the others didn't.

She wants to go to that place. The face of the men on the moon. Dead flagpole with something flapping all those years later. Did she remember right that it was garbage they left there after they took off to shoot back into the atmosphere? She imagines a pile of Styrofoam, some bags of human waste, the slippery packets of Tang squeezed and emptied. Left like ugly useless bones on the surface.

What is perfect is the coldness. The hard rock edge where it's been hit over and over by things it can't control, things such a large *environment holds. Her mind isn't big enough to encompass the enormity. It swings itself around life like a dead planet. Useless.*

There is always an image of the astronaut who is cut away from the ship. Umbilical cord emptying life into the dark star-filled sky. His white suit turning into one of those bright lights as his arms wave and then finally stop.

Why go someplace where nothing is? You go to see if your perspective is right. It surely isn't. The eight-inch black and white screen can't capture being held there on the surface only by your boots, your hands. Everything else simply gone, sucked away. She thinks of it as a landscape of grief, the entire moon a bone picked clean by sunlight. What is left to scavenge, to search for, or hunger for here?

All the children clapped when the capsule fell into the sea, leaving a fiery wake. From nowhere to somewhere. She hates heights, the flying up. Once she's over the atmosphere, clouds below her pink and blue oceans of air, she's fine. She believes in the illusion, her own illusions of safety. Not that far up, she tells herself, not at all. The landscape covered by clouds rolled and rippled like water. Once she watched the sun set over the silver wing and the dark came on, drowning them.

Buzz Aldrin sits in the hospital. He had the best care, she thinks, it wouldn't be good for the space program to have a mentally ill astronaut. He is watching his own hand light a cigarette and fill his lungs with smoke. He can't stop looking at the moon's setting, dropping low behind his skin. The moon is in him and over him rising behind the thick grated window. He just sees little pieces of it falling over him as he sits in the vinyl chair, scattering squares of light over the dull green flooring. He'd like to pray but has been where God has been. He has looked down over the earth. It was so small, a blue and green smallness.

She wants to know what it would be like to fly up to the moon and come back. She'd like a different perspective. It's not about the bravery, the deed, or the money. It's about hanging on to the umbilical cord. It's about making sure the earth doesn't pull away, breaking the threads of air that hold that dead place closely. Leaving it to circle nothing, leaving those who have traveled there alone.

When she looks out her window tonight, it is high up. Far away. Very, very cold. Out of reach and full. Round as an eye, watching.

I close my journal. There will always be sadness, I think. I've chosen to work as a psychologist and to be a writer, both callings that require courage to explore the unknown. In the Hoarder House, I found a large unframed print—art that I suspect my mother meant for me to have. It depicts a tiny mouse, holding a stick up in the air, as it balances a board with a big lion crouched on top. The background is Africa, with grasses, a few trees, and a dirt road leading toward a purpled blue sky. It's called Anger Management. After we cleaned out the house, I had it framed, and hung it over my desk in my private practice office. *Am I that mouse or that lion? And which one is my mother?*

I walk downstairs to join Marc for more coffee. As we sit together reading on the sunporch, the birds on the feeder, cardinals, blue jays, and starlings chirp loudly. The wind chime hung outside near the old magnolia gongs softly in the summer breeze. *Love is the gravity that tethers us here. Love is what gives us the strength to balance the anger.* When I was in high school, my yearbook quote under my unflattering senior photo was from James Thurber: "Every time I ask anybody for the moon, it gets larger and farther away." But the earth holds on, regardless. It's love that keeps it there.

Acknowledgements

Parts of this book appeared previously in the following publications:

A Tale of Two Primates-Opinionator New York Times (10/26/2014)
Churn-Nashville Review (#36 Winter, 2021)
Churn-Memoir Monday (12/20/2021)
What We Hold On To-The Woven Tale Press Vol.X #4 (June, 2022)
Drowning in Debris-A Daughter Faces Her Mother's Hoarding-Psychotherapy Networker (March/April 2023)

This is a work of creative nonfiction. The events are portrayed to the best of the author's memory. While she's tried to get it right, any errors or inaccuracies are hers alone and part of the story as well. Some names and details have been changed to protect the privacy of the people involved.

"Diving into the Wreck", from DIVING INTO THE WRECK: Poems 1971-1972 by Adrienne Rich. Copyright © 1973 by W.W. Norton & Company, Inc. Used by permission of W.W. Norton & Company, Inc.

From LETTERS TO A YOUNG POET by Rainer Maria Rilke, translated by M. D. Herter Norton. Copyright 1934, 1954 by W. W. Norton & Company, Inc., renewed © 1962, 1982 by M. D. Herter Norton. Used by permission of W. W. Norton & Company, Inc.

While I was working on final edits, my niece, Maddie, shared an inscription she found in a book my mother gave to me during my adolescence.

"To Deborah," it read, "Too Many Answers May Obscure a Vital Fact: Life is an unending process of looking for more *Questions*, Mom."

I hope my mother, who encouraged my writing and creativity, would understand. There will always be more questions, Mom.

With gratitude and love to my family both given and found—who have supported me and the journey of this book, particularly my sister, Melissa, and her family (Ron, Sarah, Maddie, Mike); my nieces Caitlin and Noa; my Texas sister; my brother, Andrew and his side of the family; my mother's best friend, Mrs. Lee; my "adopted little sis," Kathy; "cousin" Patty, and my oldest friend, Debbie E.

To my best friends, beta readers, and important people in my life—named and unnamed in this book (you know who you are)—who've encouraged, helped and been part of my story. Most especially: Fran, Cher, Barrie, Andi, Florence, my writing "Alterna-Group," That's What She Read-Havertown Women's Book Club, Stephanie M., Joanne F., Michelle W., Harsha, Paola, Cheryl B., Jackie L., Julie M., Jackie M., Mary B.B., Ann I., Sandy, and Dick W.

Thanks to my mother's neighbors for their kindness and care.

Thanks to the staff at The Residence at Cherry Hill who cared for my mother through the pandemic and allowed her to stay with her possessions in her studio apartment until the end.

To The Ragdale Foundation and Virginia Center for the Creative Arts for the many residencies that gave me the time and space to write parts of this book. I'm grateful for the wonderful community of friends I've created from those experiences.

To Kris Bigalk, Natasha Kane, David Groff, Alliyah Shafer, and everybody at Trio House Press for all your hard work and support of this book.

Thanks to Anne Dubuisson, my editor, cheerleader, and friend.

And for Marc, without whom, there would be no story.

About the Author

Deborah Derrickson Kossmann's essays, feature articles and poetry have been published in *The New York Times*, *Nashville Review*, *Psychotherapy Networker*, and *Solstice Magazine* to name a few. She was the winner of the Short Memoir Competition at the 2007 Philadelphia First Person Arts Festival and was awarded a Pennsylvania Council on the Arts Poetry Fellowship. When she's not working as a clinical psychologist in private practice outside Philadelphia, PA, she and her husband are devoted servants to Sofia Carmela, a cat with a whole lot of "tortitude." For more: https://www.debkossmann.com

About the Book

Lost Found Kept was designed at Trio House Press through the collaboration of:

David Groff, Lead Editor
Natasha Kane, Supporting Editor and Interior Design
Joel W. Coggins, Cover Design

The text is set in Adobe Caslon Pro.

About the Press

Trio House Press is an independent literary press dedicated to discovering, publishing, and promoting books that enhance culture and the human experience. Trio House Press adheres to and supports all ethical standards and guidelines outlined by the CLMP. For further information, or to consider making a donation to Trio House Press, visit us online at triohousepress.org.